Creativity

Creativity

From Potential to Realization

Edited by

Robert J. Sternberg
Elena L. Grigorenko
Jerome L. Singer

American Psychological Association
Washington, DC

Published by
American Psychological Association
750 First Street, NE
Washington, DC 20002
www.apa.org

To order
APA Order Department
P.O. Box 92984
Washington, DC 20090-2984
Tel: (800) 374-2721; Direct: (202) 336-5510
Fax: (202) 336-5502; TDD/TTY: (202) 336-6123
On-line: www.apa.org/books/
E-mail: order@apa.org

In the U.K., Europe, Africa, and the Middle East, copies may be ordered from
American Psychological Association
3 Henrietta Street
Covent Garden, London
WC2E 8LU England

Typeset in Goudy by Stephen McDougal, Mechanicsville, MD

Printer: United Book Press, Inc., Baltimore, MD
Cover Designer: Naylor Design, Washington, DC
Technical/Production Editor: Dan Brachtesende

The opinions and statements published are the responsibility of the authors, and such opinions and statements do not necessarily represent the policies of the American Psychological Association.

Library of Congress Cataloging-in-Publication Data

Creativity : from potential to realization / edited by Robert J. Sternberg, Elena L. Grigorenko, and Jerome L. Singer.—1st ed.
    p. cm.
Includes bibliographical references and index.
  ISBN 1-59147-120-6
 1. Creative ability. I. Sternberg, Robert J. II. Grigorenko, Elena. III. Singer, Jerome L.

  BF408.C7548 2004
  153.3'5—dc22   2003022923

British Library Cataloguing-in-Publication Data
A CIP record is available from the British Library.

Printed in the United States of America
First Edition

CONTENTS

CONTRIBUTORS

Sami Abuhamdeh, University of Chicago, Illinois

John Baer, Rider University, Lawrenceville, NJ

Ronald A. Beghetto, University of Oregon, Eugene

Mihaly Csikszentmihalyi, Claremont Graduate University, Claremont, CA

Gregory J. Feist, University of California, Davis

Howard Gardner, Harvard Graduate School of Education, Cambridge, MA

Elena L. Grigorenko, Yale University, New Haven, CT

Jacques-Henri Guignard, Université René Descartes, Laboratoire Cognition et Développement, Paris

Sheila J. Henderson, Kaiser Permanente Medical Group

James C. Kaufman, California State University at San Bernardino, Learning Research Institute

Mia Keinänen, Harvard Graduate School of Education, Cambridge, MA

Todd Lubart, Université René Descartes, Laboratoire Cognition et Développement, Paris

Jonathan A. Plucker, Indiana University, Bloomington

Michele Root-Bernstein, East Lansing, MI

Robert Root-Bernstein, College of Natural Science, Michigan State University, East Lansing

Mark A. Runco, California State University, Fullerton; University of Hawaii, Hilo

Dean Keith Simonton, University of California, Davis

Jerome L. Singer, Yale University, New Haven, CT

Robert J. Sternberg, Yale University, New Haven, CT

PREFACE

The purpose of this book is to help readers understand what it means to be creative. Thus, the principal questions it answers are, "Who is creative—and why?" and "What is creativity?" The authors discuss the attributes that lead people to be creative in fields such as the arts and letters, the sciences, and business.

The particular emphasis of the book is on the theoretical issue of whether the attributes (internal or external) that lead to creativity in one domain are the same as those that lead to creativity in another domain. Our interest is in whether the creative scientist or artist is someone who would have been creative had he or she pursued any field. In other words, is creativity a generalized attribute, as is implied by psychometric tests of creativity, or is it a domain-specific attribute, as implied by some studies of the role of knowledge in creative and other forms of expertise?

Domain-specificity theory argues that creativity can exist within a domain, but that it is not transferable to other domains. A great deal of empirical evidence supports this view, much of it from the case study approach and the cognitive approach. For example, studies of Darwin suggest that his creativity in his work depended on a complex combination of abilities, personality, motivation, work experience, and family background. The combination would not transfer, say, to art or mathematics. In a related vein, cognitive studies suggest that individuals who are creative in a given field draw on enormous knowledge bases in their domain of expertise. That knowledge would not be helpful in most other domains of work.

Domain-generality theory argues that creativity may cross over several or even many domains. Substantial empirical evidence supports this point of view, much of it from personality- and abilities-based approaches. Research using the former approach suggests that creative people consistently show certain personality or motivational traits, such as dominance, hostility, openness to experience, and determination even in the face of obstacles. These traits could lead to creativity in a variety of domains. Similarly, research from the psychometric abilities standpoint suggests that high scores on tests of creative ability, such as the Torrance, may predict creative behavior in a wide variety of fields.

The potential audience for our book is broad because the volume addresses a topic that is of potential relevance to any psychologist and to people outside the field. Practitioners need to be creative in their psychotherapy. Scientists need to be creative in designing theories and research. Educators need to be creative in their ways of teaching. There are few psychologists who do not need to be creative in their work, regardless of specialization. Moreover, the psychological study of creativity is multidisciplinary, involving approaches of social, personality, cognitive, clinical, biological, differential, developmental, educational, and other forms of psychology.

Some books on creativity are limited to a single paradigm, such as the cognitive approach or a clinical approach. Our book crosscuts fields, as noted above, including authors who specialize in social, personality, cognitive, clinical, biological, differential, developmental, and educational approaches. It also crosscuts research methods, including experimental, case-study, psychometric, biological, and analytic. Thus we believe that the book fits well into many contemporary points of view.

This book is sponsored by Division 10 (Psychology of Aesthetics, Creativity, and the Arts) of the American Psychological Association. All royalties for the book will go to Division 10.

As with any book, a number of people have made the production of the book possible. We are grateful to Gary VandenBos and Lansing Hays for contracting the book, to Alex Isgut for helping in the preparation of the manuscript, and especially to our colleagues in Division 10 of APA for their support of our work and of the field of creativity research. We hope you enjoy reading the book as much as we enjoyed editing it.

Creativity

1

HAWKING'S HAIKU, MADONNA'S MATH: WHY IT IS HARD TO BE CREATIVE IN EVERY ROOM OF THE HOUSE

JAMES C. KAUFMAN AND JOHN BAER

If Heisenberg had chosen to write poetry rather than study quantum mechanics, is it likely we would be reading his work today? Could Emily Dickinson's genius for writing poetry have led to brilliant scientific theories rather than brilliant poems had she had different interests and opportunities? These are questions we cannot really answer, because it is too late for Heisenberg and Dickinson to make such choices or to have such opportunities. What then of people still living, people who still could change fields? If Stephen Hawking renounced his scientific work to devote himself to writing music—or if he pursued both interests simultaneously—would he achieve the same renown as a composer that he has as a scientist? Could Madonna make a career change, study mathematics, and then apply the creative talents that have nurtured her musical career to the field of mathematics and find similar success in that domain? Or, on a more everyday level, is someone who is creative in one area, such as drawing, likely to be creative in other endeavors, such as writing, cooking, or solving personal problems?

When we speculate about the nature of general or domain-specific creativity, we are in essence asking if there is something (or some things) that people may possess in varying degrees that will lead them to exhibiting higher levels of creativity in everything they do—higher than they would have if they lacked these abilities. These abilities may extend to include cognitive skills, personality traits, motivational patterns, thinking styles, or even certain kinds of knowledge. Is there perhaps something we might label *c*, analogous to the *g* of intelligence, that transcends domains and enhances the creativity of a person in all fields of endeavor? And does it make sense to call someone "creative," or should attributions of creativity always be qualified in some way (e.g., "a creative storyteller" or "a creative mathematician," but not "a creative person")?

These questions go to the heart of what we mean by and understand about creativity, and creativity theories need in some way to answer these questions to be complete. That they are hard to answer goes without saying (else why this book?). The answers we give below will be seen to fall much more on the side of domain specificity[1] rather than generality, but not entirely. The answers that one discovers depend, of course, on the questions one asks. We argue that there is more than one valid question in this area, and therefore more than one valid answer.

WHAT IS CREATIVITY, AND HOW CAN WE BEST APPROACH THE QUESTION OF DOMAIN GENERALITY OR SPECIFICITY OF CREATIVITY?

When asking whether creativity is general or domain specific, we must first specify what is meant by creativity. There is some consensus here, at least at the most basic level. One popular definition that most creativity theorists endorse (Mayer, 1999) is that creativity is "the ability to produce work that is novel (i.e., original, unexpected), high in quality, and appropriate (i.e., useful, meets task constraints)" (Sternberg, Kaufman, & Pretz, 2002, p. 1). There are nonetheless unanswered important questions of exactly how novel, high in quality, or appropriate a product must be to earn recognition as creative. At the highest or genius level of creativity, where there is no doubt that the products in question deserve such recognition, few have

---

[1]The term *domain* has notoriously fuzzy boundaries, and the evidence for domain specificity of creativity includes both specificity in the sense of broadly defined cognitive domains (e.g., linguistic, mathematical, and musical) and more narrowly defined (and more numerous) task or content domains (e.g., poetry writing, story writing, painting, drawing, and collage making). The latter are what some prefer to call "micro-domains" (Karmiloff-Smith, 1992), and this kind of specificity is sometimes termed "task specificity" (see especially Baer, 1993) rather than domain specificity. Other domain-specific theories of creativity are Gardner's (1983) several "intelligences" and the "domain-relevant skills" of Amabile's (1982, 1996) componential theory (which also includes a general "creativity-relevant skills" component, as explained in the text).

achieved eminence in more than one domain, and this seems at first blush like a strong argument for domain specificity. Indeed, when creativity researchers focus on this highest level of creativity, their arguments tend to have a domain-specific flavor (Csikszentmihalyi, 1988, 1990; Gruber, 1981; Gruber & Davis, 1988; Gruber & Wallace, 1999; Policastro & Gardner, 1999; Simonton, 1994, 1999a, 1999b; Tardif & Sternberg, 1988; Wallace & Gruber, 1989; Weisberg, 1999).

But the fact that such versatile geniuses are so rare could easily be explained by the "ten year rule" (Hayes, 1989)—the fact that it takes many years of preparation before "even the most noteworthy and 'talented' individuals" (Weisberg, 1999, p. 230) can reach the level of competence necessary to achieve true excellence in any domain. These 10-plus years are typically spent in "deliberate practice and the development of expert performance" (Weisberg, 1999, p. 233)—and this is just the time needed to *prepare* oneself for the kind of paradigm-shifting creative work that may one day come to be acknowledged as the work of genius. The actual creative work follows this 10-year (or longer) period of practice and study, making the time required for such creative performance even longer. As Gruber and Davis (1988) wrote, "Perhaps the single most reliable finding in our studies is that creative work takes a long time" (p. 264).

Spending 10-plus years in dedicated study or practice in several different domains is usually impossible (or at least unlikely), and therefore the apparent lack of creators who have reached the highest levels of creativity in two or more domains can tell us little about whether the creativity-relevant skills and traits that helped them succeed so brilliantly in one field could have been applied with similar success in other, unrelated fields. As Tardif and Sternberg (1988) concluded, "although it is generally agreed that creative individuals are creative within limited domains, various explanations have been offered for why individuals differ in their propensities toward and abilities in their domains of creativity" (pp. 433–434). The question of whether the fact that creative people are typically creative in a single domain is the result of domain-specific (and possibly innate) differences in skills, traits, or modes of thinking, or of more happenstance factors such as environments that fostered specific interests or offered limited opportunities, remains open and virtually impossible to answer with certainty. Could Heisenberg have been a great poet? Probably not, but given the time required to prepare for creative productivity in a given domain (and the limits of the human life span), that's an assertion difficult to prove.

To answer the question of whether creativity is general or domain specific, therefore, we will need to consider more everyday, garden-variety creativity, in which it is at least theoretically possible that in one lifetime a person could be observed to apply the same cognitive skills or personality traits in the service of creative performance in many diverse domains. Unfortunately, this runs the risk of conflating what some have argued may be two very different kinds of creativity, the unique creativity of genius and the everyday creativity likely to be observed in laboratory studies of creativity, in which "we can have no guarantee that the sample taken includes a single person who is functioning creatively" (Gruber & Davis, 1988, p. 246). If the truly creative person were unique, this would make any conclusions based on laboratory studies of creativity inapplicable to such geniuses (Gruber & Wallace, 1999). The cognitive structures and processes that support such different levels of creativity might even be of entirely different kinds (e.g., Johnson-Laird, 1987, 1988) and might have different levels of domain-general and domain-specific processes (for a parallel argument in the study of reasoning, see Leighton & Sternberg, 2002, who argue that experts in a given domain may use far richer and more diverse reasoning strategies than novices; studies of reasoning that exclude experts might then lead to an illusory consistency, which in turn might result in theories postulating a single fundamental mechanism to explain reasoning performance rather than the varied reasoning strategies actually used by experts).

If we are to find evidence of generality, however, we have little choice but to forsake genius and examine the results of studies either of modestly creative individuals, such as practicing artists and scientists (e.g., Feist, 1999), or of the garden-variety creativity one expects in experimental studies, in which participants are selected essentially at random. In doing so, we recognize that whatever evidence for or against generality we may uncover may not apply to creativity at the paradigm-shifting or genius level.

DIFFERENT QUESTIONS, DIFFERENT ANSWERS

Research on everyday creativity can look at different aspects of creativity, such as creative personalities, creative products, or creative processes, or it may start from different frames of analysis, such as considerations of whether creativity is a social or a personal phenomenon (Mayer, 1999). It is likely that by asking different questions, researchers will find different answers, as well as different, and possibly conflicting, truths about creativity. The fact that creativity researchers are asking different questions when they approach the issue of domain generality or specificity may indeed be at the heart of much of the dispute in this area. Plucker (1998) noted that "performance assessments produce evidence of task specificity, and creativity checklists and other traditional assessments suggest that creativity is content general" (p. 180). A study by Runco (1987) exemplified this effect by using both self-report and performance-based assessments of creativity. The self-report scales, which focused on the quantity of creative activities in which participants engaged in various domains, evidenced generality of creativity across domains; but the performance assessments, which focused on the quality of creative performances in different domains, pointed to domain specificity of creativity. Is this method effect pointing to a real difference, or merely to errors in measurement or interpretation in one method or the other?

Performance assessments of creativity that have focused on the issue of domain specificity[2] have typically looked at creative products produced by participants in different domains, such as writing, art, or mathematics (Baer, 1991, 1993, 1994a, 1994b, 1996, 1998; Conti, Coon, & Amabile, 1996; Diakidoy & Constantinou, 2001; Han, 2000; Runco, 1989). Amabile's (1982) consensual assessment technique, in which groups of experts in the relevant domain independently evaluate the creativity of the artifacts (poems, stories, collages, and the like) created by participants, has been used in these studies as a way of assessing the creativity of products. This method has been shown to produce reliable and valid creativity ratings that are fairly consistent over time (Amabile, 1982, 1983a, 1996; Baer, 1994c; Baer, Kaufman, & Gentile, in press).

Performance assessment studies that have asked participants to create a variety of products in different domains have found either very small or nonexistent correlations among the creativity ratings of artifacts produced by the same participants in different domains. For example, Baer (1991) asked eighth-grade students to complete four different kinds of tasks (poems, stories, mathematical equations, and mathematical word problems), resulting in six correlations of paired tasks. Half of the correlations were positive, half negative, with a mean r of .06, and when variance attributable to IQ was removed, the mean r dropped to −.05. With fourth-gradestudents, the mean r was .01, and with a study of adults using just two tasks, r was .08. Similarly, Han (2000) found that the creative performance of 109 second-grade students whose creativity was assessed in several domains varied widely across domains and showed little evidence of domain generality. Baer (1994a) found that the creativity ratings of artifacts in different domains created by both second-grade students who had received training in divergent thinking and second-grade students who had not had such training showed little evidence of a general creativity factor.

Conti, Coon, and Amabile (1996) presented evidence for Amabile's (1983a, 1983b, 1996) componential model of creativity, which has three components: domain-relevant skills, task motivation, and creativity-relevant skills. "*Creativity-relevant skills* are those skills that contribute to performance across domains and include cognitive style, working style, and divergent think-

---

[2]Creative products must be creative within some domain; only in fiction, such as Hesse's (1943/1969) *The Glass Bead Game (Magister Ludi)*—in which he described a supradisciplinary game that managed to synthesize all areas of intellectual endeavor and allowed one to converse simultaneously in and across multiple disciplines—could a product be meaningfully deemed creative without reference to a particular field of endeavor. Studies of creative products must therefore look at products in specific domains (and be judged for creativity by appropriate experts in those specific domains), but the results of such research could as easily show domain generality (if there were positive correlations among creativity ratings across domains) as they could domain specificity (if such correlations failed to appear).

ing abilities" (Conti, Coon, & Amabile, 1996, p. 385). Their evidence for the importance of task motivation and domain-relevant skills is convincing, although it should be noted that the within-domain correlations were rather low when they asked participants to complete different *tasks* in the same domain. When, for example, they asked their college-student participants to write four stories on the basis of four different prompts, the intercorrelations were all relatively high (ranging from .21 to .64, with a mean of .452) and all but one were statistically significant, which is in line with past research (e.g., Baer, 1993, 1994c). Yet when they asked participants to do three different tasks in the same domain (make a collage, make a drawing, and make a painting), the correlations dropped quite a bit (to .15, .23, and .43, with a mean of .27). These intradomain correlations are similar to those found in past research with different tasks within the same domain (e.g., Baer 1993; Runco, 1989). Together, these results suggest the presence of both domain-specific factors and task-specific ones.

The correlations that matter for the question of domain-general factors are those *across* domains, however, and the picture is quite different here. Although they claimed to have found "some suggestive evidence of general creativity skills across quite different domains" (Conti, Coon, & Amabile, 1996, p. 388)—"suggestive" in comparison to the "compelling" (p. 388) evidence they cite for domain specificity—that evidence was very weak at best. They reported a total of seven different tasks in two domains (four verbal-domain tasks and three art-domain tasks, which were part of three different studies—two that used only verbal-domain tasks and one that used only art-domain tasks. The fact that the three studies had used many of the same participants made the cross-domain comparisons possible). None of the resulting 12 cross-domain correlation coefficients was statistically significant. Nine were positive and three were negative, with a mean r of .118. This translates to a little more than 1% of variance accounted for by all cross-domain, general creativity-relevant factors (as compared with more than 20% accounted for by domain-specific factors among very similar verbal-domain tasks and more than 7% by domain-specific factors among three different art-domain tasks). They also reported two cross-domain correlations between *average* creativity ratings on verbal- and art-domain tasks, neither of which was statistically significant. One of these correlations was .25 and the other was .00, for a mean r of .125, which accounts for only 1.6% of the variance. These 14 small and nonsignificant correlations are all of the evidence they offered as evidence of general creativity-relevant skills. Even with the possibilities of "low power, measurement error, and other sources of variation" (p. 388) that they argue may contribute to such low correlations, the complete lack of statistically significant results among the 14 relevant correlation coefficients that they reported does not make a strong argument for the existence of such factors. If one adds to this lack of significant findings their evidence that such a tiny proportion of the total variance was attributable to general creativity-relevant factors of any kind (including such potential factors as intelligence and any personality variables that may affect creativity in both domains), it is difficult to find even the "suggestive evidence" (p. 388) that they claimed for the existence of such factors. A more recent study by Amabile and colleagues (Ruscio, Whitney, & Amabile, 1998) that used three kinds of tasks from different domains (structure building, collage making, & poetry writing) confirmed this lack of significant cross-domain, general creativity-relevant factors by finding an even lower average correlation (.09) among cross-domain creativity ratings.

Studies involving performance assessments of creativity thus provide little solid evidence for general creativity-relevant factors (including skills, traits, knowledge, cognitive styles, work habits, etc.). But studies of creative personalities using creativity checklists and other traditional assessments often suggest a content general factor (e.g., Hocevar, 1976, 1979; Plucker, 1999). How might this be understood in light of the results of cross-domain performance assessment research, which argues strongly against content general factors?

One of the most commonly used tools in creative personality research is the self-report questionnaire,[3] and researchers using such personality checklists have tended toward a much more general perspective than analyses of creative products (Plucker, 1998). This may be because they are simply assessing different things. In self-report studies, researchers look at ways that people understand their own creativity (and probably that of others), and their "folk" theories of creativity are likely to color their self-assessments. As such, self-assessments offer a window into the ways that people conceptualize creativity.

We recently asked 117 college students in an educational psychology course to rate their creativity in nine areas—science, interpersonal relationships, writing, art, interpersonal communication, solving personal problems, mathematics, crafts, and bodily–physical movement—and their creativity in general (Kaufman & Baer, in press). A factor analysis of their responses for the nine domains yielded three factors: an Expressing Emotions and Communication factor that included creativity in communication, interpersonal relationships, solving personal problems, and writing; a "Hands-On" Creativity factor that included creativity in art, crafts, and bodily–physical move-

---

[3]Hocevar (1981) claimed that such self-report scales were "perhaps the most easily defensible way to identify creative talent" (p. 455), but Brown's (1989) judgment that, in assessing creativity, "self-report data and retrospective case histories are generally unverifiable" (p. 29) makes one hesitant to rely too heavily on such data. The limitations of self-report data extend well beyond creativity research, of course. In fact, questions about the validity and appropriate use of self-report data were the subject of an interesting two-day National Institutes of Health conference on "The Science of Self-Report: Implications for Research and Practice" (Azar, 1997; Rowe, 1997), where both basic problems with self-report data (such as poor recall and both intentional and unintentional distortions by participants) and ways to improve its validity were discussed. For the purposes of this chapter we are accepting on face value the results of self-report data and trying to interpret those results, but we believe it important to note potential validity concerns.

ment; and a creativity in Math and Science factor. Self-ratings of creativity in general had positive correlations with all domain self-ratings, ranging from .03 for math and .24 for science to .55 for crafts and .62 for art. The correlation of self-ratings of creativity in general with Factor 2 (Hands-On Creativity) was .67; with Factor 1 (Expressing Emotions and Communication), the correlation with creativity in general was .38; and with Factor 3 (Math and Science), .02.

What these students (most of whom were young women studying to become elementary school teachers) seemed to be telling us is that their notion of what it means to be creative is closely associated with being creative in arts and crafts, slightly less associated with being creative in communication, and very little related to being creative in math or science. Would the results be the same if we asked a group of science fair participants the same questions? Might they connect creativity in general with creativity in math and science far more than these students? It seems likely that they would.

Our participants appeared already to have an implicit and readily accessible category or definition of *general creativity*: they had no trouble understanding our question, "How creative would you say you are in general?" and their responses to the nine domain questions tell us a great deal about their conception of what it means to be creative in general, an implicit definition that might vary from group to group. Other researchers have found that different groups define creativity in general, as well as different kinds of creativity, somewhat differently. For example, Runco (1990) asked artists and nonartists to nominate characteristics they associated with artistic, scientific, and everyday creativity and found that each group came to some consensus in their attributions of traits associated with each kind of creativity, but that there was both great disparity in the adjectives they chose for each of the three kinds of creativity and fairly great disparity between the lists generated by artists and nonartists. He also asked teachers and parents to list adjectives from the Adjective Check List (Gough & Heilbrun, 1980) that they associated with creativity in general, and the two groups came up with two rather different lists. Gluck, Ernst, and Unger (2002) found that even among successful creators in a single domain (art), those working in different media had different conceptions and personal definitions of creativity—definitions that they shared with other artists in the same media, but not with artists working in different media (e.g., painters vs. graphic designers).

Sternberg (1985) found that the implicit theories of creativity of professors of art, business, philosophy, and physics overlapped significantly, as they did also with the implicit theories of creativity of laypersons. For example, creative people, according to both diverse experts and laypersons, are likely to demonstrate a willingness to act in unconventional ways, to be inquisitive, and to be intuitive. There were also differences among the specialists in their theories of creativity, however. For example, the art professors in the sample emphasized imagination, originality, and risk taking more than the business professors, who were more likely to stress the importance of coming up with and exploring new ideas, whereas the philosophy professors stressed the ability to play with new ideas and to classify ideas more than the physics professors, who showed a special concern with the ability to find order in chaos, with inventiveness, and with the creative aspects of problem solving. Laypersons' implicit theories of creativity "seem to be an amalgamation of these different views without the specializations that appear in the implicit theories of individuals from particular fields of endeavor" (p. 624). Among all groups, implicit theories of creativity also overlapped significantly with implicit theories of intelligence and wisdom.

People appear to have ideas about what traits and skills are associated with creativity in general and creativity in different domains, and they share these conceptions with others with similar backgrounds, but the fact that different groups of people have different ideas about which traits and skills go with which kinds of creativity should lead us to wonder what validity these conceptions might have. Runco's (1990) two studies were reported as part of an article assessing the validity of the general concept of ideational abilities as important components of creative thinking, and he concluded that "perhaps there is an ideational component for each of the intelligences discussed by Gardner (1983)" (p. 248).

Feist (1999) reported that "certain personality traits consistently covary with creativity, yet there are some domain specificities" (p. 289). He reported some differences in the traits of creative artists and creative scientists—that is, there were trait lists for artists and scientists that had no overlap (e.g., creative scientists tend to be much more conscientious than artists, and creative artists tend to have a much more affective orientation than scientists)— but he also found that creative people in both art and science shared some traits: They tend to be "open to new experiences, less conventional and less conscientious, more self-confident, self-accepting, driven, ambitious, dominant, hostile, and impulsive" (p. 290). His lists, like those of Runco (1990), suggest both domain-specific traits and domain-general traits.

We believe there is reason to question how truly domain-general are the domain-general traits that Feist (1999) and others have found, as we explain below. But first we need to summarize what we believe we can say with confidence on the basis of creative personality research: People have beliefs about what it means to be creative in general, and what it means to be creative in different domains. Whatever their validity, implicit beliefs about creativity are important (Runco, 1990; Sternberg, 1985). They are real— they "need to be discovered rather than invented because they already exist, in some form, in people's heads" (Sternberg, 1985, p. 608)—and they "act as prototypes against which behavior is compared, and they may be involved whenever an individual makes a decision about his or her behavior or the behavior of another" (Runco, 1990, p. 235). As Sternberg (1985) noted, "despite the seeming omnipresence of standardized tests in our society, by far the largest proportion of evaluation of people's abilities are informal and observational . . . . People use their implicit theories to make these judgments" (p. 621). Our implicit theories of creativity matter because they are part of us and because they influence deeply the ways we think about creativity and about the creative behavior (or not so creative behavior) of ourselves and other people.

Is the fact that they matter the same as saying that implicit theories of creativity present true pictures of the structure of creativity, as it exists and functions operationally? Or course not. What people believe about natural phenomena affects their thinking and behavior, but misconceptions about the sun going around the earth did not change the truth of what was actually happening. People's beliefs about creativity are interesting, and they matter, but unless they jibe with other evidence regarding content generality—such as studies based on performance assessments of creativity—they should not be taken as evidence for it.

HOW DOMAIN-SPECIFIC SKILLS AND TRAITS MAY APPEAR TO BE DOMAIN GENERAL

Creative processes are presumably what creative people use to produce creative products (Finke, Ward, & Smith, 1992; Guilford, 1967; Guilford & Hoepfner, 1971; Koestler, 1964; Nickerson, 1999; Torrance, 1988). As such, they could be thought of as go-betweens between the creative people who possess and use the processes and the creative products that result from their use. From the creative person perspective, they constitute the skills or traits that make people creative (and thus are part of the definition of creative people); from the perspective of creative products, one infers their existence from the products that they are instrumental in or associated with creating. The psychometric tradition has worked hard to isolate these skills, but in the final analysis if one is to validate claims regarding creative processes, one must associate creative processes in some way with either creative products or creative people (e.g., Cropley, 1972; Kogan & Pankove, 1974; Plucker, 1998, 1999; Plucker & Renzulli, 1999; Runco, 1986, 1990; Torrance, 1972a, 1972b, 1990). For this reason, studies of creative processes necessarily overlap studies of either creative persons or creative products.

Some ways one might describe a creative person (e.g., intelligence) may be more general in nature, whereas others (e.g., possessing extensive domain-relevant knowledge) tend to be more domain specific. Many other skills or traits associated with creativity might appear on the surface to be domain general (e.g., divergent thinking ability, task motivation, openness to experience, tolerance of ambiguity) but may in fact be domain specific.

Let us start with intelligence. The question of the relationship between intelligence and creativity has been a contentious one in psychology (see, e.g., Getzels & Jackson, 1962; McNemar, 1964; Wallach, 1971; Wallach & Kogan, 1965a, 1965b), but most psychologists agree that there is some relationship, whether it is a case of (a) two partially overlapping sets of abilities that share some common ground, (b) two sets of abilities that are distinct only in the sense of one being a subset of the other, or (c) a single set of abilities that have come to be known by different terms (Sternberg & O'Hara, 2000). We agree that intelligence, however conceptualized, has some relationship with creativity, and that intelligence has domain-general properties. In fact, one piece of evidence for this comes from some of the performance assessment studies cited above, in which the already-low correlations of creativity ratings across domains decreased still further when variance attributable to intelligence test scores was removed (Baer, 1991, 1993). However, to the extent that these two constructs overlap one another, we leave those shared abilities to those who study and assess intelligence and the disputes within that field regarding specificity and generality. We are interested in the area in which the two concepts do not overlap: the part of creativity that is independent of intelligence and has effects in addition to those attributable to intelligence.

Our question then is whether there are some general-purpose, creative-thinking skills (or traits) that we might call c, analogous to g in being applicable to virtually all creativity-relevant tasks, but distinct from g: some general creativity-relevant factor that accounts for differences in creativity across domains above and beyond whatever contribution g makes. The evidence presented above about performance assessments of creativity suggests little room for a factor representing general creativity-relevant skills or traits, and yet there are some that come up again and again as important factors contributing to creativity, such as divergent thinking ability, tolerance of ambiguity, and risk taking (Plucker & Renzulli, 1999); openness to new experiences, unconventionality, self-confidence, self-acceptance, and ambitiousness (Feist, 1999); and motivation and thinking styles (Sternberg & Lubart, 1999). How can we make sense of this?

It is possible that a skill or trait that appears to be general may in fact be domain or even task specific. Using motivation as an example, Amabile (1983a, 1983b, 1996) has demonstrated quite convincingly that intrinsic motivation is associated with creativity in every domain in which researchers have assessed its effects. But even in Amabile's model, which includes general, all-purpose creativity-relevant skills, "task motivation operates at the most specific level" (Amabile, 1996, p. 79)—more specific even than the domain-specific skills her theory posits, and nothing at all like a domain-general skill. "In terms of impact on creativity, motivation may be very specific to particular tasks within domains" (Amabile, 1996, pp. 79–80).

A skill or trait can be very general in the sense that we understand it as a single thing and yet it may operate on a very domain-specific (or even task-specific) level. Just as someone may have a great deal of intrinsic motivation when it comes to writing poetry but none at all when it comes to solving scientific puzzles (or vice versa), so it may be with other seemingly domain-transcending skills and traits. Baer (1993) proposed a task-specific theory of divergent thinking, going a step beyond Runco's (1990) suggestion that ideational thinking be thought of as domain specific along the lines of Gardner's (1983) intelligences. He demonstrated that it was possible to teach such narrowly applicable divergent-thinking skills so as to increase creativity on one task but not on other tasks, even if the different tasks were in the same verbal domain, such as writing poetry and writing stories (Baer, 1996). In the same way, self-confidence, ambition, openness to experiences, and so forth, may be domain-specific skills that are convenient to think of as the same on one level for the sake of convenience and because they are quite similar. Yet on the level of cognitive operations, these superficially similar skills and traits may be totally unlike one another. Heisenberg was probably much more self-confident and open to new experiences in the area of physics than in poetry; Madonna is presumably far more ambitious and a greater risk taker in music than in mathematics.

DOES IT MAKE SENSE TO REFER TO SOME PEOPLE AS "CREATIVE"?

Referring to people as "creative" may still be appropriate in many contexts, even if creativity is domain specific. Even if creativity across domains were randomly distributed among people, some people would nonetheless be more creative than others by virtue of being creative in more relevant domains, and therefore more creative than others who were creative in fewer domains. Similarly, within a given contextual meaning of *creative*—the definition of which may vary greatly across different groups, as say between a group of scientists and a group of chefs—some people may show more of the skills and traits and behaviors thought in that group to demonstrate creativity. For example, producing interesting and testable theories might be associated with creativity in one group, whereas producing delicious and beautiful soufflés might be associated with creativity in another (indeed, see Balazs, 2001, for a discussion of creativity in chefs). Anyone who can creatively engage in the activities that matter to a group will appropriately be deemed a creative person by the members of that group, but this does not in any way suggest that these creative people will be viewed as creative in other contexts in which different implicit definitions of creativity are operational.

Unlike g, however, the existence of which is supported by a considerable body of evidence, the evidence for c, and thus for any content-general creativity-relevant skills or traits, is weak. It may make sense in many contexts to refer to people as creative, and there are many ideas shared by many diverse groups of people about what it means to be creative. As noted previously, there are also many skills and traits that contribute to creative performance in many domains; thus it makes sense to group together under single labels, such as divergent thinking ability, openness to new ideas, or willingness to take risks. But that is not the same as saying there exist actual creativity-enhancing cognitive skills or personality traits that operate in the same ways across all, or even most, domains. Could Hawking apply the same creative thinking skills and traits that helped make him a brilliant astrophysicist with similar success to writing poetry? As for Madonna, could she study math with the same rigor she applies to her artistic craft and be a successful mathematician? We admit that certainty is impossible, but the answer appears to be no. Hawking and Madonna should keep their day jobs.

REFERENCES

Amabile, T. M. (1982). Social psychology of creativity: A consensual assessment technique. *Journal of Personality and Social Psychology, 43,* 997–1013.

Amabile, T. M. (1983a). *The social psychology of creativity.* New York: Springer-Verlag.

Amabile, T. M. (1983b). The social psychology of creativity: A componential conceptualization. *Journal of Personality and Social Psychology, 45,* 357–376.

Amabile, T. M. (1996). *Creativity in context: Update to the social psychology of creativity.* Boulder, CO: Westview.

Azar, B. (1997, January). Poor recall mars research and treatment. *The APA Monitor, 28*(1), 1, 29.

Baer, J. (1991). Generality of creativity across performance domains. *Creativity Research Journal, 4,* 23–39.

Baer, J. (1993). *Divergent thinking and creativity: A task-specific approach.* Hillsdale, NJ: Erlbaum.

Baer, J. (1994a). Divergent thinking is not a general trait: A multi-domain training experiment. *Creativity Research Journal, 7,* 35–46.

Baer, J. (1994b). Generality of creativity across performance domains: A replication. *Perceptual and Motor Skills, 79,* 1217–1218.

Baer, J. (1994c). Performance assessments of creativity: Do they have long-term stability? *Roeper Review, 7*(1), 7–11.

Baer, J. (1996). The effects of task-specific divergent-thinking training. *Journal of Creative Behavior, 30,* 183–187.

Baer, J. (1998). The case for domain specificity in creativity. *Creativity Research Journal, 11,* 173–177.

Baer, J., Kaufman, J. C., & Gentile, C. A. (in press). Extension of the consensual assessment technique to nonparallel creative products. *Creativity Research Journal.*

Balazs, K. (2001). Some like it haute: Leadership lessons from France's great chefs. *Organizational Dynamics, 30,* 134–148.

Brown, R. T. (1989). Creativity: What are we to measure. In J. A. Glover, R. R. Ronning, & C. R. Reynolds (Eds.), *Handbook of creativity* (pp. 3–32). New York: Plenum Press.

Conti, R., Coon, H., & Amabile, T. M. (1996). Evidence to support the componential model of creativity: Secondary analyses of three studies. *Creativity Research Journal, 9,* 385–389.

Cropley, A. J. (1972). A five-year longitudinal study of the validity of creativity tests. *Developmental Psychology, 6,* 119–124.

Csikszentmihalyi, M. (1988). Society, culture, and person: A systems view of creativity. In R. J. Sternberg (Ed.), *The nature of creativity* (pp. 325–339). New York: Cambridge University Press.

Csikszentmihalyi, M. (1990). The domain of creativity. In M. A. Runco & R. S. Albert (Eds.), *Theories of creativity* (pp. 190–212). Newbury Park, CA: Sage.

Diakidoy, I. A., & Constantinou, C. P. (2001). Response fluency and task specificity. *Creativity Research Journal, 13,* 401–410.

Feist, G. J. (1999). Influence of personality on artistic and scientific creativity. In R. J. Sternberg (Ed.), *Handbook of creativity* (pp. 273–296). New York: Cambridge University Press.

Finke, R. A., Ward, T. S., & Smith, S. M. (1992). *Creative cognition: Theory, research, and applications.* Cambridge, MA: MIT Press.

Gardner, H. (1983). *Frames of mind: The theory of multiple intelligences.* New York: Basic Books.

Getzels, J. W., & Jackson, P. W. (1962). *Creativity and intelligence: Explorations with gifted children.* New Brunswick, NJ: Transaction Books.

Gluck, J., Ernst, R., & Unger, F. (2002). How creatives define creativity: Definitions reflect different types of creativity. *Creativity Research Journal, 14,* 55–67.

Gough, H. G., & Heilbrun, A. B., Jr. (1980). *The adjective checklist manual.* Palo Alto, CA: Consulting Psychologists Press.

Gruber, H. E. (1981). *Darwin on man: A psychological study of scientific creativity* (2nd ed.). Chicago: University of Chicago Press.

Gruber, H. E., & Davis, S. N. (1988). Inching our way up Mt. Olympus: The evolving-systems approach to creative thinking. In R. J. Sternberg (Ed.), *The nature of creativity* (pp. 243–270). New York: Cambridge University Press.

Gruber, H. E., & Wallace, D. B. (1999). The case study method and evolving systems approach for understanding unique creative people at work. In R. J. Sternberg (Ed.), *Handbook of creativity* (pp. 93–115). New York: Cambridge University Press.

Guilford, J. P. (1967). *The nature of human intelligence.* New York: McGraw-Hill.

Guilford, J. P., & Hoepfner, R. (1971). *The analysis of intelligence.* New York: McGraw-Hill.

Han, K. S. (2000). Varieties of creativity: Investigating the domain-specificity of creativity in young children. *Dissertation Abstracts International Section A: Humanities and Social Sciences, 61,* 1796.

Hayes, J. R. (1989). Cognitive processes in creativity. In J. A. Glover, R. R. Ronning, & C. R. Reynolds (Eds.), *Handbook of creativity* (pp. 135–146). New York: Plenum Press.

Hesse, H. (1969). *The glass bead game (Magister Ludi).* (R. Winston & C. Winston, Trans.). New York: Holt, Rinehart & Winston. (Original work published 1943)

Hocevar, D. (1976). Dimensionality of creativity. *Psychological Reports, 39,* 869–870.

Hocevar, D. (1979). The unidimensional nature of creative thinking in fifth-grade children. *Child Study Journal, 9,* 273–278.

Hocevar, D. (1981). Measurement of creativity: Review and critique. *Journal of Personality Assessment, 45,* 450–464.

Johnson-Laird, P. N. (1987). Reasoning, imagining, and creating. *Bulletin of the British Psychological Society, 40,* 121–129.

Johnson-Laird, P. N. (1988). Freedom and constraint in creativity. In R. J. Sternberg (Ed.), *The nature of creativity* (pp. 202–219). New York: Cambridge University Press.

Karmiloff-Smith, A. (1992). *Beyond modularity: A developmental perspective on cognitive science.* Cambridge, MA: MIT Press.

Kaufman, J. C., & Baer, J. (in press). Sure, I'm creative–but not in math! Self-reported creativity in diverse domains. *Empirical Studies of the Arts.*

Koestler, A. (1964). *The act of creation.* London: Hutchison.

Kogan, N., & Pankove, E. (1974). Long-term predictive validity of divergent-thinking tests. *Journal of Educational Psychology, 66,* 802–810.

Leighton, J. P., & Sternberg, R. J. (2002). Thinking about reasoning: Is knowledge power? [Electronic version.] *The Korean Journal of Thinking & Problem Solving, 12*(1), 5–25.

Mayer, R. E. (1999). Fifty years of creativity research. In R. J. Sternberg (Ed.), *Handbook of creativity* (pp. 449–460). New York: Cambridge University Press.

McNemar, Q. (1964). Lost: Our intelligence? Why? *American Psychologist, 19,* 871–882.

Nickerson, R. S. (1999). Enhancing creativity. In R. J. Sternberg (Ed.), *Handbook of creativity* (pp. 392–430). New York: Cambridge University Press.

Plucker, J. A. (1998). Beware of simple conclusions: The case for the content generality of creativity. *Creativity Research Journal, 11,* 179–182.

Plucker, J. A. (1999). Reanalyses of student responses to creativity checklists: Evidence of content generality. *Journal of Creative Behavior, 33,* 126–137.

Plucker, J. A., & Renzulli, J. S. (1999). Psychometric approaches to the study of human creativity. In R. J. Sternberg (Ed.), *Handbook of creativity* (pp. 35–61). New York: Cambridge University Press.

Policastro, E., & Gardner, H. (1999). From case studies to robust generalizations: An approach to the study of creativity. In R. J. Sternberg (Ed.), *Handbook of creativity* (pp. 213–225). New York: Cambridge University Press.

Rowe, P. (1997, January). The science of self-report. *APS Observer, 10*(1), 3, 35–38.

Runco, M. A. (1986). Predicting children's creative performance. *Psychological Reports, 59*, 1247–1254.

Runco, M. A. (1987). The generality of creative performance in gifted and nongifted children. *Gifted Child Quarterly, 31*, 121–125.

Runco, M. A. (1989). The creativity of children's art. *Child Study Journal, 19*, 177–190.

Runco, M. A. (1990). Implicit theories and ideational creativity. In M. A. Runco & R. S. Albert (Eds.), *Theories of creativity* (pp. 234–252). Newbury Park, CA: Sage.

Ruscio, J., Whitney, D. M., & Amabile, T. M. (1998). Looking inside the fishbowl of creativity: Verbal and behavioral predictors of creative performance. *Creativity Research Journal, 11*, 243–263.

Simonton, D. K. (1994). *Greatness: Who makes history and why.* New York: Guilford Press.

Simonton, D. K. (1999a). Creativity from a historiometric perspective. In R. J. Sternberg (Ed.), *Handbook of creativity* (pp. 116–133). New York: Cambridge University Press.

Simonton, D. K. (1999b). *Origins of genius.* New York: Oxford University Press.

Sternberg, R. J. (1985). Implicit theories of intelligence, creativity, and wisdom. *Journal of Personality and Social Psychology, 49*, 607–627.

Sternberg, R. J., Kaufman, J. C., & Pretz, J. E. (2002). *The creativity conundrum.* New York: Psychology Press.

Sternberg, R. J., & Lubart, T. I. (1999). The concept of creativity: Prospects and paradigms. In R. J. Sternberg (Ed.), *Handbook of creativity* (pp. 3–15). New York: Cambridge University Press.

Sternberg, R. J., & O'Hara, L. A. (2000). Intelligence and creativity. In R. J. Sternberg (Ed.), *Handbook of intelligence* (pp. 609–628). New York: Cambridge University Press.

Tardif, T. Z., & Sternberg, R. J. (1988). What do we know about creativity? In R. J. Sternberg (Ed.), *The nature of creativity* (pp. 429–440). New York: Cambridge University Press.

Torrance, E. P. (1972a). Career patterns and peak creative achievements of creative high school students twelve years later. *Gifted Child Quarterly, 16*, 75–88.

Torrance, E. P. (1972b). Predictive validity of the Torrance tests of creative thinking. *Journal of Creative Behavior, 6*, 236–252.

Torrance, E. P. (1988). Creativity as manifest in testing. In R. J. Sternberg (Ed.), *The nature of creativity* (pp. 43–75). New York: Cambridge University Press.

Torrance, E. P. (1990). *The Torrance tests of creative thinking: Norms-technical manual.* Bensenville, IL: Scholastic Testing Service.

Wallace, D. B., & Gruber, H. E. (Eds.). (1989). *Creative people at work: 12 cognitive case studies*. New York: Oxford University Press.

Wallach, M. A. (1971). *The intelligence/creativity distinction*. Morristown, NJ: General Learning Press.

Wallach, M., & Kogan, N. (1965a). *Modes of thinking in young children*. New York: Holt, Rinehart & Winston.

Wallach, M., & Kogan, N. (1965b). A new look at the creativity-intelligence distinction. *Journal of Personality, 33*, 348–369.

Weisberg, R. W. (1999). Creativity and knowledge: A challenge to theories. In R. J. Sternberg (Ed.), *Handbook of creativity* (pp. 226–250). New York: Cambridge University Press.

2

EVERYONE HAS CREATIVE POTENTIAL

MARK A. RUNCO

Creativity is notoriously difficult to define and measure. This is probably because it is complex, with various forms of expression, and because it is overdetermined, with multiple potential influences. Creativity is certainly not the same thing as intelligence or giftedness. Like creativity, these may involve problem solving, but sometimes it is better to look at creativity as a kind of self-expression, and sometimes it involves problem finding in addition to problem solving (see Runco, 1994a). In this sense, creativity is distinct from other forms of talent.

Probably the only thing on which everyone agrees is that creativity involves originality. This does not imply that creativity is merely a kind of originality; originality is necessary but not sufficient for creativity. Sadly, the agreement on originality leads directly to another question. After all, originality requires a careful definition, just as creativity did. Fortunately, originality is amenable to operational definition. Originality can, for example, be defined in terms of statistical infrequency. Original things are uncommon. They might be unique, or they might merely be unusual—the difference is a matter of degree. Originality is also suggested by novelty. These characteristics can be objectively determined. If only one person out of 1,000 produces a particular solution to a particular problem, that specific solution can be objectively defined as unique and therefore original.

This view that creativity must involve originality has several practical implications. For one, it suggests that original behavior has value. Clearly, it is useful for individuals in any society to recognize conventions, and frequently to conform, for this is a large part of what allows a society or even a small group to communicate and cooperate. Yet some of the time there is no moral, legal, or ethical reason for conformity, and it may be that nonconformity can lead to original and useful behaviors. Both conventional behavior and original behavior have value, though perhaps at different times.

This chapter assumes that there is value in creativity and originality, and in a manner of speaking attempts a very modest demonstration. You might say I am attempting to practice what I briefly preached: Very likely my answer to the question of who is creative (which is explicit in the title to this chapter) will be an uncommon one. I trust the reader will consider the value of this perspective, even if it muddies the scientific waters. As we will see, the objectivity required by the scientific method is more easily found if we focus on individual differences, and in particular on unambiguous cases of creativity, namely famous creative persons. If we focus on eminent individuals, there is a high level of agreement, and whence objectivity.

What exactly is the uncommon answer to which I am referring? The question was, "who is creative?" And the answer is, "everyone." Everyone is creative.

In this chapter I intend to support that position. For the most part, I will apply the theory of *personal creativity* as justification. In the first part of this chapter I review the existing theory of personal creativity. I also draw from the research on mental models in an attempt to diagram the process underlying personal creativity. Because this is the first time I have attempted to apply the theory of personal creativity specifically to the distribution issue that is implied by the "who is creative?" question, in the next section of this chapter I explore individual differences and universals: If everyone is creative, there should be identifiable universals. In the third section of this chapter I attempt to demonstrate that personal creativity can be objectively studied, and that the assumptions of this theory are consistent with those which are quite common in the sciences, and in particular in psychometrics and measurement theory. In this light we will not lose anything scientifically if we recognize that everyone—not just the eminent or unambiguously productive—is creative.

PERSONAL CREATIVITY

Elsewhere I defined personal creativity, suggesting that it is "*manifested in the intentions and motivation to transform the objective world into original interpretations, coupled with the ability to decide when this is useful and when it is not*" (Runco, 1996, p. 4). I devoted that earlier article to exploring the key features of personal creativity, namely *transformational capacity*, *discretion*, and *intentionality*.

What is most important for present purposes is that the interpretive and transformational bases of personal creativity are universal or nearly universal. Transformations are apparent whenever an individual constructs a new understanding. We do not merely absorb experience; we filter and select it. That is the connection between the transformational capacity and interpretation. Piaget (1976) claimed that "to understand is to invent" (the title of his book, actually), and his theory—and much of the more recent views of cognition—support the role of interpretations and personal constructions of meaning. Universality is implied by the fact that interpretations are a part of most everyone's experiences. Surely not everyone performs creatively, nor is anyone creative all of the time. Highly creative people often rely on rote interpretations, for example, and some people find them more comfortable and easier than original ones, and thus rely primarily on them.

Interpretation is not the only important aspect of creative efforts. The individual needs to invest the time and effort, and this assumes some sort of interest and motivation. It also assumes that the individual is willing to explore and postpone closure. This is because creative insights are often not the first things that come to mind; they are remote (Mednick, 1962; Runco, 1986). Thus the individual may need to construct an interpretation that is merely the first step down a potentially meaningful chain of ideas and potential solutions. Note, then, that we have several things besides the interpretive capacity involved in the process (i.e., willingness to postpone closure, motivation). Ego strength should be added to this list because creative ideas are always original, and this means they may be surprising or risky. Not everyone will appreciate them because they are original and unexpected. The creative individual may need ego-strength to withstand pressures to conform and to forego original ideas in favor of more conventional ones.

Practically speaking, this line of thought may suggest that we exclude the transformational (interpretive) bases of creative potential from our enhancement and measurement efforts. After all, interpretive capacity is universally distributed. Perhaps, then, we need not worry about them or waste our time with them. Perhaps there will be a more notable payoff if enhancement and educational efforts focus on those other factors, namely ego-strength, motivation, and openness. But there is something associated with interpretations that would benefit from education and the like. It is suggested by the discretionary aspect of personal creativity and is summarized by the idea that the individual not only can transform experience into a meaningful interpretation but also knows when to do so, and when not to do so. This discretionary process is essentially decision making, and no doubt it would benefit from opportunities like those involved in other decision making. Kohlberg's (1987) theory of moral reasoning also involves judgments and decisions, and a number of programs have been designed to help children learn about their own decision making. These might be adapted to judgments about when to be original and when not to be original.

This reference to Kohlberg (1987) may remind us that the theory of personal creativity recognizes children's efforts as original. They too construct original interpretations. They do not always convince others of the value of their insights, but the insights are often a part of children's imaginative play, and as such there is no function required, no need to convince anyone of anything. Similarly, children may not be productive; but products are unimportant for personal creativity. They may also be unimportant for everyday creativity (Runco & Richards, 1998).

The recognition of potential—by the definition of personal creativity, and by educators, for that matter—is vitally important. If we want to have the most bang for our buck, for instance, we should not work with individuals who are already behaving in a creative fashion, but should instead work with individuals who have potential but are not yet in a position to actually perform in a creative manner. Potential and actual performance (and productivity) are mutually exclusive of each other. If someone (gifted child or otherwise) is productive, then they are productive—there is no need to consider their potential. Conversely, if they are not yet productive, they may have potential, but they are not productive. In this sense the individual is one or the other and cannot be both.

As noted above, productivity is too often viewed as a requisite part of creativity. These theories of productivity (see Runco, 1995) each assumed that creative work had value to some audience, or had impact, or changed the way a group or society as a whole thought. It is not just productivity that is the problem, then, but the assumption that creativity is necessarily social and consensual (Runco, 1999a). Productivity per se is probably included in so many contemporary definitions because it allows objectivity, and therefore certainty of measurement. It also allows those responsible for identification or assessment to avoid the numerous problems that follow from subjective assessments.

One of the problems with productivity is that it relies on information about unambiguous cases (e.g., Picasso, Einstein), but this information might in turn lead us to believe that certain factors, shared by those cases, are critical for the development of talent. But research like this begins with individuals who are productive and then moves backwards. It cannot, therefore, tell us much with any certainty about the development of persons who did not begin by being productive. We cannot identify these persons by relying on productivity. If nothing else, we cannot make very general generalizations from the research on unambiguous cases to ambiguous cases.

Another problem with product definitions and approaches is that they are not very psychological. People are not studied; objects (again, e.g., works of art or publications) constitute the subject matter. At most, psychological descriptions and explanations are inferred from productivity patterns. In this sense product approaches rely just as much on inference as on studies of potential (which infer performance in the form of predictions).

There is an ethical and moral issue at hand. As Toynbee (1964) put it:

> It is obviously the outstandingly able individual's moral duty to make a return to society by using his unfettered ability in a public-spirited way and not just for selfish purposes. *But society, on its side, has a moral duty to ensure that the individual's potential ability is given free play.* (p. 5, emphasis added)

A MODEL OF PERSONAL INTERPRETATIONS

Cognitive integration models may provide one means for representing the process that underlies personal interpretations and personal creativity. Simplifying a great deal, imagine someone who is faced with an open-ended problem. That person's decision about which idea to pursue (cognitively and behaviorally) is likely to be multivariate; several factors may come into play. Picture each of these in an equation, with the result being the final decision. That equation could look something like this:

Decision = Factor 1(A) + Factor 2 (B) + Factor 3 (C). . . . Factor N (Z)

The parenthetical elements represent the weight (or importance) that that particular individual gives to each specific factor in that particular situation. Again, I am simplifying, but suppose you have a creative individual who is in the classroom and has an opportunity to answer the divergent thinking (open-ended) question, "Can you name strong things?" with the answer "Superman." This individual may consider factors such as (a) the teacher's reaction, (b) his or her best friend's reaction, (c) the other students' reaction, and (d) his sense of pride or appreciation of original thinking. A creative student may dismiss the possibility that the peers will laugh at his idea ("Superman") because it is a cartoon character and therefore immature. In the equation above, the weight given to that factor would be negligible. The student may give his best friend's reaction a slightly higher weight, and a slightly higher one yet to his or her own pride, but give a large weight to the teacher's reaction. Another child, who has an equivalent cognitive capacity to the first student, may take the same factors into account but weight them differently. This second student may weigh the reaction by the other students most heavily, and although he or she considers "Superman" as one possible answer to the question of Strong Things, this child is more likely to answer with a more conventional and unoriginal idea. Obviously decisions like this may change depending on situations, and either of these students may change the originality of their ideation depending on what factors are relevant and how they each weigh the relevant factors.

Perhaps most important in this simple equation and mental model is that decisions are multivariate and a function of both factors and weights.

This may be why we are sometimes surprised by the thinking, interpretations, and creativity (or lack thereof) of other people. We may assume that they are cognizant of certain factors because we are. Or we may assume that they will think like we do because we know how important certain things are—but they then surprise us! That surprise may result from the fact that the other person formulates his or her own interpretation and does so by taking factors into account that we do not or by weighing factors differently from the way that we ourselves do. Parents may appreciate this explanation if they have ever wondered, "How could my child do that?" These parents may be certain that the child is taking X, Y, and Z into account—after all, those things might be similar to events from previous experiences. Yet those factors may not be important to a child. This is why I gave an example with peers just above; sometimes preadolescents or adolescents surprise parents by what they do, and it may be because in this age the weight given to fitting in and being a part of one's peer group is much higher than those given to family values and the things that have been considered when the adolescent was younger. This equation may explain why parents occasionally ask their children, "What were you thinking?" They know that their own children are aware of certain things (certain factors), but what they do not know is how the child weighs those things or how those weights may change as the child grows older.

The fourth grade slump (Runco, 1999b) may reflect a change in weighing tendencies. Indeed, creative insights probably either reflect the individual's weighing originality, independent thinking, or surprise heavily, and rote, unoriginal, conventional thinking must reflect the individual's weighing appropriateness, getting along with others, and so on most heavily. Contrarians probably weigh uniqueness as all-important, and persons who are creative by generating ideas with what Bruner (1962) called "effective surprise" clearly weight both originality and fit when interpreting options. For more detailed explanations of cognitive integration, and evidence that it occurs (and occurs differently in different age groups), consult Anderson (1980) or Dawes (1979).

OBJECTIVITY AND CREATIVE POTENTIAL

The product approach to creativity may appear to offer more objectivity than theories like that describing personal creativity. Yet psychometric theory recognizes discrepancies, like those we may see between potential and performance. Consider the following description by Sprinthall (2000):

> To a statistician, the word error equals deviation and does not imply a mistake. Hence, a standard error always refers to a standard deviation, or a value designating the amount of variation of the measures around the

mean. It was originally called "error" by the German mathematician Karl Fredrich Gauss, the father of the normal curve. In the early 19th century, Gauss had used the term error to describe the variations in the measure of "true" physical qualities, such as the measurement error made by astronomers in determining the true position of a star at any given moment in time. The idea behind the current use of the concept of the "standard error" was largely formulated during the latter half of the nineteenth century by Sir Francis Galton (1822–1911). Galton noted that a wide variety of human measures, both physical and psychological, conform graphically to the Gaussian, bell-shaped curve. Galton used this curve not for differentiating true values and false values but as a method of evaluating population data on the basis of their members' variation from the population mean. Galton saw with steady clarity the importance of the normal curve in evaluating measures of human traits. Thus, to Galton, error came to mean deviation from the average, not falsity or inaccuracy. The greater the error among any set of measures, then, the greater their deviation from the mean, and the lower their frequency of occurrence. Said Galton, "there is scarcely anything so apt to impress the imagination of the wonderful form of cosmic order expressed by the law of frequency of error. The law would have been personified by the Greeks and deified, if they had known of it." (pp. 145–146)

The reason I quote Sprinthall in such detail is because he covers not only deviation and measurement but also the normal curve. Each of these topics is directly relevant to this chapter. The normal curve, for instance, is assumed in theories like those of the present chapter, namely that creativity (or at least creative potential) is widely distributed. A wide distribution does not in any way suggest that everyone is equal; it merely suggests that the trait or capacity is found through the full range of human genotypes. Here it is *creative potential* that is so widely distributed.

The other specific issue in the lengthy quotation above is that of error as deviation. I would suggest that the measurement error described above, and in all statistical and psychometric textbooks, can be applied here in the sense that any one observation of an individual's creativity is not going to be perfectly indicative of his or her true creative potential. This is a vitally important point for the theory of personal creativity because it assumes that we can look to potential and do not need to go overboard with objectivity. Exaggerated objectivity takes us to a creative-products perspective and away from creative persons, and further away from creative potentials. By definition, creative potential is not expressed. If it is expressed it becomes actual performance, which is exclusive of potential. There will always be a discrepancy, then, between performance (what we observe) and true creative potential. That discrepancy is acceptable in statistical terms, and in psychometric terms, and it should be acceptable in theories of creativity. Indeed, as Sprinthall (2000) and other statisticians explicitly note, error is to be expected. You cannot get around it. You might minimize it by avoiding certain sources of error, but deviation, and therefore error, are a part of science (and life!). Again, the critical point is that it is perfectly acceptable to have a discrepancy between performance and potential, and therefore acceptable to develop theories that acknowledge potential and do not relegate it in favor of actual observed performances.

This view is consistent with a suggestion I put forth some time ago. When I first made the suggestion, it did not seem too grand, but I have come to find out it does support the position of the current chapter. I am referring to a suggestion that we stop using the term *creativity*. I proposed that *creativity* is too ambiguous a term for the sciences. Of course I am not suggesting that we terminate our investigation of creativity, but that we do not use the noun *creativity* and only use the term in its adjectival form. We would then investigate and discuss creative *performance*, creative *potential*, creative *behavior*, creative *personality*, creative *products*, and so on. This approach would ensure that we do not confuse creative potential with something that is very different: namely, actual creative performance. I should, then, reword my claim: Everyone has creative *potential*. That is probably much easier to accept. It certainly is consistent with a large number of psychological theories, including those of Kohlberg (1987) and Piaget (1976), for they often emphasize potential (and the related concept of competence) and assume that actual performance will naturally occur (see also Duska & Whelan, 1975).

CONCLUSIONS

Several key questions guided the production of this volume. These can be addressed in a fairly precise fashion now that I have outlined the theory of personal creativity.

First is the question that apparently led to the design of this volume. The editors asked, "What do you mean by *creativity?*" The ideas in this chapter might be applied here such that creative persons are capable and interested in applying their interpretive capacities and will put effort into constructing original interpretation of experience. They probably do so regularly, many times each day, but they may also bring this interpretive tendency to bear on notable problems. What is most important is that the interpretive capacity is universal, but it is only an indication of potential; creative performance requires more. Actual performance requires motivation (Amabile, in press; Runco, 1994b) and ego-strength (Barron, 1998; Runco, 1996), just to name two important requirements. Expert-level performance probably also requires a large knowledge base, although here we need to recognize that knowledge can be inhibitive (Rubenson & Runco, 1995). Clearly the answer to the question of what is meant by creativity depends on whether you are talking about creative potential (which is universal and generalized) or creative performance. To the question "What attributes lead to creativity in various fields of endeavors?" we can look to universals (e.g., interpretive skill, ego-strength) and individual differences (e.g., information within the specific field).

Then there is the question of enhancement. The theory of personal creativity outlined in this chapter implies that enhancement efforts are potentially very effective. They can even take someone with moderate potential and provide the strategies and necessary skills, the result being that this individual actually performs at a higher level than someone who has more potential but is disinterested or not strategic in his or her efforts. This assumes that the two individuals have ranges of potential that overlap, but the range of a person's creative potential is probably fairly large, and overlap is likely. Note that domains are relevant here, for many individuals may not be interested in applying themselves (and fulfilling potential) because they have not found a domain that captures their interest. Potential goes unfulfilled.

Creativity is extremely valuable to individuals and society as a whole. It is related to productivity, adaptability, and health, and it benefits individuals, institutions, and societies. For this reason, I believe that we should be willing to take reasonable risks. These may be necessary because by dealing with potential, we could make mistakes. We could be wrong that the individual will eventually perform in an unambiguously creative manner. Of course, I would call it a victory even if that individual does not actually impress anyone with creative insights but instead merely fulfills some of his or her creative potential.

People are often willing to take a greater risk if they have little to lose and a smaller risk if they have a great deal to lose. Turning this on its head, I am merely suggesting that the potential payoffs in studying creativity, for enhanced productivity, adaptability, and health would support investigations even if creative potential is not an objective and certain thing—even if it is just a personal thing.

REFERENCES

Amabile, T. (in press). Within you, without you. In M. A. Runco & R. S. Albert (Eds.), *Theories of creativity* (Rev. ed.). Cresskill, NJ: Hampton Press.

Anderson, N. H. (1980). Information integration theory in developmental psychology. In F. Wilkening, J. Beden, & T. Trabasso (Eds.), *Information integration by children* (pp. 1–45). Hillsdale, NJ: Erlbaum.

Barron, F. (1998). *No rootless flower*. Cresskill, NJ: Hampton Press.

Bruner, J. (1962). The conditions of creativity. In J. Bruner (Ed.), *Beyond the information given: Studies in the psychology of knowing* (pp. 208–217). New York: Norton.

Dawes, R. (1979). The robust beauty of improper linear models in decision making. *American Psychologist, 34,* 571–582.

Duska, R., & Whelan, M. (1975). *Moral development: A guide to Piaget and Kohlberg.* New York: Paulist Press.

Kohlberg, L. (1987). The development of moral judgment and moral action. In L. Kohlberg (Ed.), *Child psychology and childhood education: A cognitive developmental view.* New York: Longman.

Mednick, S. A. (1962). The associative basis of the creative process. *Psychological Review, 69,* 220–232.

Piaget, J. (1976). *To understand is to invent.* New York: Penguin.

Rubenson, D. L., & Runco, M. A. (1995). The psychoeconomic view of creative work in groups and organizations. *Creativity and Innovation Management, 4,* 232–241.

Runco, M. A. (1986). Flexibility and originality in children's divergent thinking. *Journal of Psychology, 120,* 345–352.

Runco, M. A. (1994a). Conclusions regarding problem finding, problem solving, and creativity. In M. A. Runco (Ed.), *Problem finding, problem solving, and creativity* (pp. 272–290). Norwood, NJ: Ablex.

Runco, M. A. (1994b). Creativity and its discontents. In M. P. Shaw & M. A. Runco (Eds.), *Creativity and affect* (pp. 102–123). Norwood, NJ: Ablex.

Runco, M. A. (1995). Insight for creativity, expression for impact. *Creativity Research Journal, 8,* 377–390.

Runco, M. A. (1996, Summer). Personal creativity: Definition and developmental issues. *New Directions for Child Development, 72,* 3–30.

Runco, M. A. (1999a). Creativity need not be social. In A. Montuori & R. Purser (Eds.), *Social creativity* (Vol. 1, pp. 237–264). Cresskill, NJ: Hampton.

Runco, M. A. (1999b). The fourth-grade slump. In M. A. Runco & Steven Pritzker (Eds.), *Encyclopedia of creativity* (pp. 743–744). San Diego, CA: Academic Press.

Runco, M. A., & Richards, R. (Eds.). (1998). *Eminent creativity, everyday creativity, and health.* Norwood, NJ: Ablex.

Sprinthall, R. (2000). *Basic statistical analysis* (6th ed.) Boston: Allyn & Bacon.

Toynbee, A. (1964). Is America neglecting her creative minority? In C. W. Taylor (Ed.), *Widening horizons in creativity* (pp. 3–9). New York: Wiley.

3

THE ARTISTIC PERSONALITY: A SYSTEMS PERSPECTIVE

SAMI ABUHAMDEH AND MIHALY CSIKSZENTMIHALYI

"Why do people think artists are special? It's just another job."
—Andy Warhol (1975, p. 178)

When considering the relationship between personality and a given occupation or vocation, we usually assume the relationship remains invariant over time. One might assume, for instance, that the temperament and traits that distinguished military leaders in the 5th century BCE would be the same traits as those belonging to warriors in the Middle Ages, or in our own times. Yet the changes throughout history in the social and economic status of soldiers, and in the technology of warfare, suggest that the personalities of men (or women) attracted to a military career will be quite different in each period.

This variability is very obvious in the case of artists. Until the end of the 15th century in Europe, when even the greatest artists were considered to be merely craftsmen and when works of art required the collaboration of several individuals, the typical artist did not display the eccentric, fiercely independent qualities of the "artistic personality" that we now take for granted. In the words of an eminent sociologist of art, "The artist's studio in the early Renaissance is still dominated by the communal spirit of the mason's lodge and the guild workshop; the work of art is not yet the expression of an independent personality" (Hauser, 1951, pp. 54–55).

By the middle of the 16th century, however, several artists had become celebrities, in part, because now that painting in oils on canvas was the favorite medium of expression they could work alone, and also because their status had been elevated by such stars as Michelangelo, Leonardo, and Raphael. Thus, Vasari, who in 1550 published the biographies of the "most eminent artists" in Italy, complained that nature had given the artists of his time "a certain element of savagery and madness, which, besides making them strange and eccentric . . . revealed in them the obscure darkness of vice rather than the brightness and splendor of those virtues that make men immortal" (Vasari, 1550/1959, p. 22).

The popular idea of artistic temperament embodied in Vasari's view went through several transformations in the past five centuries, but many of its basic traits have endured. One of the most prominent American painters of the past generation, Jackson Pollock, is a good illustration of that "savagery and madness" Vasari complained about. He spent most of his 44 years battling alcoholism, depression, and self-doubt (Solomon, 1987), and his stormy marriage to artist Lee Krasner was a source of unrelenting torment. When Pollock painted, he did it with a passion bordering on madness, hurling paint across the canvas in an all-out blitzkrieg of emotion, determined to give life to his singular vision.

Psychological studies suggest that artists are emotional (Barron, 1972), sensitive, independent, impulsive, and socially aloof (Csikszentmihalyi & Getzels, 1973; Walker, Koestner, & Hum, 1995), introverted (Storr, 1988), and nonconforming (Barton & Cattell, 1972). But how pervasive are these traits among successful artists—the personalities who actually shape the domain of art? Is there really such a thing as a timeless, constitutional artistic personality?

In this chapter we propose that the notion of the "artistic personality" is more myth than fact. Although it describes some of the traits that distinguish aspiring artists at certain times under certain conditions, these traits are in no sense required to create valuable art at all times, in all places. We argue that artistic creativity is as much a social and cultural phenomenon as it is an intrapsychic one. And because the social and cultural constraints on the artistic process vary significantly across time and place, the nature of the artistic personality will vary accordingly. When the predominant style or styles of a period change—from Abstract Expressionism to Op Art, Conceptual Art, Photorealism, let us say—so will the personalities of the artists.

We begin with an overview of the theoretical framework that guides this chapter—the systems model of creativity.

THE SYSTEMS MODEL OF CREATIVITY

Creativity has traditionally been viewed as a mental process, as the insight of an individual. The majority of past psychological research on creativity, accordingly, has concentrated on the thought processes, emotions, and motivations of individuals who produce novelty: the "creative personality." However, beginning with the observations of Morris Stein (Stein, 1953, 1963) and continuing with the extensive data presented by Dean Simonton (1988, 1990) showing the influence of economic, political, and social events on the rates of creative production, it has become increasingly clear that variables external to the individual must be considered if one wishes to explain why, when, and from where new ideas or products arise and become established in a culture (Gruber, 1988; Harrington, 1990).

The systems model proposes that creativity can be observed only in the interrelations of a system made up of three main elements. The first of these is the *domain*, which consists of information—a set of rules, procedures, and instructions for action. To do anything creative, one must operate within a domain. Art is a domain, and the various styles and movements within art can be considered subdomains.

The second component of a system is the *field*, which includes all the individuals who act as gatekeepers to the domain. It is their job to decide whether a new idea or product should be added to the domain. In the world of art, the field consists of the art critics and art historians, the art dealers and art collectors, and the artists themselves. Collectively, this group selects the art products that become recognized as legitimate art.

The final component of the system is the *individual*. In the systems model, creativity occurs when a person makes a change in the information contained in a domain, a change that will be selected by the field for inclusion in the domain.

As this overview of the systems model suggests, the nature of the creative individual—and therefore the artistic personality—is dependent on the nature of the domain and field in which the individual operates. Therefore, to gain a meaningful assessment of the artistic personality, we must pay attention to these other two components of the system. We begin with the domain.

The Domain of Art

During the premodern era, the domain of art was relatively homogeneous in its vocabulary. It consisted almost entirely of figurative works recalling images of religious, philosophical, or historical significance that were widely shared by most members of society. With the arrival of modernism, however, an explosion of artistic styles and movements broadened the boundaries of art considerably. This "de-definition of art" (Rosenberg, 1972) has continued during the postmodern era, at warp speed, rendering all tidy definitions of art obsolete.

To illustrate the relationship between the content of artwork and the personality of the artist, we use a classification scheme based on two dimensions of stylistic content, *representational versus abstract* and *linear versus painterly* (see Figure 3.1).[1] These two dimensions are among a set of five critical

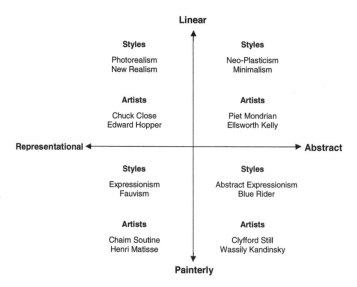

Figure 3.1. The domain of modern and contemporary painting can be described by two continuous dimensions, *representational–abstract* and *linear–painterly*. Examples of artists and styles for each of the quadrants are given.

dimensions of stylistic content first proposed by the art historian Heinrich Wolfflin (1929), and later validated by empirical research (e.g., Cupchik, 1974; Loomis & Saltz, 1984) as important for differentiating artistic styles. The first dimension, *representational versus abstract*, refers to the degree to which a particular artwork imitates an external reference; the second dimension, *linear versus painterly*, represents the degree to which the content of an artwork is characterized by precisely controlled line and distinct figures (i.e., linear) as opposed to loosely handled paint and relatively undefined form (i.e., painterly).[2]

The diversity of stylistic content represented by the two dimensions within the domain of painting are the outward manifestations of a corresponding diversity in artistic processes and artistic experience. First, let us consider the representational–abstract dimension. Artists painting in a predominantly representational manner have clear external references toward which they can direct their artistic activity—a person, an object, a scene, or any and all combinations. Artists are able to accurately monitor their progress by comparing their work with these external references. Indeed, the success of the work is highly dependent on the artist making such comparisons repeatedly and skillfully.

For those artists working in a nonrepresentational manner, the creative process differs considerably. There is little or no objective referent toward which artists can guide their activity, no clear challenges and goals to pursue.

---

[1]For practical reasons, we limit our discussion of the domain of art to Western painting.
[2]Clearly, the two dimensions of the classification system are not completely independent. The more "painterly" a style is, for example, the less "representational" it is likely to be.

Whereas the artistic process for the representational artist is highly structured, driven by constraints imposed by the task of representation, abstract artists must actively impose structure on the artistic process, relying on feelings or concepts to guide the process. Susan Rothenberg, who works in a predominantly abstract style, commented on this formidable challenge: "I struggle with it all the time, and a straightforward portrait would be a kind of anchor. I envy Lucian Freud and Chuck Close [two artists with highly representational styles], waking up every morning and knowing what they're going to do" (Kimmelman, 1998, p. 178).

The linear–painterly dimension is also associated with significant variety in artistic process and experience. For the artist who paints in a linear style, the artistic process must be exact and focused. Attentional resources are necessarily directed outward, away from the self, toward the technical demands of the task. Because of this, the process tends to be associated with secondary-process cognition (Fromm, 1978)—rational and reality-oriented—and devoid of strong emotion. In contrast, the artist who paints using the looser brushstrokes of painterly styles is not bound by the rigid stylistic constraints of the linear style, and is therefore able to allow primary-process cognition—free-associative, irrational, and often emotional—to drive the process. As a result, the creative process is often more improvisational in nature.

The significant relationship among style and experience is exemplified by comparing the following two accounts of the artistic process. The first account is by Clyfford Still, one of the original Abstract Expressionists, and the second is by Chuck Close, a Photo Realist famous for his mural-sized, eerily lifelike portraits.

> A great free joy surges through me when I work . . . with tense slashes and a few thrusts the beautiful white fields receive their color and the work is finished in a few minutes. (Like Belmonte [the bullfighter] weaving the pattern of his being by twisting the powerful bulls around him, I seem to achieve a comparable ecstasy in bringing forth the flaming life through these large areas of canvas. And as the blues or reds or blacks leap and quiver in their tenuous ambience or rise in austere thrusts to carry their power infinitely beyond the bounds of the limiting field, I move with them and find a resurrection from the moribund oppressions that held me only hours ago.) Only they are complete too soon, and I must quickly move on to another to keep the spirit alive and unburdened by the labor my Puritan reflexes tell me must be the cost of my joy. (Lucie-Smith, 1999, p. 184)

Clearly, the artistic process for Clyfford Still was an expressive, intensely personal experience. Contrast this with the artistic process of Chuck Close, as described by his biographers, Lisa Lyons and Robert Storr (1987):

> Propped on an easel to his left are the griddled photographs he refers to as he paints; a shelf on the right carries a telephone and two other important pieces of equipment: a television and a radio/cassette deck. The

background noise they provide helps him to maintain that subtle degree of detachment he needs from the tedious activity of building an image, part by part, with machine-like precision. In the past, Close listened to (but did not watch) television almost constantly while working, becoming in the process a connoisseur of morning game shows and afternoon soap operas. Their slow-paced soundtracks are "of such a mundane nature that you don't really get engaged," he once said. "It's like having a dumb friend in the room. It just chatters away and you don't have to respond to it."

Personality Implications

That significantly different artistic processes exist within the domain of art has significant implications for attempts to define the nature of the artistic personality. More specifically, it suggests that the kinds of traits optimally suited to the creation of art will be dependent on the specific kind of art being created. For example, an artist who is extroverted, sociable, and moved by external norms would not be well-suited to create introspective work, as it requires a special sensitivity to private inner events. Conversely, an introverted artist would have a hard time being noticed if the prevailing style of the domain consisted in polished representations of the objective world.

Although past research on the relationship between artistic style and personality has been relatively sparse, the results of these studies support the idea of a significant relationship between the personality of the artist and the type of art he or she produces. Dudek and Marchand (1983) found a strong correspondence between artists' painting styles and the degree to which they exhibited cognitive defenses and controls. Artists who had lower cognitive defenses and controls (assessed using the Rorschach test) tended to paint in a loosely controlled, painterly manner, whereas artists who were more rigid in their psychological defenses painted in a more formal, linear style. In a study that examined the relationship between personality and the representational–abstract dimension, Loomis and Saltz (1984) found that "rational cognitive styles" were associated with representational artistic styles, whereas "irrational cognitive styles" were associated with abstract styles. Furthermore, extroverts tended to have representational styles, whereas introverts tended to have more abstract styles.

Perhaps the most compelling empirical support for a significant relationship between the personality of an artist and his artistic style comes from a study by Ludwig (1998). He compared the lifetime rates of mental disorder among artists whose work was primarily *formal* (emphasizing structural, compositional, or decorative elements) with rates of mental disorder among artists whose work was primarily *emotive* (emphasizing self-expression).[3] Results

---

[3] In the study, Ludwig also classified the works of certain artists as "symbolic." Because we do not use this classification category in the present chapter, Ludwig's findings relating to symbolic styles are not discussed here.

were dramatic: the incidence of lifetime mental disorder among the artists in the emotive category was more than three times the incidence of mental disorder among artists in the formal category—22% versus 75%, respectively ($p < .001$).

These results point to a significant relationship between the personality of the artist and the stylistic content of the art he or she produces. Next, we examine the field's role in shaping the personality traits that are characteristic of recognized artists.

The Field of Art

> "We are not the masters of what we produce. It is imposed upon us."
> —Henri Matisse (Seuphor, 1961, p. 16)

Artists have traditionally been perceived as individuals working in relative isolation, free to follow their creative urges. "Like most geniuses," wrote Ambrose Vollard, friend and biographer of Degas, "[Degas] was essentially independent of events, persons, and places, refusing to be limited by time and disregarding as unimportant everything which did not include and enrich his work"(Vollard, 1986, p. 5).

A consideration of the forces at work suggests a less romantic image. One does not become an artist simply by making art. To earn a living and develop a self-concept as a bona fide artist distinct from a dilettante, one must be legitimated by the appropriate art institutions. Only when the artist's work has been recognized by the *field* of art—the critics, historians, dealers, collectors, curators, and fellow artists—can the artist continue to focus his or her energies on creating art.

So what does the art world look for? An artwork will only be accepted as significant if it provides a meaningful extension (aesthetic, political, moral, etc.) to the catalogue of past artistic achievements, the so-called "grand narrative" of art. The greater the contribution to the story, the more significant the work is judged to be. "The imperative to make abstract art comes from history," wrote the famous critic Clement Greenberg in 1940, when Abstract Expressionism was just beginning to take hold of the art world, "and the artist is held in a vise from which at the present moment he can escape only by surrendering his ambition and returning to a stale past" (Greenberg, 1940, p. 310).

If an artist creates artwork that does not fulfill the needs of the field, that artist will be dismissed or ignored. Leon Golub, who like so many other artists spent a significant amount of his career living and working in New York, commented on the pressures often felt by artists and created by the field pursuing its rigid agenda:

> The critics were angry about my art. New York seemed impenetrable. I was devastated by some of the reactions, so we [Golub and his wife, artist

Nancy Spero] decided to leave because, frankly, we didn't have whatever it took to fight New York and the atmosphere of that time. There was, and still is, a force in New York, you see, that pushes art in certain directions—ideologically, rhetorically, and rather strongly. (Kimmelman, 1998, p. 178)

Because of the field's perpetual need for novelty, the field's aesthetic preference is guaranteed to change constantly. Within a given artistic style, this change is characterized by, among other things, an increase in complexity and unpredictability (Martindale, 1990). These changes maintain the field's interest in a given style, warding off habituation and boredom. When the style has exhausted its potential for interest, the field will be actively looking for works that hold promise for ushering in a new paradigm.

Consider the emergence of Pop Art in the late 1950s. The first Pop Art paintings appeared at a time when interest and faith in Abstract Expressionism was on the wane. Warhol's mass-produced paintings were not only novel in concept, they also provided a meaningful contrast to the highly expressive paintings of Pollock, de Kooning, and other leading Abstract Expressionists. In other words, Abstract Expressionism created the opportunity for Pop Art to emerge. It is unlikely that Pop Art would have appeared at another point in the history of art.

The nature of the art field's selection process has two important implications for the current topic under consideration, the artistic personality. The first is that, at any given point in time, there will be a constellation of personality traits that are optimally suited to create the kind of art the field will recognize as significant. The nature of these traits will be strongly determined by the nature of the domain. For example, if an abstract, painterly style such as Abstract Expressionism is reigning in the art world, emotional, introverted artists will have the advantage; if a realistic, linear style such as Social Realism is in vogue, more extroverted, unemotional dispositions will be favored. It is important to note, however, that the stylistic qualities of movements often change significantly during a movement's life span, so that different personality traits will be adaptive depending on the developmental stage of the movement (Kubler, 1962). For example, original, nonconforming types will flourish more during the early stages of a movement, when the task is to lay new foundations, rather than the later stages, when the task is to elaborate and refine already existing symbols and themes.

The second implication of the field's selection process, already suggested by the first, is that the artistic personality is not a stable, timeless personality type. As the field's taste for art changes, so too will the types of personalities creating the art that will be accepted as significant. Though it may have been adaptive at one point in history for artists to possess the traits associated with the archetypal "artistic personality"—introverted, nonconforming, socially aloof, and so forth—there is no reason to believe that these traits will continue to be adaptive, or even that they are adaptive in today's art world.

Indeed, a longitudinal study conducted by Getzels and Csikszentmihalyi (1976) suggests many of these traits are a recipe for failure in the contemporary art world.

A LONGITUDINAL STUDY OF ARTISTIC DEVELOPMENT AND ARTISTIC SUCCESS

The study involved 281 students at the prestigious Art Institute of Chicago. During the first phase of the study, the artists completed several personality questionnaires and engaged in problem-finding and problem-solving tasks designed to assess various dimensions of creativity. Twenty years later, 64 of the original 281 students were contacted. The primary focus of this second phase of the study was to identify and understand the factors that were most predictive of artistic success.

The picture that emerged was unexpected. Out of the handful of artists that did achieve some artistic success, the traits that distinguished them from their unrecognized peers were more characteristic of Wall Street marketing executives than what we have come to associate with artists. Compared with their less successful peers, these artists were more sociable, practical, and career-driven (Csikszentmihalyi, Getzels, & Kahn, 1984). "Unless you are a social beast," said one of the artists, "it is naïve to think you are going to make it." They also demonstrated a willingness to sacrifice personal expressivity in the service of artistic recognition. Instead of ignoring the business aspects of the art world, or pretending that they did not exist, the successful artists acknowledged, accommodated, and even embraced them. One artist put it this way: "Usually you can judge somebody's career orientation and ability in building a career by how good their career is. It has nothing to do with their art, it has everything to do with how they can build a career and who they know" (Freeman, 1993, p. 115).

Consider Jim, the most successful artist of the sample. Like the handful of other successful artists in the group, Jim had an acute understanding of how the business side of the art world worked. He tailored his art to accommodate it. "You need to have a monotheistic thing on the surface for business reasons," he pointed out. "This is not Versace. This is Robert Hall. It's on the racks, like small, medium, and large. These are made to order." Jim held no illusions about where his art fit into the system: "[Art] exists as a vehicle for criticism and writing" (Freeman, 1993, p. 193).

In art school, students whose traits resembled that of the archetypal artistic personality tended to be viewed by their teachers as very original and creative. But when students left school, those who lacked the extroversion, aggressiveness, and a knack for promoting themselves that attracted the attention of critics, gallery owners, and media tended to disappear from the art scene, never to be heard of again. Simpson (1981) went so far as to suggest that the "artistic mystique" has been perpetuated more by unsuccessful artists than successful artists, as a defense against artistic failure.

So we see that many of the traits traditionally associated with the artistic personality—nonconforming, socially aloof, impulsive—are incompatible with artistic success in the contemporary art world. The loft, the exhibition channels, the galleries, the New York art scene are all necessary steps a serious artist must be able and willing to negotiate. Yet these steps to success run counter to a large array of values and traits young artists hold dear and were encouraged to believe in. Today's art world is extremely inhospitable to the romantic image of the artist.

CONCLUSION

The systems perspective of the artistic personality admits that individual traits may be necessary for a person to be recognized as creative, but that these cannot be predicted a priori. The specific individual traits associated with the artistic personality will depend on characteristics of the other two subsystems, the domain of art and the field of art. A person who becomes a painter in a period when Abstract Expressionism is the reigning style will be more likely to be recognized if he or she possesses the emotional, imaginative, and introverted qualities that are well-suited for the creation of abstract, expressionistic art. Likewise, in a period when Photo Realism is in vogue, a cool, rational, and outward-oriented person will be more likely to make a contribution to the domain. Given the constantly evolving nature of both the domain of art and the field of art, the idea of the artistic personality as a timeless, constitutional personality type is therefore an improbable proposition.

The preceding analysis suggests that a construct as broad as the *artistic personality* may be of limited value if addressing questions related to individual differences in artistic creativity. Consider, for example, the relationship between psychopathology and artistic creativity. Though it seems reasonable to suggest a link between the psychological torment of artists like Frida Kahlo, James Ensor, and Vincent Van Gogh and their heavily affect-laden art, such a relationship in areas that allow for less self-expression (e.g., Photo-Realism, Minimalism, etc.) is highly questionable. Indeed, it is hard to imagine how psychopathology would be anything but a distraction.

It is important to keep in mind that our analysis has focused on one area of art, painting. In the highly diversified, "radical pluralism" (Danto, 1998)[4] of today's postmodern art world, painting constitutes just one of many media available to artists, ranging from audio and video installations to the human body to the natural landscape. Given that each of these me-

---

[4]Also referred to, less favorably, as the "post-Warholian nightmare" (Morgan, 1992, p. xvii).

dia involves unique artistic processes, we should expect the range of traits found among artists today to be even greater than our analysis in this chapter suggests.

Finally, it should be clear from all we have said that the same argument holds for any other profession or occupation. A biologist like Friedrich von Humboldt (1769–1859) was an explorer, adventurer, and naturalist; a century and a half later, E. O. Wilson (1929–) complains that the hegemony of molecular biology has transformed the domain into an abstract laboratory discipline (Csikszentmihalyi, 1996). It is unlikely that the personality of individuals attracted to biology in Humboldt's time would be the same as those who join the field now. The links between a domain and the personality of those who work in it are not rigidly forged but change organically as the domain itself changes with time.

REFERENCES

Barron, F. (1972). *Artists in the making.* New York: Seminar Press.

Barton, K., & Cattell, H. (1972). Personality characteristics of female psychology, science and art majors. *Psychological Reports, 31,* 807–813.

Csikszentmihalyi, M. (1996). *Creativity.* New York: HarperCollins.

Csikszentmihalyi, M., & Getzels, J. W. (1973). The personality of young artists: An empirical and theoretical exploration. *British Journal of Psychology, 64*(1), 91–104.

Csikszentmihalyi, M., Getzels, J. W., & Kahn, S. P. (1984). *Talent and achievement* (Report). Chicago: Spencer and MacArthur Foundations.

Cupchik, G. C. (1974). An experimental investigation of perceptual and stylistic dimensions of paintings suggested by art history. In D. E. Berlyne (Ed.), *Studies in the new experimental aesthetics* (pp. 235–257). New York: Wiley.

Danto, A. (1998). *After the end of art: Contemporary art and the pale of history.* Princeton, NJ: Princeton University Press.

Dudek, S. Z., & Marchand, P. (1983). Artistic style and personality in creative painters. *Journal of Personality Assessment, 47*(2), 139–142.

Freeman, M. (1993). *Finding the muse.* Cambridge, England: Cambridge University Press.

Fromm, E. (1978). Primary and secondary process in waking and in altered states of consciousness. *Journal of Altered States of Consciousness, 4,* 115–128.

Getzels, U. J. W., & Csikszentmihalyi, M. (1976). *The creative vision: A longitudinal study of problem finding in art.* New York: Wiley.

Greenberg, C. (1940). Towards a newer Laocoon. *Partisan Review, 3,* 296–310.

Gruber, H. (1988). The evolving systems approach to creative work. *Creativity Research Journal, 1*(1), 27–51.

Harrington, D. M. (1990). The ecology of human creativity: A psychological perspective. In M. A. Runco & R. S. Albert (Eds.), *Theories of creativity* (pp. 143–169). Newbury Park, CA: Sage.

Hauser, A. (1951). *The social history of art.* New York: Vintage.

Kimmelman, M. (1998). *Portraits: Talking with artists at the Met, the Modern, the Louvre, and elsewhere.* New York: Random House.

Kubler, G. (1962). *The shape of time.* New Haven: Yale University Press.

Loomis, M., & Saltz, E. (1984). Cognitive styles as predictors of artistic styles. *Journal of Personality, 52*(1), 22–35.

Lucie-Smith, E. (1999). *Lives of the great twentieth century artists.* London: Thames & Hudson.

Ludwig, A. (1998). Method and madness in the arts and sciences. *Creativity Research Journal, 11*(2), 93–101.

Lyons, L., & Storr, R. (1987). *Chuck Close.* New York: Rizzoli.

Martindale, C. (1990). *The clockwork muse.* New York: Basic Books.

Morgan, Robert. (1998). *The end of the art world.* New York: Allworth Press.

Rosenberg, H. (1972). *The de-definition of art.* Chicago: University of Chicago Press.

Seuphor, M. (1961). *Abstract painting: Fifty years of accomplishment, from Kandinsky to the present* (H. Chevalier, Trans.). New York: Harry Abrams.

Simonton, D. K. (1988). Age and outstanding achievement: What do we know after a century of research? *Psychological Bulletin, 104,* 163–180.

Simonton, D. K. (1990). Political pathology and societal creativity. *Creativity Research Journal, 3*(2), 85–99.

Simpson, C. R. (1981). *SoHo: The artist in the city.* Chicago: University of Chicago Press.

Solomon, D. (1987). *Jackson Pollock: A biography.* New York: Simon & Schuster.

Stein, M. I. (1953). Creativity and culture. *Journal of Psychology, 36,* 311–322.

Stein, M. I.(1963). A transactional approach to creativity. In C. W. Taylor & F. Barron (Eds.), *Scientific creativity* (pp. 217–227). New York: Wiley.

Storr, A. (1988). *Solitude: A return to the self.* New York: Free Press.

Vasari, G. (1959). *Lives of the artists.* Oxford, England: Oxford University Press. (Original work published 1550)

Vollard, A. (1986). *Degas, an intimate portrait.* New York: Dover.

Walker, A. M., Koestner, R., & Hum, A. (1995). Personality correlates of depressive style in autobiographies of creative achievers. *Journal of Creative Behavior, 29*(2), 75–94.

Warhol, A. (1975). *The philosophy of Andy Warhol.* San Diego: Harcourt.

Wolfflin, H. (1929). *Principles of art history: The problem of the development of style in later art* (7th rev. ed.). New York: Dover.

4

THE GENERALITY–SPECIFICITY OF CREATIVITY: A MULTIVARIATE APPROACH

TODD LUBART AND JACQUES-HENRI GUIGNARD

There is currently a debate about the nature of creativity. Is creativity a generalized ability that will lead to original thinking regardless of the task domain? Does creativity involve a set of domain-specific creative abilities (e.g., creativity in art, literature, business, science, etc.)? Within a domain, such as art, is it appropriate to speak of task-specific creative abilities; should we distinguish creativity in painting from creativity in sculpture, or creativity in sculpture with clay from creativity in sculpture with metal? Although it may seem paradoxical, we argue that the answer to each of these questions is "yes." Drawing on a multivariate approach to creativity, we suggest that creativity is partly a generalized ability, partly a set of domain-specific abilities, and partly a set of task-specific abilities.

WHAT IS CREATIVITY?

In general, creativity can be defined as the capacity to produce novel, original work that fits with task constraints (Lubart, 1994). Work refers to all types of ideas and productions. This work must be novel in the sense that it goes beyond a replication or copy of that which exists. The extent to which the work produced is novel can vary from being original only for the person who completed the work (this is the notion of reinventing ideas known already in the larger social context) to being original for a limited social group, to being original for all of humanity. Furthermore, within a given domain, there are different ways that an idea may be novel, or original. For example, it may (a) reiterate a known idea in a new way, (b) move a field forward along its current trajectory, (c) move a field forward in a new direction, or (d) lead to an integration of diverse trends in a field (Sternberg, Kaufman, & Pretz, 2002). In addition to novelty, the second defining component of creativity concerns the extent to which a proposed idea fits with constraints. We distinguish creative ideas from bizarre ideas, which are also novel, because creative ideas take into account the parameters of a situation, the constraints. Novel productions that are in some way useful in a given context are, thus, creative.

Contextual factors may modulate this general definition of creativity. For example, depending on the field of endeavor, the weight given to the two defining components of creativity—novelty and constraint satisfaction—varies. The field of art may be characterized by a strong emphasis on the novelty criterion and relatively little weight given to the constraint satisfaction criterion. For creativity in science and business settings, novelty and constraint satisfaction may be equally important. Similar contrasts in the relative importance of different parts of the definition of creativity may occur within a given domain, such as literary composition, with differences in the weight of novelty and constraint satisfaction varying across poetry, short stories, historical novels, and journalistic texts. The same kind of variations may occur within a task such as poetry composition, with differences between creativity in blank verse and creativity in sonnets or Haiku poems.

A recent study of artists' definitions of creativity showed both similarities and differences between "free" artists, such as painters and sculptors, and relatively "constrained" artists, such as architects or designers (Glück, Ernst, & Unger, 2002). Sixty-four Austrian artists completed a questionnaire concerning their definitions of creativity and the relative importance of various attributes of creative products. The free artists reported on average that originality and functionality (useful, technically correct, fulfilling its purpose) were both somewhat important with a slight advantage for originality; for the constrained artist group, the functionality component of creativity was markedly more important than the originality component.

For the domain specificity–generality debate, we can see that the definition of creativity lays the seeds for some generality of creativity (both novelty and constraint satisfaction are involved in general), as well as some domain- and task-level nuances in the specific definition of creativity. We can speak about creativity in general but we can also speak about field- or task-dependent "creativities."

WHAT ATTRIBUTES LEAD TO CREATIVITY?

Recent work concerning the attributes necessary for creativity has suggested that a combination of cognitive, conative, and environmental attributes are important. In general these proposals are called multivariate, componential, or confluence approaches because several attributes must converge to yield creative behavior. Theories vary on the nature of the components for creativity as well as the way that the components work together and interact with each other. Consider two proposals.

According to Amabile (1996), there are three components for creativity: domain-relevant skills, creativity-relevant processes, and task motivation. Domain-relevant skills include knowledge, technical skills, and special talents relevant to the task domain. For example, domain-relevant skills for creativity in science may be factual knowledge about a problematic phenomenon, technical skills for laboratory procedures, and a special talent for mental imagery. Creativity-relevant processes include a cognitive style that facilitates coping with complexity and breaking one's mental set during problem solving, the use of heuristics for generating novel ideas (e.g., trying a counterintuitive idea when stuck on a problem), and a work style characterized in part by persistence and sustained attention to a task. Task motivation involves an individual's reasons for engaging in a task and the person's attitude toward the task to be accomplished. Intrinsic motivation, considered important for creativity, arises from inherent qualities of a task, such as the challenge that the task offers. Extrinsic motivation, which arises from sources exterior to the task (such as a reward for task completion), tends to have a negative influence on creativity. However, extrinsic motivators may have a positive effect on creativity under certain circumstances (e.g., if a high level of intrinsic motivation is present). An individual's level on the three components determines that person's creative performance on a task. In terms of the generality–specificity issue, the creativity-relevant processes are considered to apply to all tasks for which creativity is sought, whereas the domain-relevant skills and task motivation components show greater domain and task specificity.

Sternberg and Lubart (1995), in their investment approach, proposed that creativity requires a confluence of six distinct but interrelated resources. A creative person is one who possesses the necessary resources and uses these resources to "buy low" (pursue ideas that are new or out of favor but have potential) and, after developing these ideas, to "sell high" (presenting the production publicly, at the right moment for the production to be appreciated). These resources for creativity are specific aspects of intelligence, knowledge, cognitive styles, personality, motivation, and environmental context. Three intellectual abilities important for creativity are the synthetic ability to define and represent problems in new ways, the analytic ability to recognize which ideas are worth pursuing, and the practical ability to "sell" one's work to others—that is, to persuade them of the value of the new work. Divergent thinking, or the capacity to generate many diverse ideas from a given starting point, as well as evaluative ability are also important. With regard to knowledge, some knowledge is necessary to make a contribution to a field but too much knowledge can result in an entrenched perspective (seeing a problem in terms of old schemas). For thinking styles, a preference for thinking in novel ways of one's own choosing and a preference for working with the big picture rather than the details are considered important for creativity. Creativity-relevant personality attributes include perseverance, willingness to take risks, willingness to tolerate ambiguity, openness to new experiences, and individuality. The motivation for creativity may be either intrinsic or extrinsic as long as the motivator energizes a person to work and allows the person to keep his or her attention focused on the task. Finally, the environment is considered a resource for creativity because it can provide physical or social stimulation to help generate ideas and to nurture these ideas. The environment additionally evaluates creativity through social judgment.

With regard to the confluence of resources, Sternberg and Lubart (1995) propose that creativity involves more than a simple sum of an individual's level on each of the components for creativity. First, there may be thresholds for some components (e.g., knowledge) below which creativity is not possible, regardless of an individual's level on the other components. Second, partial compensation may occur between the components in which strength on one component (e.g., motivation) may counteract weakness on another component (e.g., knowledge). Third, although each component contributes in its own way to creativity, a component is always acting in the presence of other components and this coaction can lead to interactive effects. For example, high levels on both intelligence and motivation could multiplicatively enhance creativity.

A person's set of resources yields a potential for creativity. According to the investment theory, some components for creativity are domain or task specific, such as knowledge, whereas other components are more generally applicable across domains, such as the intellectual ability to selectively combine information using analogies or metaphors. Factor-analytic results concerning the structure of intellectual abilities, which suggest a multifactorial hierarchical organization of capacities, are relevant to the generality–specificity debate for creativity. Indeed, if the realm of intellectual abilities contains (a) some very generalized capacities, notably factor g, which Spearman considered to be the ability to find relations among diverse elements; (b) group factors such as verbal ability and spatial ability; and

(c) more specific factors, such as language comprehension ability and language production ability, then it would be logical that creativity is also partly domain general and partly domain specific because creativity involves these intellectual capacities that are themselves partly general and partly specific. In addition, at least some of the personality attributes considered important for creativity have themselves domain-specific forms. An example is the trait of risk taking, which is best characterized as a set of domain-specific risk-taking tendencies. Lubart and Sternberg (1995) found that hypothetical scenario-based measures of risk taking in artistic, literary, and general-life domains correlated weakly among themselves, indicating a relative domain specificity for risk taking. Furthermore, creative performance in a drawing composition task correlated with risk taking in art-related scenarios but not with literary or general-life scenarios (parallel findings were observed for a creative story task which related to risk taking in literary scenarios rather than artistic or general-life ones).

ARE THESE ATTRIBUTES THE SAME ACROSS FIELDS OR DO THEY DIFFER DEPENDING ON THE FIELD?

In the previous section, we noted that some attributes involved in creativity, such as risk taking, may have domain specific forms. Thus, the trait of risk taking that may be important for creativity in each domain actually refers to a set of more specific traits: for example, risk taking in artistic settings, risk taking in scientific endeavors, or risk taking in social interactions. Other attributes, such as selective comparison ability (i.e., analogical, metaphorical thinking) are proposed to be more general in nature. Thus the mix between some attributes that have domain specific forms such as risk taking and other attributes that are general can explain the partial domain specificity of creative capacity.

Now consider another piece of the generality–specificity puzzle. Do fields, and tasks with a given field, require the same cognitive and conative attributes for creative work? For example, do the fields of art, science, literature, business, and others all require selective encoding, selective comparison, selective combination, divergent thinking, idea evaluation ability and other skills? Do these fields all require the same profile of personality traits: risk taking, openness to experience, perseverance, and others? Are these abilities and traits important to the same degree in each field?

To answer these questions we need to examine the similarities and differences between work in varying fields, or between different tasks within a given field. Each field, and each task within a field, needs to be characterized by a descriptive profile of cognitive and conative variables that are important for creativity. For example, we could imagine that artistic endeavors require, in particular, selective encoding, selective combination, visual imagery, as well as other abilities. In contrast, literary endeavors (such as poetry) may require specially selective comparison (metaphor generation), selective combination, and auditory imagery. If these two lists of required abilities are correct, then we can understand why creativity in artistic tasks and creativity in literary tasks will correlate only partially.

We can imagine two tasks within the same domain that have nearly identical profiles of required abilities and traits for creativity. Creativity scores for these tasks will correlate strongly. In contrast, it is also possible to have two tasks that have very different sets of required skills for creativity, leading to a weak correlation. This kind of task analysis is essentially missing in the literature and limits our ability to predict creativity in a given task as well as to understand why creativity scores correlate for certain tasks and not for others. Thus, task analyses can show a profile of needed abilities for each task, and at a more general level, a profile for each field or domain. There may be a hierarchical clustering arrangement of tasks in terms of their creativity requirements. It can be added that a complete task description will not only include the list of cognitive and conative attributes involved in a task, but also their relative importance and the way that these attributes enter the process of task execution. It is possible that two tasks, such as designing an advertisement for a magazine page and designing an advertisement for a billboard, require the same abilities and traits but place a slightly different emphasis on certain of these abilities or require that the abilities intervene in the work process at slightly different moments due to the size differences between artwork in a magazine and artwork on a billboard.

The empirical evidence of correlations between creativity in different fields and between creativity in different tasks with the same field suggest that some pairs of tasks may have essentially no overlap in their requirements for creativity (nearly zero correlation) whereas other pairs of tasks may show considerable similarity (moderately strong correlations of .70 suggesting approximately 50% of shared characteristics). A classic study by Gray (1966) examined 2,400 historically eminent creative people and found that only 2% showed creative accomplishments in diverse domains, such as art and literature, and 17% of the sample showed creative work in related domains, such as painting and sculpture. This investigation suggests a strong degree of task specificity in the requirements for creative performance across fields and even across tasks within a given field. There may, however, be a further parameter at play, namely expertise level. It is possible that the required abilities and traits for a small degree of creativity in a task are not the same as the required abilities and traits for a high level of creative performance. In other words, eminent levels of creativity may require a different cognitive and conative profile than more "run-of-the mill" levels of creativity in the same task. This possibility will further contribute to the specificity of creativity at eminent levels of performance.

According to confluence models, a person's profile across several components may fit more or less closely the requirements of a given task, and this leads to variations in the level of creative performance across domains. Thus, the level of creative performance depends on both the individual's resources and the requirements of the task that is undertaken.

ARE THESE ATTRIBUTES PREDISPOSED GENETICALLY OR DO THEY DEVELOP OVER THE LIFE SPAN?

Drawing on research on intelligence and personality, we propose that the attributes involved in creativity have, at least to some extent, genetic substrates (Petrill, 2003). However, research suggests that notable cognitive and conative development relevant to creativity occurs throughout the life span.

Concerning development of creativity in children, the family environment may provide cognitive (e.g., intellectual stimulation) and affective (e.g., emotional security) support for creativity (Harrington, Block, & Block, 1987). For example, families that provide stimulating settings with many books, magazines, and cultural activities foster intellectual abilities, knowledge acquisition and, perhaps, traits such as openness to new experiences (Simonton, 1984). Carl Rogers (1954) suggested that a warm, secure family will serve as a base from which risk taking can be attempted. Other work has explored a social–cognitive dimension of the family environment and the nature of parental rules for their children's daily life. Children from families with flexible rules tend to have greater creativity than children from families with rigid rules, regardless of socioeconomic level (Lubart & Lautrey, 1998; Lubart, Mouchiroud, Tordjman, & Zenasni, 2003).

In addition to the family setting, the school environment plays a crucial role in the development of creativity, or its lack of development in many cases. Often schools emphasize convergent thinking: that is, finding the correct answer to problems proposed by the teacher. Sometimes, however, divergent thinking is encouraged and children are allowed to struggle with ill-defined problems. Teachers serve as role models for children and may value or devalue the expression of creative ideas in the classroom. The emphasis on certain intellectual tasks at school may also contribute to the emergence of a generalized verbal ability at the end of elementary school; this could explain a temporary phase of dedifferentiation (generality) of creative divergent thinking abilities at 10- to 12-years old, which then evolves toward less correlated, more specific capacities (Mouchiroud & Lubart, 2002). In terms of knowledge, information is often transmitted in a compartmentalized way, with an emphasis on the specificity of knowledge rather than links across different content areas.

Additionally, school serves as an important context for socialization and personality development. Consider, for example, the trait of risk taking. Clifford (1988) examined children's risk taking and failure tolerance in academic situations. She asked children at various grade levels (8- to 12-year-olds) to solve problems of their own choice in verbal, mathematics, and other academic domains. The problems were clearly labelled as being appropriate for average children of various ages (age 6- to 14-years-old). Fourth-grade children selected problems that were approximately 6 months below their ability level; fifth graders selected problems that were on average 1 year below their level, and for sixth graders differences reached up to 1.5 years between real age and the age level of the problems selected. This shows that children were increasingly risk averse with age, which is smart for getting good grades in school. In line with the investment approach to creativity (Sternberg & Lubart, 1995), many people are not creative because they are unwilling to pursue unknown or little valued ideas, they do not want to take a risk and "buy low." Being creative is, in part, a philosophy of life, which is acquired through childhood experiences.

Beyond the local, school setting, the macroscopic social environment influences the development of creative potential in numerous ways (Lubart, 1999). For example, cultural activities such as concerts, artistic expositions, museums, and television shows on diverse topics can all contribute to children's creative development. Historiometric studies have shown that the presence of eminent role models (such as great scientists or writers) in one generation (g) tends to predict the creative accomplishments of future generations (g + 1, g + 2) in the same domain (Simonton, 1984, 1996).

Concerning adult development, we observe variations in creativity over the life span with regard to productivity, originality, and the nature of the work produced (Lubart & Sternberg, 1998). These developmental trends can be traced to a combination of biopsychosocial factors. For example, the intellectual processes involved in creative performance are subject to both positive and negative age influences. On the positive side, problem definition, strategy selection, and selective comparison and combination can become more efficient with experience (Berg & Sternberg, 1985). Also, dialectical thinking is believed to develop with age and may contribute to the harmony and decreased tension that characterizes certain late-life creative contributions (called "old-age style"; Lubart & Sternberg, 1998). On the negative side, age is associated with a biologically driven, generalized slowdown of information processing, which could cause changes in productivity of creative work.

Conation (including personality and motivation) may also play a key role in life span changes of creativity. For example, there is a tendency for increased cautiousness with age (Botwinick, 1984). Elderly participants showed a tendency to avoid risk in hypothetical situations by refusing to endorse the risky course of action "no matter what the probability" of success. On cognitive tests, elderly participants prefer to omit answers rather than guess incorrectly and, if possible, choose problems that offer a high probability of success (Okun & di Vesta, 1976). Motivation may be especially linked to life-span-related trends in the social system of career advancement and retirement policies (Mumford & Gustafson, 1988). A few studies have shown changes in the level of specific motivations, which may affect creative productivity, such as shifts in achievement motivation with age (Kausler, 1990; Veroff, Reuman, & Feld, 1984).

CAN CREATIVITY BE TRAINED?

Studies on the development of creativity and creativity-relevant attributes suggest that training is possible, at least to some degree. Most work has focused on divergent thinking exercises. For example, Baer (1996) examined whether divergent thinking exercises in one domain have beneficial effects in another domain. He focused on creativity in producing poems and short stories. Participants who received divergent thinking training concerning poetry writing produced more creative poems than a control group who did not receive training. However, the divergent thinking training group did not outperform the control group on a story composition task. The creativity of poems and stories was rated by judges using a consensual assessment technique.

These results suggest that there may be small transfer effects but that divergent thinking training is largely domain or task specific. This finding is consistent with the idea that many creativity-relevant abilities are partially domain specific. Of course divergent thinking is only one ability among others that are involved in creativity. Thus, training programs that focus on one or a small number of abilities are bound to yield limited effects on the development of creativity. Given the somewhat specific nature of creativity, the most effective creativity training programs will be those tailored to enhance creativity in a specific domain, and even better in a specific task (Baer, 1998). A complete training program would seek to enhance all components involved in creativity (both cognitive and noncognitive ones). Additionally, creativity training could be tailored to each person after determining which components are not at their optimal level for the individual given the requirements for being creative in a specific task. Training includes teaching people which kinds of thinking are important during one phase of a task and which are important during a later phase of a task.

HOW CAN THESE ATTRIBUTES BE ASSESSED?

On the basis of the tenets of multivariate models of creativity, potentially creative individuals can be identified by measuring each component necessary for creativity. Cognitive components can be measured by specialized tasks that isolate specific abilities relevant to creativity. For example, we have used insight problems to measure selective encoding ability, and counterfactual analogy problems to measure selective comparison skills (Lubart & Sternberg, 1995). Also, domain-specific divergent thinking tests measure one of the cognitive components for creativity (however, these tests are sometimes considered as measures of creativity itself, which is an error in our point of view). Broad intellectual assessments, such as IQ tests will not be very informative because they contain several tasks that are not particularly relevant to creative thinking. Personality traits and motivation can be measured by self-report questionnaires focusing on relevant variables, such as risk taking, openness to new experiences, or intrinsic and task-focused motivation. It is also possible to use hypothetical scenario-based measures or objective personality tests to measure traits such as domain-specific risk taking (Lubart & Sternberg, 1995). Once the components have been assessed, an individual can be described as having a componential profile that will be more or less ideal for creativity. As described earlier, the optimal profile for creativity is hypothesized to differ, at least to some extent, for each specific task and for each domain of work (e.g., visual art, literature, science). Ideally, the identification of potentially creative people should involve a comparison between an individual's profile over the set of components for creativity and the profile of components needed for creativity in a particular task.

Two of the main assessment techniques for measuring creativity itself are self-report creative activity questionnaires and performance-based evaluations. We consider these different types of assessments and the typical results obtained concerning the specificity–generality of creativity below.

In self-report creative activity questionnaires, people are asked to recall creative accomplishments in diverse settings (home, school, work, extravocational contexts) over several years of activity. This kind of measure is worthwhile because it captures real-life creative acts in self-chosen domains. For Kaufman and Baer (2002), self-assessment offers a window into the ways that people conceptualize their own creativity; this representation may be centered on a general ability notion of creativity and depends, of course, on each individual's personal definition of creativity, which may be more or less stringent. Hocevar (1976) found moderate correlations among self-report indexes of creativity in various domains, suggesting a common factor among his measures. Reanalyzing archival data collected with self-report scales, Plucker (1999) pointed out evidence for both a strong content-general factor (that could explain 40–50% of the variance) and nonnegligible variance that could be explained by specific factors. Of course, one of the main psychometric difficulties with these scales is the unverifiable, subjective nature of people's reported creative accomplishments, and the potential for biases, such as halo effects in self-reports (Brown, 1989).

For performance-based assessments, people are asked to produce a work in a limited amount of time, which is then evaluated by a panel of judges.

The work may be a story, a poem, a drawing, a collage, an advertisement, or other products. For these tasks, a given topic or limited set of topics and materials may be imposed. Judges, often expert in the domain examined, evaluate the work produced and give a score of creativity, using a standardized scale (such as a 7-point scale from low to high creativity; see Amabile, 1996). Several studies have examined the correlations between creativity scores when people complete several performance-based tasks (Amabile, 1996; Lubart & Sternberg, 1995). The results tend to show low-to-moderate intertask relations. For example, Baer (1994) measured creativity in story writing and poetry composition tasks in a sample of 128 eighth-grade students. Expert judges evaluated the creativity of the productions and observed a relatively weak correlation ($r = .19$, $p < .05$). In one of our studies (Lubart & Sternberg, 1995), 48 adults completed 8 tasks (2 stories, 2 drawings, 2 advertisements, 2 societal problem-solving tasks). The correlations between tasks from the same domain, such as two story-writing tasks, varied from .37 ($p < .05$) to .67 ($p < .001$). The correlations between tasks from different domains varied from .23 (ns) to .62 ($p < .001$) (median $r = .36$, $p < .05$; Lubart & Sternberg, 1995).

Thus, it seems that performance-based evaluations provide results favoring a domain-specific view of creative behaviors, whereas the use of self-report inventories lead to a more general-oriented conception of creativity (Plucker, 1998). These findings illustrate the complexity of assessing creativity and its specificity or generality.

CONCLUSIONS

One of the controversial issues in creativity research is whether one's creativity is domain specific or domain general. We propose that different components of creativity may have different levels of generalization, but also that these components develop throughout one's life. The relative importance of the components as well as their interaction at a moment of one's life must be considered. This leads to questions about the origin of creativity. At an early stage of life, does every individual have potential to produce a creative answer in response to a stimulus? Is a baby, just discovering the world, constantly creating behaviors and new concepts (Ayman-Nolley, 1999)? Does this general form of creativity become increasingly specified in childhood and adulthood?

From this point of view, the question is not to determine if creativity is domain specific or not, but when it becomes specific, and what components are domain specific and what components are general. This issue has particular importance in the field of education. Some periods of development may be best for promoting general creative achievement, and during other periods it may be best to focus on specific creative activities. Also there are implications for the assessment of creative potential in children. As Han and

Marvin (2002) note, the use of multiple assessment in diverse domains and performance-based assessments within real learning contexts is essential to assess properly the different kinds of creative abilities. The issues raised in this chapter, over the long term, may contribute to building a new model of creativity based on a hierarchical factor structure, with both general and specific components contributing to observed creative performance.

REFERENCES

Amabile, T. M. (1996). *Creativity in context*. Boulder, CO: Westview.

Ayman-Nolley, S. (1999). A Piagetian perspective on the dialectic process of creativity. *Creativity Research Journal, 12(4)*, 267–275.

Baer, J. (1993). *Creativity and divergent thinking: A task-specific approach*. Hillsdale, NJ: Erlbaum.

Baer, J. (1994). Generality of creativity across performance domains: A replication. *Perceptual and Motor Skills, 79*, 1217–1218.

Baer, J. (1996). The effects of task-specific divergent-thinking training. *Journal of Creative Behavior, 30*, 183–187.

Baer, J. (1998). The case for domain specificity of creativity. *Creativity Research Journal, 11(2)*, 173–177.

Berg, C. A., & Sternberg, R. J. (1985). A triarchic theory of intellectual development during adulthood. *Developmental Review, 5*, 334–370.

Botwinick, J. (1984). *Aging and behavior* (3rd ed.). New York: Springer Publishing Company.

Brown, R. T. (1989). Creativity: What are we to measure? In J. A. Glover, R. R. Ronning, & C. R. Reynolds (Eds.), *Handbook of creativity* (pp. 3–32). New York: Plenum Press.

Clifford, M. M. (1988). Failure tolerance and academic risk-taking in ten to twelve year old students. *British Journal of Educational Psychology, 58(1)*, 15–27.

Glück, J., Ernst, R., & Unger, F. (2002). How creatives define creativity: Definitions reflect different types of creativity. *Creativity Research Journal, 14(1)*, 55–67.

Gray, C. E. (1966). A measurement of creativity in western civilization. *American Anthropologist, 68*, 1384–1417.

Han, K. S., & Marvin, C. (2002). Multiple creativities? Investigating domain-specificity of creativity in young children. *Gifted Child Quarterly, 46(2)*, 98–109.

Harrington, D. M., Block, J. H., & Block, J. (1987). Testing aspects of Carl Rogers's theory of creative environments: Child-rearing antecedents of creative potential in young adolescents. *Journal of Personality and Social Psychology, 52*, 851–856.

Hocevar, D. (1976). Dimensionality of creativity. *Psychological Reports, 39*, 869–870.

Kaufman, J. C., & Baer, J. (2002). Could Steven Spielberg manage the Yankees? Creative thinking in different domains. *The Korean Journal of Thinking & Problem Solving, 12*(2), 5–14.

Kausler, D. H. (1990). Motivation, human aging and cognitive performance. In J. E. Birren & K. W. Schaie (Eds.), *Handbook of the psychology of aging* (3rd ed., pp. 171–182). San Diego, CA: Academic Press.

Lubart, T. I. (1994). Creativity. In E. C. Carterette & M. P. Friedman (Series Eds.) & R. J. Sternberg (Vol. Ed.), *The handbook of perception and cognition: Vol. 12. Thinking and problem solving.* New York: Academic Press.

Lubart, T. I. (1999). Creativity across cultures. In R. J. Sternberg (Ed.), *Handbook of creativity* (pp. 339–350). New York: Cambridge University Press.

Lubart, T. I., & Lautrey, J. (1998, July). *Family environment and creativity.* Paper presented at the 15th biennial meetings of the International Society for the Study of Behavioral Development, Berne, Switzerland.

Lubart, T. I., Mouchiroud, C., Tordjman, S., & Zenasni, F. (2003). *Psychologie de la créativité* [Psychology of creativity]. Paris: Colin.

Lubart, T. I., & Sternberg, R. J. (1995). An investment approach to creativity: Theory and data. In S. M. Smith, T. B. Ward, & R. A. Finke (Eds.), *The creative cognition approach* (pp. 271–302). Cambridge, MA: MIT Press.

Lubart, T. I., & Sternberg, R. J. (1998). Creativity across time and place = lifespan and cross-cultural perspectives. *High Ability Studies, 9*(1), 59–74.

Mouchiroud, C., & Lubart, T. I. (2002). Social creativity: A cross-sectional study of 6- to 11-year-old children. *International Journal of Behavioral Development, 26*(1), 60–69.

Mumford, M. D., & Gustafson, S. B. (1988). Creativity syndrome: Integration, application, and innovation. *Psychological Bulletin, 103*, 27–43.

Okun, M. A., & di Vesta, F. J. (1976). Cautiousness in adulthood as a function of age and instructions. *Journal of Gerontology, 31*, 571–576.

Petrill, S. (2003). The development of intelligence: Behavioral genetic approaches. In R. J. Sternberg, J. Lautrey, & T. Lubart (Eds.), *Models of intelligence: International perspectives* (pp. 81–89). Washington, DC: American Psychological Association.

Plucker, J. A. (1998). Beware of simple conclusions: The case for content generality of creativity. *Creativity Research Journal, 11*, 45–53.

Plucker, J. A. (1999). Reanalyses of student responses to creativity checklists: Evidence of content generality. *Journal of Creative Behavior, 33*(2), 126–137.

Rogers, C. (1954). Toward a theory of creativity. *International Society for General Semantics, 11*, 249–260.

Simonton, D. K. (1984). *Genius, creativity and leadership.* Cambridge, MA: Harvard University Press.

Simonton, D. K. (1996). Individual genius within cultural configurations: The case of Japanese civilization. *Journal of Cross Cultural Psychology, 27*, 354–375.

Sternberg, R. J., Kaufman, J. C., & Pretz, J. E. (2002). The propulsion model of creative contributions applied to the arts and letters. *Journal of Creative Behavior, 35*(2), 75–101.

Sternberg, R. J., & Lubart, T. I. (1995). *Defying the crowd: Cultivating creativity in a culture of conformity.* New York: Free Press.

Veroff, J., Reuman, D., & Feld, S. (1984). Motives in American men and women across the adult life span. *Developmental Psychology, 20,* 1142–1158.

5

THE EVOLVED FLUID SPECIFICITY OF HUMAN CREATIVE TALENT

GREGORY J. FEIST

It is a very appealing, and ultimately firmly American, notion that a creative person could be creative in any domain he or she chose. All the person would have to do would be to decide where to apply her or his talents and efforts, practice or train a lot, and *voilà*, you have creative achievement. On this view, talent trumps domain and it really is somewhat arbitrary in which domain the creative talent is expressed. Indeed, we often refer to people as "creative" not as a "creative artist" or "creative biologist."

I argue that this is a rather naive and ultimately empirically false position and that creative talent is in fact domain specific, and that with a few exceptions creative achievement is limited within an individual to usually one or two (sometimes maybe three) domains. There are some generalized mental strategies and heuristics that do cut across domains, but creativity and talent are usually not among the domain-general skills. Next I argue for evolved domains in seven areas (psychology, physics, biology, number, linguistics, music, and aesthetics), and then how creative talent is expressed within rather than across each of these domains. In other words, creative talents get expressed along the lines of evolved domains. First things first, however: What is creativity?

CONSENSUS IN HOW CREATIVITY IS DEFINED

Many people outside of the field, and even some inside it, like to cling to the romantic notion that creativity is inherently mysterious (which it is), ineffable (which it can be), and therefore amorphous and poorly defined (which it is not). Most every researcher who studies creativity agrees that two criteria are necessary and neither alone is sufficient: novelty and usefulness (Amabile, 1996; Feist, 1998; Guilford, 1950; MacKinnon, 1970; Simonton, 1988b; Sternberg, 1988). Usefulness, of course, is not meant in merely the pragmatic sense but rather in the broader sense that incorporates aesthetic, technical, literary, scientific, and economic usefulness, to name just a few of the major categories.

DOMAINS OF MIND

Among other evolutionary forces (such as genetic drift and recombination), natural and sexual selection pressures have been predominant in predisposing the human mind toward certain kinds of sensations and functions. These functions are specific mechanisms and domains that solve specific problems. Domains are universal and part of human nature and they concern knowledge of the social (people), animate (animals) and inanimate (physical objects) worlds; being able to count, quantify (number), communicate (language) our ideas about these worlds; appreciating and creating aesthetically pleasing arrangements of visual images (aesthetics); and being sensitive to and appreciative of rhythm, pitch, and timing in sounds (music). The domain categories are anything but arbitrary, but rather are intimately tied to our survival and reproductive success.

Domains of mind have some degree of physical–neuroanatomical status but are primarily conceptual and heuristic. As defined by Gelman and Brenneman (1994), a domain is a "given set of principles, the rules of their application, and the entities to which they apply" (p. 371). The principles are interrelated and are specific to a class of entities (cf. Karmiloff-Smith, 1992). Domains are not to be confused with modules, for the latter are encapsulated information units that process inputs (perceptions) (cf. Fodor, 1983; Karmiloff-Smith, 1992; Sperber, 1994). Modules are perceptual and domains are conceptual. Various authors have proposed anywhere from three to eight domains, with four being the most common number. In Table 5.1 I have organized these general trends and put forth my own proposal for seven distinct domains, based on six criteria: archeological, comparative psychological, universal, developmental, giftedness, and neuroscientific.

Implicit Psychology: The Social–Emotional Domain

One of the most fundamental aspects of being human is our social structure and complexity. We are constantly confronted with problems of inter-

TABLE 5.1
Proposed Domains of Mind by Various Authors

Author	Psychology	Self	Physics	Biology	Linguistics	Mathematics	Art	Bodily	Music
				Implicit folk domain					
Gopnik, Meltzhoff & Kuhl (1999)	Knowing people		Knowing things		Knowing language				
Carey & Spelke (1994)	Person reasoning		Physical objects		Language	Number (sets)			
Karmiloff-Smith (1992)	Psychologist		Physicist		Linguist	Mathematician	Notator		
Mithen (1996)	Social (psychology)		Technical (physics)	Natural history (biology)	Linguistic (linguistics)				
Parker & McKinney (1999)	Social		Physical objects		Linguistic	Logical–mathematical			
Pinker (1997)	Intuitive psychology		Intuitive physics	Intuitive biology	Linguistics	Intuitive mathematics			
Feist (2001, in press)	Psychology		Physics (Physical objects-spatial)	Biology (natural history)	Linguistics (language)	Math (numerical)	Art (aesthetics)		Music
Gardner (1983, 1999)	Interpersonal	Intrapersonal	Spatial	Natural history	Language	Logical–mathematical	Spatial	Bodily–kinesthetic	Musical

personal relations: from sexual behavior to child rearing, from friendship alliances to kinship-based altruism, from emotion and facial recognition to deception and cooperation. Very briefly, implicit psychology consists first and foremost of social preferences seen in newborns as young as hours old: namely an intuitive and automatic preference for humans (especially the face) over other animal forms. With development we see several specific abilities involving interaction between people: for instance, the ability to recognize and infer the mental and emotional states in oneself and in other members of one's species even if these beliefs and emotions differ from one's own. Imitation, pretend play, false-belief, deception, mental attribution, joint attention, and self-awareness are some of the specific manifestations of theory of mind. The social-psychological domain also involves self-knowledge and self-concept. What is meant by implicit psychology is very similar to what E. L. Thorndike (1920) referred to as "social intelligence," Howard Gardner (1983, 1999) referred to as the "personal intelligences" (inter- and intrapersonal), and what Peter Salovey and John Mayer referred to as "emotional intelligence" (Salovey & Mayer, 1990; cf. Goleman, 1995). The social sciences (psychology, sociology, anthropology, and economics) originate from this domain of mind.

Implicit Physics: Physical Objects and Spatial Relations

Physical knowledge concerns the inanimate world of physical objects (including tools); their movement, positioning, and causal relations in space; and their inner workings (machines). Because the tool-use element is a large component of physical knowledge, some archeologists refer to this domain as "technical intelligence" (cf. Byrne, 2001; Mithen, 1996). An "implicit physics" is also seen in children's automatic sense that physical objects obey different rules than living things (inanimate versus animate rules). Inanimate objects fall to the ground and do not get up. It consists of the ability to solve problems of tool use (wood versus stone; simple versus complex) and mental and physical manipulation of inanimate objects of different materials, as well as an implicit understanding of physics (gravity, inertia, and dynamics of objects). Moreover, spatial knowledge and skills are involved in the physical objects domain.

Implicit Biology: Natural History

This domain consists first of the knowledge that the world consists of animate things that differ from inanimate (the flip-side to physics). Some things are living and breathing and move by themselves; we call them animals. Some things fall to the ground and do get up (assuming they did not fall from too great a height). Moreover, some things are alive and grow but stay in the same place (plants). Indeed, biology and physics are part of the same innate and built-in sense that the world is divided into things that move and grow and things that do not, and that these classes of things obey different rules. Implicit biology also includes the ability to solve problems concerning natural resources, namely food acquisition (hunting, scavenging, foraging, mental maps of landscape); classifying plants (for food and medicine) as well as animals and their behavior; and knowing which landscapes are resource-rich and fertile. The biological sciences (natural history, botany, zoology, biology, genetics, etc.) are extensions of this domain of knowledge.

Implicit Mathematics: Numerosity and Seriation

There is compelling evidence for including a numerical or quantitative domain of mind. Unless we have a lesion in the left parietal lobe, we all have a sense of numerosity; we intuitively, automatically know that there are 3 or 5 of something (one-to-one correspondence) and that one series is larger or smaller than another; we are born with this ability and it takes no learning, but is supplemented of course with cultural knowledge. Numerosity allows us to automatically use (add and subtract) positive whole numbers. Formal math ultimately stems from this implicit domain.

Implicit Musical Ability: Music

Music is the capacity to produce, perceive, and appreciate rhythmic and melodic sounds that evoke an emotional response in oneself and others. It can also be defined as the ability to perceive changes in pitch to be harmonically or rhythmically related (Gelman & Brenneman, 1994). As one ethnomusicologist wrote recently, "All of us are born with the capacity to apprehend emotion and meaning in music, regardless of whether we understand music theory or read musical notation" (Tramo, 2001, p. 54). Much evidence from brain specificity, universality, ethnomusicology, the development of musical preference and ability, and archeology argues for music being an evolved domain of the human mind. Music and dance stem from this domain.

Implicit Linguistics: Language

Linguistic ability is the ability to use meaningful sounds to communicate with others and understand abstract symbols. As linguists have pointed out (e.g., Bloom, 1998), language essentially consists of three components: phonology (physical expression of language, usually through sounds), morphology (words and word-parts), and syntax (the combination of words and phrases). It also involves the intuitive ability to acquire syntactical and semantic rules of language as well as the ability to use sentences spontaneously, novelly, and flexibly. The science of linguistics as well as creative writing and literature stem from this implicit domain of knowledge.

Implicit Aesthetics: Art

The visual art domain is the production of and appreciation and preference for particular visual forms, figures, and color combinations over others (Aiken, 1998; Barrow, 1995; Dissanayake, 1992; Gardner, 1983; Karmiloff-Smith, 1992; Miller, 2000; Orians, 2001; Orians & Heerwagen, 1992). Aesthetics inherently involves emotional response of like–dislike and as several emotion theorists have argued, emotions have evolved as adaptive signals for how one is doing and one's well-being (Lazarus, 1991; LeDoux, 1996). Indeed, a sense of aesthetics is an inevitable outcome of our sense of safety, order, and well-being (Bradshaw, 2001; Feist, 2001; Orians, 2001; Orians & Heerwagen, 1992). Aesthetics is seen in most every domain of life and over every sensory modality, but is most readily apparent in the visual arts. The visual arts (drawing, painting, photography, and sculpting) stem from this domain.

Criteria for an Evolved Domain

Any detailed discussion of the evidence for choosing these seven domains as evolved domains of mind is beyond the scope of this chapter and can be found elsewhere (cf. Feist, in press; Gardner, 1983; Mithen, 1996; Parker & McKinney, 1999). Nevertheless a brief overview of such criteria is warranted. To call something a domain requires specific criteria, otherwise it risks being an arbitrary enterprise. It is not arbitrary and there are at least seven criteria, the majority of which must be met if a capacity is to earn the label *domain of mind*: archeological, comparative, developmental, universal, precocious and prodigious talent (giftedness), neuroscientific, and genetic. In short, nothing less than the convergent interdisciplinary evidence from archeology, primatology, developmental psychology, anthropology, giftedness-education, neuroscience, and genetics is required to classify something as an evolved domain of mind.

First, there is the *archeological fossil record*. What do the human fossil record (bones) and tools and artifacts (stones) tell us of the evolution of mind in general and of domains of mind in particular? Yet it is important to keep in mind that the stone and bone evidence is inherently conservative, for two reasons. First, because of the lack of fossilization of key brain structures, and second because what we know now will always be less than we know after later discoveries are unearthed. As long as we understand that what we now know from fossil evidence will only be added to in the future, we will realize that our current inferences will almost always be underestimates of what our ancestors' capacities truly were. Nevertheless, stones and bones are a critical and necessary piece of the puzzle. But they are just one piece.

Second, we must have *comparative evidence* of domains from our living primate relatives, in particular in the Great Apes (chimps, bonobos, gorillas, orangutans), Old World Monkeys (baboons and macaques), and New World Monkeys (e.g., cebus, rhesus, capuchins). Darwin, George Ramones, and Lloyd Morgan in the 19th century and Köhler, Yerkes, and Harlow in the first half of the 20th century have been key figures in providing key insights into the evolution of primate intelligence. Both the relative strengths and weaknesses in the intellectual abilities of different taxa have been documented and compared by experimental as well as observational research, often from a Piagetian perspective (see Parker & McKinney, 1999). Such analysis tells us much about the common evolutionary past we share with our closest relatives and when certain cognitive capacities may have first started to evolve.

Third, *developmental psychology* must provide evidence that these capacities are relatively automatic and easy to learn. In other words, infants and children all over the world must perform these tasks spontaneously. Just to give a flavor for what kinds of things we now know about infants and what they prefer and are capable of: They are attracted to the human face more than most other stimuli, respond to facial emotional expression of others, distinguish sounds and voices and start to imitate those sounds, are surprised by impossible physical or numeric events, and prefer consonant music to dissonant music as young as 4 months of age. Toddlers and young children intuitively and automatically learn grammar, syntax, and semantics, develop a sense of self, and learn what other people know or feel. The fact that these capacities develop automatically and spontaneously suggests that natural and sexual selection (and other nonselection forces) have gradually produced a nervous system to do such things, much the way an eye has been built to accurately perceive one's environment.

Fourth, the capacities *must be universal*, that is, seen in every culture at most every time, to be considered a domain. Anthropologists have been at the forefront of supplying us with knowledge of the cultural similarities and differences that exist and have existed in terms of folk knowledge and representation of social interaction, physical object knowledge, natural history and taxonomic classification, quantity and seriation, language, music and dance, and art, ornamentation and aesthetics.

Fifth, to exist as an independent set of principles applied to a specific class of entities, evidence must also come from research on *precocious talent and prodigies*. One would expect, if domain-based skills were part of our ancestral past, and were relatively automatic, spontaneous, and universal, that these domains would be areas in which extreme talent and giftedness should be exhibited. Precocious and prodigious talent exists in each of the major domains of mind, but cultural outlets exist primarily for the spatial–mechanical (chess and machines and computers), mathematical, linguistic, bodily–kinesthetic, and musical domains.

The sixth criterion for domain specificity is *neuroscience*. Historically much of the neuroscience evidence came from disease or injury and took the form of case reports. There are many case studies of people through accident or disease who lose, for instance, the ability to recognize faces or facial expression, maintain joint attention (autism), count, understand language, or speak. As initial and exploratory lines of investigation, neuropathology cases are important, but they must be supplemented by more systematic research on noninjured and nondiseased people. With the advent of brain imaging techniques over the past 30 years, in particular positron emission tomography (PET) in the 1970s and functional magnetic resonance imaging (fMRI) in the 1990s, we now know much more about the distinct brain regions that are involved in different cognitive tasks of normal functioning adults.

The last category of evidence for domain specificity is as much latent as it is actual: namely *genetics*. Much is being learned about human genetics on a daily basis, thanks to the Human Genome Project, but the degree of complexity between genes and behavior precludes easy causal paths and understanding of mechanisms involved in complex psychological behavior such as thought, motivation, and personality. All genes do is code for protein synthesis and then these proteins become all the cellular, neurochemical, and neuroanatomical structures of the body. Moreover, cognitive processes result from "quantitative genetic traits": that is, they are expressed on a continuum rather than in discrete categories with many, many genes involved in the neuroanatomical structures and neurochemistry behind these traits (Clark & Grunstein, 2000). The Human Genome Project promises to uncover some of the missing pieces of the genetics puzzle, but that is probably years, if not decades, away.

DOMAIN SPECIFICITY OF CREATIVE TALENT

My argument about specificity of creative talent is rather straightforward: Creative talent is expressed in each evolved implicit domain and is specific to its domain rather than general. Individuals tend to have talent in one or sometimes two related domains, but seldom across more than two domains and never across all domains. In other words, there are seven distinct domains of creative talent, with three involving science, one involving math, and three involving art. The scientific domains of creative talent are the physical sciences, the biological sciences, and the social sciences. The artistic domains of creative talent are literature, the visual arts, and music. I review the key specific aspects of each domain of talent and some evidence that its giftedness is manifested early in life, during childhood or adolescence.

I focus on scientific creativity first. The kind of science one is interested in and has talent for, whether physical, biological, or social, is determined by one's cluster of domain-specific talents. To be gifted in the physical–inanimate world is one thing, in the biological and natural history world another, and in the social and interpersonal world yet another. One may see crossover ability in biology and psychology but almost never in physics and psychology, unless it is a relatively nonsocial form of psychology, such as psychophysics.

The first major domain of scientific talent is the social sciences, which is composed of talent and ability in the interpersonal and intrapersonal realms. More specifically, such talent consists of possessing outstanding faculty in theory of mind (recognizing and understanding the motives, feelings, and thoughts of others), self-knowledge, impulse control, and emotion regulation. Social-psychological precocity no doubt exists, as when young children exhibit a gift for joint attention, knowing what others are actually thinking and feeling, or can regulate and control interpersonal conflict with great tact and aplomb.

Relatively little research has been conducted on giftedness and talent in the social intelligence domain, partly because it cannot be assessed through pen and paper methodology. One of Howard Gardner's colleagues, however, Thomas Hatch (1997) has written about these skills among kindergarten-aged children at play, and argues that children with interpersonal and social skills are the leaders and diplomats of the playground. They have talents for responding to the thoughts and feelings of their fellow playmates and can regulate their own desires and impulses. These children organize groups, mediate conflict, have empathy, and are team players. Similarly, Schmitt and Grammar (1997) argue that the most socially skilled and successful children are not simply the most cognitively complex ones, but rather those who know how to produce the most desired and often simplest outcomes. If people are talented at social–emotional intelligence, they may become leaders or well-liked by peers, but they seldom win awards and talent recognition contests because there are none. Gifted programs are mostly geared toward language, math, science, and music, but not interpersonal talent. Some schools, however are beginning to include social–emotional skills in their curriculum, such as the Self Science curriculum at the Nueva School (Goleman, 1995). It is interesting to speculate whether many of our best psychotherapists and even political leaders showed precocious gifts in the area of social–emotional intelligence and mediating interpersonal conflicts in early childhood. Clearly more longitudinal research is needed on this topic.

The disability in social intelligence is much more dramatic and tragically evident than its talent. On an individual level, social disability is manifested in terms of autism and on a social level it is manifested in terms of antisocial personality disorders and impulsive explosions of fits of rage and violence. Goleman (1995) referred to the latter as "emotional high-jacking," and unfortunately it is the kind of behavior that makes the newspapers because of its destructiveness. Both of these disorders, autism and impulse control problems, are associated with abnormal frontal lobe function (Pincus,

1999; Stone, Baron-Cohen, & Knight, 1998; Stuss, Gallup, & Alexander, 2001).

The next domain of scientific talent is the physical domain. Various lines of evidence, sometimes direct and sometimes indirect, converge on the conclusion that physical scientists from very early in life have temperaments and personalities that are thing- rather than people-oriented. Supporting this domain-specific view of talent, Baron-Cohen and his colleagues have found that engineers, mathematicians, and physical scientists score much higher on measures of high-functioning autism and Asperger's syndrome than nonscientists, and that physical scientists, mathematicians, and engineers are higher on nonclinical measures of autism than social scientists (Baron-Cohen, Wheelwright, Stone, & Rutherford, 1999; Baron-Cohen, Wheelwright, Skinner, Martin, & Clubley, 2001). This result may be a more extreme expression of the general phenomenon, but it does suggest that physical scientists may have temperaments that orient them away from the social and toward the inanimate; their interest and ability in science is then just one expression of this orientation. Moreover, autistic children are more than twice as likely as nonautistic children to have a father or grandfather who was an engineer (Baron-Cohen, Wheelwright, Stott, Bolton, & Goodyer, 1997; Baron-Cohen, et al., 1998).

Giftedness in the physical–technical domain is seen most readily in the area of physics, mechanics, chess, and computer science, which tap in to the spatial and mechanical elements of physical knowledge (Cranberg & Albert, 1988; Rimland & Fein, 1988). Chess is one example of a visual–spatial ability that manifests its extreme talent often very early in life, with future masters sometimes becoming national champions at the age of 12 or 14 (Cranberg & Albert, 1988). Indeed, "only in chess, music, and mathematics have profound, original insights been contributed by preadolescents" (Cranberg & Albert, 1988, p. 167).

Extreme creative talent in theoretical physics, like chess, pure math, and lyric poetry, is also likely to peak earlier than in some other fields of study, such as biology, geology, history, and philosophy (Lehman, 1953; Moulin, 1955; Simonton, 1988a). It is not uncommon for major theoretical contributions in physics to be made in one's 20s, with Einstein being the most obvious but not only case, and the general peak of productivity occurring during the late 20s or early 30s (Simonton, 1988a). Although not often happening after age 30, extreme creative achievement in theoretical physics before age 20 (extreme precocity) also is not very common (Charness, 1988; Lehman, 1953). This stands in contrast to chess, pure math, and music.

As mentioned above, an intriguing connection with physical giftedness is the fact that special talents in mechanics and space are often manifested in autistic children (Baron-Cohen et al., 1997; Baron-Cohen et al., 1998; Rimland & Fein, 1988). For instance, some autistic children are experts at mechanics, being able to take clocks, radios, and other machines apart and put them back together without error. In at least one recorded instance, an autistic boy could determine with a high degree of accuracy an object's dimensions, such as a room, fence, or driveway. With objects smaller than 20 feet, he was accurate within ¼ inch (Rimland & Fein, 1988).

People who have natural history or biological science talent have a different orientation than those with social or physical science talent. They gravitate toward, show interest in, and have well-developed knowledge of plant and animal classification as well as plant and animal behavior and habitat. Those with talent for the natural world are less thing-oriented than physical scientists and less people-oriented than social scientists. As Gardner (1999) wrote:

> Biographies of biologists routinely document an early fascination with plants and animals and a drive to identify, classify, and interact with them; Darwin, Gould, and Wilson are only the most visible members of this cohort. Interestingly, these patterns are not echoed in the lives of physical scientists who, as children, more often explored the visible manifestations of invisible forces (like gravity or electricity) or played with mechanical or chemical systems. (pp. 50–51)

In other words, children who are talented in this domain spend much of their time in nature observing, collecting, and classifying—that is creating taxonomies. One of the more interesting observations about Darwin is by all accounts, including his own, his lack of intellectual precocity: He was a most unremarkable child intellectually. The only distinguished talent he seemed to manifest by adolescence was for identifying natural objects (Howe, 1999).

The psychologists Eleanor Rosch and Carolyn Mervis (Mervis & Rosch, 1981; Rosch, 1975) have conducted perhaps the best-known work on the psychology of natural object classification and taxonomy. The fundamental idea is that categorizations of natural objects are neither arbitrary nor equivalent. That is, humans do not have every logically possible category of thing, otherwise we would have the category "four-legged animals with fur and mouths and move about primarily by flying": This category is logically possible but naturally impossible. Attributes are correlated not randomly combined. Humans only form categories of real flora and fauna groups actually found in their locale. Furthermore, some objects are better exemplars (more prototypical) of a category than others, a sparrow being more representative of *bird* than penguin. The world over, natural categories are represented on a continuum (nonequivalently) rather than discretely. Finally, categorization develops universally in a hierarchy, with basic levels being acquired first in childhood: For example, "fastest" and "most likely to be given names" (e.g. Berlin, 1972; Daehler, Lonardo, & Bukatko, 1979; Rosch, Mervis, Gray, Johnson, & Boyes-Braem, 1976). The problem with categorization research, however, is that it has ignored individual differences in talent for categorizing natural objects. That is, not one relevant citation came up in PsycINFO under the combined terms "categorization and giftedness" or "categorization and talent."

Next is mathematical talent—that is, facility with abstract quantitative reasoning. Some children begin to display incredible mathematical computational and reasoning skills as early as 2 or 3 years old and by 10 years of age are already performing complex mathematical calculations (Bell, 1937; Kanigel, 1991; Wiener, 1953). The list of historical examples of inherent precocious mathematical genius is long and impressive: Pascal, Newton, Leibniz, Laplace, Gauss, Boole, Wiener, Ramanujan, and Feynman to name but a few of the truly outstanding examples (Bell, 1937; Gleick, 1992; Kanigel, 1991; Wiener, 1953).

More systematically, however, one of the largest studies ever of mathematical ability was started by Julian Stanley in 1971 at Johns Hopkins University titled the Study of Mathematically Precocious Youth (SMPY). In the tradition of Terman (1925) and Cox (1926), Stanley and his colleagues studied very large but select samples of mathematically precocious young people, the most extreme form of whom they defined as scoring at or above 700 on the math portion of the SAT (SAT-M) before age 13 (Stanley, 1988; Stanley, Keating, & Fox, 1974). That this is an extremely selective criterion is beyond dispute: only 4% of male college-bound high school seniors and fewer than 1% of female college-bound high school seniors score 700 or higher on the SAT-M, and Stanley's sample consisted of preadolescents. In general, this sample of extreme mathematically precocious has continued to excel in their careers. Stanley (1988) argued for the predictive value of extreme mathematical precocity:

> ... these young students seem to have the potential to become the nation's superstars in pure and applied mathematics, computer science, electrical engineering, physics, and other fields that depend heavily on great quantitative aptitude. Quite a few of the 292 [who scored 700 on the SAT-M] appear well on the way toward excellence in such fields. (p. 206)

Using the SMPY sample, Benbow and her colleagues have presented data showing that precocious ability predicts achievement in high school (Benbow & Minor, 1986; Benbow & Stanley, 1982) and in college (Lubinski & Benbow, 1994). Approximately 90% go on to get bachelor's degrees, slightly less than 40% get master's degrees, and about 25% receive doctorates. These figures are well above the base rates for such degrees (with 23%, 7%, and 1% being the national figures respectively). Furthermore, longitudinal research has shown that those who went into math or science careers scored in the 90th percentile on math achievement tests in high school (Wise, Steel, & MacDonald, 1979). But as Farmer (1988) pointed out, only 42% of the male and 22% of the female extremely precocious students went on to choose science or math graduate programs (cf. Benbow, 1988; Benbow & Lubinski, 1993). In short, only 25% of the extremely gifted math sample continue in science and math through graduate school, and even fewer are retained in science and math careers. Whatever the life and career outcomes, one thing is certain: Mathematics is a domain in which extreme and precocious talent manifests itself in a small portion of the population.

The first domain of artistic talent and creativity to be discussed is music. Just as mathematical talent is manifested early in life, so too is musical talent. In fact, Gardner (1983) argues this is the earliest of all creative talents to be expressed: "Of all gifts with which individuals may be endowed, none emerges earlier than musical talent" (p. 99). Of course, the most famous case of this is Mozart, who played violin and clavier at age 3 and composed minuets at age 6 and symphonies at age 9 (Morelock & Feldman, 1999).

A few attempts have been made to study musical precocity more systematically. Influenced by the work of Gardner and Feldman, Freeman (1999) interviewed 24 musically precocious boys and asked questions concerning the existence and importance of "crystallizing experiences." Crystallizing experiences are singular, remarkable, and memorable experiences that often come in the form of sudden insight or epiphany (Walters & Gardner, 1986). These experiences have the function of being life altering, where in one moment one's purpose in life is revealed. Freeman's study was exploratory and qualitative, but the importance of crystallizing experiences to the musically precocious was clear. Almost to a person, each boy recounted an experience in which their musical talents were revealed to them in such a way that from that point forward music took on profound and even spiritual importance for them. They had to have music in their lives from that moment forward.

However, it is important to point out, just as is true of mathematical precocity and prodigiousness, early childhood talent in music by no means is a necessary or a sufficient condition for adult creative achievement. It is often the case that the musically most-accomplished adults do not begin to set themselves apart in any significant way until middle adolescence, and even here there are hundreds if not thousands of similarly talented musicians (Sosniak, 1990). It is also true that being a musical prodigy or even being precocious does not guarantee or even predict to a high degree adult creative achievement (Howe, 1999; Howe, Davidson, Moore, & Sloboda, 1995).

An interesting bit of evidence for domain specificity of musical ability comes from Williams syndrome, a somewhat opposing disorder from autism. People with Williams syndrome often have talent in music, face recognition, and are hypersociable and friendly, and yet have severe impairment in math and spatial domains. For instance, absolute pitch occurs in approximately 1 out of 10,000 people in the general population, but was seen in 5 out of 5 Williams syndrome individuals (Lenhoff, Perales, & Hickok, 2001). More often, individuals with Williams syndrome demonstrate normal overall talents in music, such as rhythm production or music performance, but also report higher levels of liking music and a greater range of emotional responses to music compared with control children (Don, Schellenberg, & Rourke, 1999; Levitin & Bellugi, 1998).

Next in the artistic domain comes linguistic talent and creativity. Linguistic ability is composed of various distinct forms of talent that map onto the standard components of language: Ability to understand and use nuanced meanings of words (semantics) and sensitivity and facility with the sound of word-strings (phonology) as well as rules of order (syntax). Verbal precocity can take many different forms, from precocious speaking in infancy, to precocious literacy (reading and writing), to precocious and talented written expression. Precocious speech in infancy as it turns out does not predict precocious literacy (Crain-Thoreson & Dale, 1992) or other domains of precocity (Robinson, Dale, & Landesman, 1990). A higher level of linguistic talent is seen in real-world creative achievement. Linguistic talent and creativity is usually not as obvious and distinct early in life as it is in mathematics and music, but it does manifest itself by late adolescence or early adulthood, especially in poetry (Simonton, 1975).

The last domain of artistic talent involves the visual arts, drawing, painting, sculpting, and photography. Again, as is true with other areas of precocious talent, artistic talent in childhood has not been the topic of large numbers of studies, case study or otherwise. A few major figures of art were either child prodigies or precocious, Toulouse-Lautrec (Pariser, 1995) and Picasso (Gardner, 1993) being the most notable examples of child prodigies who went on to world-class adult creative achievement. However, such cases of prodigies becoming creative adults are the exception rather than the rule. One of the most fascinating if not disturbing cases of artistic childhood prodigies is the case of Nadia (Selfe, 1995). An autistic savant, Nadia started producing incredibly sophisticated drawings at age 3 years 6 months and by age 6 years was creating drawings that were beyond even most adult artists in terms of perspective, movement, and orientation. By the age of 9 and 10 years she had garnered much notoriety and many considered her abilities to be "genius-level" accomplishments. Unfortunately, Nadia's story does not have a happy ending. By late adolescence her incredibly talented drawings had stopped and by her mid-20s she was never spontaneously drawing anything and what she did produce on demand was completely stereotyped, without feeling or perspective, much like a typical 3- or 4-year-old. Selfe speculates that both Nadia's very modest growth in language abilities (corresponding with her enrollment in a school for autistic children) and the death of her mother in mid- to late adolescence probably were factors in her artistic decline. Hou and colleagues (2000) described case studies of six artistic savants with autism, all of whom showed little variation in artistic theme and none of whom understood art theory. Hou and colleagues argue that the autistic characteristics (attention to visual detail, ritualistic–compulsive repetition, and single-focused attention) coupled with specific neuroanatomical substrate activity directly contribute to their artistic talents.

A few researchers have explored the topic of childhood expressions of artistic talent systematically. For instance, Rostan (1997) studied artistic talent development in 60 children from ages 5–11 years who were enrolled in a private art-enrichment program. The participants were videotaped while they solved art problems and professional artists then evaluated the drawings on knowledge, novelty, and ideation. Among the findings were that the most expressive and best-composed drawings were rated as most novel and that novelty was curvilinearly related to age. Additionally, Porath and Arlin (1997) reported unique and novel use of spatial representations in a group of artistically gifted children, aged 4 to 10 years. Karmiloff-Smith (1992) examined the development of drawing and notation in nongifted children and concluded that its progress is driven more by internal factors than external ones and the children become more and more capable of explicit representation with development. Finally, it is of note that some variability in artistic talent corresponds with specific neuroanatomical activity and deficits, often in the frontal and occipital regions (Gardner, 1982; Hou et al., 2000; Ramachandran & Hirstein, 1999). Even more remarkable is the development of artistic talent in previously nonartistically talented patients who experience frontotemporal dementia (Miller et al., 1998).

In summary, the domains of talent and creativity map quite directly onto the evolved domains of mind. Individuals tend to show talent early in life in one of the seven evolved domains and adult creative achievement (not always or even usually by the precocious and prodigy) also is channeled into these domains. Moreover, it is rare for one individual to have real talent and creativity in more than one domain, and if they do it tends to be in two related domains such as social–linguistic or mathematical–physical–musical.

To be clear, I am not arguing for complete specificity. It is well known that talent and creativity in some domains do overlap and covary. Indeed spatial ability is quite crucial to artistic (visual art) creativity as well as physical, mathematical, and musical ability, and so it could be considered a component to all of these domains. If this is so, it would suggest that perhaps a core set of relatively general cognitive processes play a role in different domains, such as visual representation (others being recall and processing speed). It also may suggest two general ways in which ideas are represented, namely verbal and nonverbal, with spatial thought being crucial to nonverbal representation, whether it be visualizing objects, mathematical ideas, musical notes, or images and patterns.

One general principle of talent is its highly positively skewed distribution in the population. That is, rather than being normally distributed, talent (in the form of real creative achievement) is expressed by a very few individuals, and creative output disproportionately comes from a small percentage of people, such that if graphed the distribution forms an inverted J. Authors who have discussed this phenomenon argue for a multiplicative function of talent (Jensen, 1996; Simonton, 2000; Walberg, Strykowski, Rovai,

& Hung, 1984). That is, talent is based on the convergence of many normally distributed domains that are each necessary but not sufficient for creative achievement. Because the outcome is multiplicative, if a person is missing even one talent domain then creative potential is zero. That is, creative achievement occurs if, and only if, one has all of the requisite components at at least a moderately high level. This may also explain the lack of predictive relationship between childhood precocity and prodigiousness and adult creative achievement: So many things can happen between childhood and adulthood to make one critical component functionally disappear (not pass a certain threshold) that real achievement is unlikely even in the most gifted.

PERSONALITY DIFFERENCES BETWEEN
ART AND SCIENCE DOMAINS

Personality differences among creative people have been examined at a relatively global level in that artists have been compared with scientists, but few studies have compared personality traits of highly creative people within each domain of the arts and sciences. Therefore, my review of the personality literature will focus on the art–science distinction.

Although there are common traits of personality across the artistic and scientific domains (both are introverted, arrogant, driven, open, and flexible), there also are some key personality differences between creative artists and creative scientists (Feist, 1998, 1999). Compared with creative scientists, artists appear to be more anxious, emotionally labile, and impulsive. More generally, therefore, the artistically creative person appears to have a disposition toward intense affective experience (Andreasen & Glick, 1988; Bamber, Bill, Boyd, & Corbett, 1983; Csikszentmihalyi & Getzels, 1973; Gardner, 1973; Getzels & Csikszentmihalyi, 1976; Jamison, 1993; Ludwig, 1995; Richards, 1994; Russ, 1993). To quote Russ (1993), "One of the main differences between artistic and scientific creativity may be the importance of getting more deeply into affect states and thematic material in artistic creativity" (p. 67). To the extent that art is more often an introspective journey and science more of an externally focused one (see Gardner, 1973), it is not surprising that artists would be more sensitive to and expressive of internal emotional states than scientists. This is not to say that the creative process in art is exclusively emotional and in science exclusively nonemotional. Research suggests that is not the case (Feist, 1991). The discovery stages of scientific creativity are often very intuitive and emotional, just as the elaboration stages of artistic creativity can be very technical and tedious. Yet dispositionally, artists and scientists generally do tend to differ on the degree to which they are sensitive to their own and other people's emotional states.

The second core set of unique characteristics of the artistic personality can be classified as low socialization and low conscientiousness. Although it is true that low socialization and nonconformity are traits of both creative artists and scientists (Barron, 1963, 1972; Cattell & Drevdahl, 1955; Csikszentmihalyi & Getzels, 1973; Hall & MacKinnon, 1969; Helson, 1971; Kemp, 1981; Ochse, 1990), the form that nonconformity takes may be different in the two professions. Artists and not scientists, for instance, tend to be much lower than the norm on personality scales for "socialization," "communality," "tolerance," and "responsibility" and higher on the "radical" scale (e.g., Barron, 1972; Csikszentmihalyi & Getzels, 1973; Domino, 1974; Drevdahl & Cattell, 1958; Kemp, 1981; Zeldow, 1973). The low socialization and responsibility scores are indicative of people who very much question, doubt, and struggle with social norms. Perhaps artists are more actively nonconformist or asocialized than scientists, who may be less overt in their nonconformity. Consistent with the idea that scientists are less actively nonconforming than artists, scientists in general tend to be more conscientious and orderly than nonscientists (Kline & Lapham, 1992; Rossman & Horn, 1972; Schaefer, 1969; Wilson & Jackson, 1994). If one considers that traits such as "organized," "planful," "not careless," and "not slipshod" make up the conscientiousness dimension (John, 1990), it is not surprising that scientists would be higher on the dimension than artists.

As mentioned above, one limitation with the research on personality and scientific and artistic creativity is that it is not specific to different kinds of scientists and different kinds of artists but rather covers artists and scientists in general. Very little if any research has compared the personality dispositions of natural, biological, and social scientists to examine whether the more social the scientist the more sociable his or her personality. Of most interest would be developmental research that examined whether a preference for things is evident early in life for future physical scientists and likewise whether a preference for people is evident early in life for future social scientists. The next line of research for the personality psychology of science is to explore differences in personality among physical, biological, and social scientists. My hunch is that the physical scientists as a group will be more introverted and thing-oriented (i.e., have more developed implicit physical domain knowledge) than the biological scientists, who in turn will be less sociable and extraverted than social scientists.

IMPORTANCE OF FLUID INTEGRATION BETWEEN DOMAINS FOR CREATIVE THOUGHT

Our minds may have evolved domain-specific talents, but they are not simply a handful of capacities that have nothing to do with one another. As cognitive archeologist Stephen Mithen (1996, 1998) has argued, the truly remarkable feature of modern humans is our ability to have ideas and solutions to problems that cross domain boundaries. In other species of hominoid and hominid, problem-solving strategies do not permeate between domains. As far as we now know from the archeological and comparative records, only the mind of modern humans has had the capacity to rather fluidly move between domains—that is to form creative associations (Donald, 1991; Mithen, 1996; Parker & McKinney, 1999). This creative ability to apply ideas from one domain to another, more than language or tool making, may be what distinguishes us most as a species. For instance, we have integrated knowledge of the physical world with the social world and created body paints or jewelry to signify identity or status. No other species of hominid or hominoid, including our closest ancient relative, Neanderthal, has shown such a capacity. In fact, each art form involves some technical foundation that one must master to become proficient in that medium, and then apply it to another domain, whether it is the physics of pigment combination and spatial orientation in visual art or the musical technique of piano, guitar, violin, and so forth. Even the craft of literature involves combining linguistic skills with social-psychological insight. In short, we are a creative species precisely because we have the cognitive capacity to apply knowledge from one domain to a distinctly different domain. We are the only species with art, science, religion, literature, music, each of which requires integration from at least two domains. One of the things that makes creative talent so rare is that it requires simultaneously both very specialized knowledge and very broad knowledge that can fluently, if not unconsciously, cross domain boundaries (Feist, 2001).

Such flexible integration of and fluidity between domains is not inconsistent with domain-specific creative talent, for it still is solving a specific problem in a specific domain. It is not that a chemist is likely to ever create a master painting or create a new form of psychotherapy, but that creative chemists are creative because they can cull from other domains and have some knowledge and familiarity with a wide range of topics and apply that knowledge to the physical domain. Talent resides in a domain or cluster of domains but brings in knowledge and principles from other domains. That may well be what distinguishes a creative person in a given domain from a less creative one: The former is ideationally fluent and has a wide range of ideas and a large knowledge base and is open to novel ideas and experiences. Each of these traits has been shown to increase the possibility that a creative combination will be formed (Barron, 1963; Feist, 1998; Simonton, 1999).

Understanding the evolution of the human mind tells us much of what the mind does and what it is capable of. One of the things it tells us is the human mind is not a generalized tabula rasa but rather an active organizer of sensory experience with many domain-specific problem-solving mechanisms dedicated to solving specific social, physical, biological, numeric, aesthetic, linguistic, and musical problems. Historically, much of social science has assumed human nature to be blank and completely socially and culturally malleable (cf. Pinker, 2002; Tooby & Cosmides, 1992). An evolutionary perspective, conversely, suggests that the human mind in general and individual minds in particular develop along at least seven specified paths, each with its own particular talents and limitations. Such a view goes a long way in explaining the specific expressions of creative talents along specific scientific and artistic lines. It is not a coincidence that creative talent gets expressed in physical science, biological science, social science, mathematics, literature, art, and music. These are the domains of mind important in our ancestral past and they have developed over the millennia from very implicit and folk forms of knowledge to the systematic, formal, and explicit modes of thought that they are today.

An evolutionary perspective also provides a framework for understanding the neurophysiological and psychological mechanisms that make up these domains and what their criteria are. Creative talent tends to fall along domain-specific lines and any one individual is fortunate if he or she has the combination of inherent skills and encouraging environmental conditions to facilitate creative achievement in one domain—a combination that results from genetic and environmental interactions as seen in the Darwinian process of early neural development in the brain (Deacon, 1997; Edelman, 1987) and its related phenomenon brain plasticity (Bennett, Rosenzweig, & Diamond, 1969; Bennett, Diamond, Krech, & Rosenzweig, 1996; Deacon, 1997; Renner & Rosenzweig, 1987). An individual's creative talents are generally channeled into a few specific domains by their inherited genotype (i.e., what others may call "God-given talents"), but whether they fulfill their innate and domain-specific talent is a function of many complex environmental forces, including training, practice, and encouragement (or lack of active discouragement) from key figures in their life. Understanding the evolution of the human mind also tells us the brain of *Homo sapiens* is uniquely complex and flexible in its ability to form associations between domains. Such fluid integration between domains is the foundation for human creativity and has much to say about why art, science, and religion are unique behaviors limited to our species, and why talent in any given domain tends to be limited to certain individuals of our species.

REFERENCES

Aiken, N. E. (1998). *The biological origins of art.* Westport, CT: Praeger.

Amabile, T. M. (1996). *Creativity in context: Update to the social psychology of creativity.* New York: Westview Press.

Andreasen, N. C., & Glick, I. D. (1988). Bipolar affective disorder and creativity: Implications and clinical management. *Comprehensive Psychiatry, 29,* 207–216.

Bamber, J. H., Bill, J. M., Boyd, F. E., and Corbett, W. D. (1983). In two minds—arts and science differences at sixth-form level. *British Journal of Educational Psychology, 53,* 222–233.

Baron-Cohen, S., Bolton, P., Wheelwright, S., Short, L., Mead, G., Smith, A., & Scahill, V. (1998). Autism occurs more often in families of physicists, engineers, and mathematicians. *Autism, 2*, 296–301.

Baron-Cohen, S., Wheelwright, S., Skinner, R., Martin, J., & Clubley, E. (2001). The autism-spectrum quotient (AQ): Evidence from Asperger syndrome/high-functioning autism, males and females, scientists and mathematicians. *Journal of Autism and Developmental Disorders, 31*, 5–17.

Baron-Cohen, S., Wheelwright, S., Stone, V., & Rutherford, M. (1999). A mathematician, a physicist, and a computer scientist with Asperger syndrome: Performance on folk psychology and folk physics tests. *Neurocase, 5*, 475–483.

Baron-Cohen, S., Wheelwright, S., Stott, C., Bolton, P., & Goodyer, I. (1997). Is there a link between engineering and autism? *Autism, 1*, 101–109.

Barron, F. (1963). *Creativity and psychology health.* New York: Van Nostrand.

Barron, F. (1972). *Artists in the making.* New York: Seminar Press.

Barrow, J. D. (1995). *The artful universe.* Boston: Little, Brown.

Bell, E. T. (1937). *Men of mathematics.* New York: Simon & Schuster.

Benbow, C. P. (1988). Sex differences in mathematical reasoning ability in intellectually talented preadolescents: Their nature, effects, and possible causes. *Behavioral and Brain Sciences, 11*, 169–183.

Benbow, C. P., & Lubinski, D. (1993). Psychological profiles of the mathematically talented. Some sex differences and evidence supporting their biological basis. In G. R. Bock & K. Ackrill (Eds.), *The origins and development of high ability* (pp. 44–66). Chichester, England: Wiley.

Benbow, C. P., & Minor, L. L. (1986). Mathematically talented males and females and achievement in the high school sciences. *American Educational Research Journal, 23*, 425–436.

Benbow, C. P., & Stanley, J. C. (1982). Consequences in high school and college of sex differences in mathematical reasoning ability: A longitudinal perspective. *American Educational Research Journal, 19*, 598–622.

Bennett, E. L., Diamond, M. C., Krech, D., & Rosenzweig, M. R. (1996). Chemical and anatomical plasticity of brain. *Journal of Neuropsychiatry and Clinical Neurosciences, 8*, 459–470.

Bennett, E. L., Rosenzweig, M. R., & Diamond, M. C. (1969, February 21). Rat brain: Effects of environmental enrichment on wet and dry weights. *Science, 163*, 825–826.

Berlin, B. (1972). Speculations on the growth of ethnobotanical nomenclature. *Language and Society, 1*, 63–98.

Bloom, P. (1998). Some issues in the evolution of language and thought. In D. D. Cummins & C. Allen (Eds.), *The evolution of mind* (pp. 204–223). New York: Oxford University Press.

Bradshaw, J. L. (2001). Ars brevis, vita longa: The possible evolutionary antecedents of art and aesthetics. *Bulletin of Psychology and the Arts, 2*, 7–11.

Byrne, R. W. (2001). Social and technical forms of primate intelligence. In F. B. M. de Waal (Ed.), *Tree of origin: What primate behavior can tell us about human social evolution* (pp. 147–172). Cambridge, MA: Harvard University Press.

Carey, S., & Spelke, E. (1994). Domain specific knowledge and conceptual change. In L. A. Hirschfeld & S. A. Gelman (Eds.), *Mapping the mind: Domain specificity in cognition and culture* (pp. 169–200). Cambridge, England: Cambridge University Press.

Cattell, R. B., & Drevdahl, J. E. (1955). A comparison of the personality profile (16PF) of eminent researchers with that of eminent teachers and administrators, and the general population. *British Journal of Psychology, 46*, 248–261.

Charness, N. (1988). Expertise in chess, music, and physics: A cognitive perspective. In L. K. Obler & D. Fein (Eds.), *The exceptional brain: Neuropsychology of talent and special abilities* (pp. 399–426). New York: Guilford Press.

Clark, W. R., & Grunstein, M. (2000). *Are we hardwired? The role of genes in human behavior.* Oxford, England: Oxford University Press.

Cox, C. (1926). *Genetic studies of genius: Vol. II. The early mental traits of three hundred geniuses.* Stanford, CA: Stanford University Press.

Crain-Thoreson, C., & Dale, P. S. (1992). Do early talkers become early readers? Linguistic precocity, preschool language, and emergent literacy. *Developmental Psychology, 28*, 421–429.

Cranberg, L. D., & Albert, M. L. (1988). The chess mind. In L. K. Obler & D. Fein (Eds.), *The exceptional brain: Neuropsychology of talent and special abilities* (pp. 156–190). New York: Guilford Press.

Csikszentmihalyi, M., & Getzels, J. W. (1973). The personality of young artists: An empirical and theoretical exploration. *British Journal of Psychology, 64*, 91–104.

Daehler, M. W., Lonardo, R., & Bukatko, D. (1979). Matching and equivalence judgments in very young children. *Child Development, 50*, 70–79.

Deacon, T. (1997). *The symbolic species: The co-evolution of language and the brain.* New York: Norton.

Dissanayake, E. (1992). *Homo aestheticus: Where art comes from and why.* New York: Free Press.

Domino, G. (1974). Assessment of cinematographic creativity. *Journal of Personality and Social Psychology, 30*, 150–154.

Don, A. J., Schellenberg, E. G., & Rourke, B. P. (1999). Music and language skills of children with Williams syndrome. *Child Neuropsychology, 5*, 154–170.

Donald, M. (1991). *Origins of the modern mind: Three stages in the evolution of culture and cognition.* Cambridge, MA: Harvard University Press.

Drevdahl, J. E., & Cattell, R. B. (1958). Personality and creativity in artists and writers. *Journal of Clinical Psychology, 14*, 107–111.

Edelman, G. (1987). *Neural Darwinism.* New York: Basic Books.

Farmer, H. S. (1988). Predicting who our future scientists and mathematicians will be. *Behavioral and Brain Sciences, 11*, 190–191.

Feist, G. J. (1991). Synthetic and analytic thought: Similarities and differences among art and science students. *Creativity Research Journal, 4,* 145–155.

Feist, G. J. (1998). A meta-analysis of the impact of personality on scientific and artistic creativity. *Personality and Social Psychological Review, 2,* 290–309.

Feist, G. J. (1999). Personality in scientific and artistic creativity. In R. J. Sternberg (Ed.), *Handbook of human creativity* (pp. 273–296). Cambridge, England: Cambridge University Press.

Feist, G. J. (2001). Natural and sexual selection in the evolution of creativity. *Bulletin of Psychology and the Arts, 2,* 11–16.

Feist, G. J. (in press). *The origins of science: An introduction to the psychology of science.* New Haven, CT: Yale University Press.

Fodor, J. A. (1983). *The modularity of mind: An essay on faculty psychology.* Cambridge, MA: MIT Press.

Freeman, C. (1999). The crystallizing experience: A study of musical precocity. *Gifted Child Quarterly, 43,* 75–84.

Gardner, H. (1973). *The arts and human development: A psychological study of the artistic process.* New York: Wiley.

Gardner, H. (1982). *Art, mind & brain: A cognitive approach to creativity.* New York: Basic Books.

Gardner, H. (1983). *Frames of mind: The theory of multiple intelligences.* New York: Basic Books.

Gardner, H. (1993). *Creating minds: An anatomy of creativity.* New York: Basic Books.

Gardner, H. (1999). *Intelligence reframed: Multiple intelligences for the 21st century.* New York: Basic Books.

Gelman, R., & Brenneman, L. (1994). First principles can support both universal and culture-specific learning about number and music. In L. A. Hirschfeld & S. A. Gelman (Eds.), *Mapping the mind: Domain specificity in cognition and culture* (pp. 369–390). New York: Cambridge University Press.

Getzels, J. W., & Csikszentmihalyi, M. (1976). *The creative vision.* New York: Wiley.

Gleick, J. (1992). *Genius: Richard Feynman and modern physics.* New York: Pantheon Books.

Goleman, D. (1995). *Emotional intelligence.* New York: Bantam Books.

Gopnik, A., Meltzoff, A. N., & Kuhl, P. K. (1999). *The scientist in the crib: Minds, brains, and how children learn.* New York: Morrow.

Guilford, J. P. (1950). Creativity. *American Psychologist, 5,* 444–454.

Hall, W. B., & MacKinnon, D. W. (1969). Personality inventory correlates of creativity among architects. *Journal of Applied Psychology, 53,* 322–326.

Hatch, T. (1997). Friends, diplomats, and leaders in kindergarten: Interpersonal intelligence in play. In P. Salovey & D. J. Sluyter (Eds.), *Emotional development and emotional intelligence: Educational implications* (pp. 70–92). New York: Basic Books.

Helson, R. (1971). Women mathematicians and the creative personality. *Journal of Consulting and Clinical Psychology, 36,* 210–220.

Hou, C., Miller, B. L., Cummings, J. L., Goldberg, M., Mychack, P., Bottino, V., & Benson, D. F. (2000). Artistic savants. *Neuropsychiatry, Neuropsychology, and Behavioral Neurology, 13,* 29–38.

Howe, M. J. A. (1999). Prodigies and creativity. In R. J. Sternberg (Ed.), *Handbook of creativity* (pp. 431–446). New York: Cambridge University Press.

Howe, M. J. A., Davidson, J. W., Moore, D. G., & Sloboda, J. A. (1995). Are there early childhood signs of musical ability? *Psychology of Music, 23,* 162–176.

Jamison, K. R. (1993). *Touched with fire: Manic-depressive illness and the artistic temperament.* New York: Free Press.

Jensen, A. R. (1996). Giftedness and genius: Crucial differences. In C. Benbow & D. J. Lubinski (Eds.), *Intellectual talent: Psychometric and social issues* (pp. 393–411). Baltimore: Johns Hopkins University Press.

John, O. P. (1990). The "Big Five" factor taxonomy: Dimensions of personality in the natural language and in questionnaires. In L. A. Pervin (Ed.), *Handbook of personality research and theory* (pp. 66–100). New York: Guilford Press.

Kanigel, R. (1991). *The man who knew infinity: A life of the genius Ramanujan.* New York: Scribner.

Karmiloff-Smith, A. (1992). *Beyond modularity: A developmental perspective on cognitive science.* Cambridge, MA: MIT Press.

Kemp, A. (1981). The personality structure of the musician. I. Identifying a profile of traits for the performer. *Psychology of Music, 9,* 3–14.

Kline, P., & Lapham, S. L. (1992). Personality and faculty in British universities. *Personality and Individual Differences, 13,* 855–857.

Lazarus, R. S. (1991). *Emotion and adaptation.* New York: Oxford University Press.

LeDoux, J. (1996). *The emotional brain: The mysterious underpinnings of emotional life.* New York: Simon & Schuster.

Lehman, H. C. (1953). *Age and achievement.* Princeton, NJ: Princeton University Press.

Lenhoff, H. M., Perales, O., & Hickok, G. (2001). Absolute pitch in Williams syndrome. *Music Perception, 18,* 491–503.

Levitin, D. J., & Bellugi, U. (1998). Musical abilities in individuals with Williams syndrome. *Music Perception, 15,* 357–389.

Lubinski, D., & Benbow, C. P. (1994). The study of mathematically precocious youth: The first three decades of a planned 50-year study of intellectual talent. In R. F. Subotnik & K. D. Arnold (Eds.), *Beyond Terman: Longitudinal studies of giftedness and talent* (pp. 255–281). Norwood, NJ: Ablex.

Ludwig, A. M. (1995). *The price of greatness.* New York: Guilford Press.

MacKinnon, D. W. (1970). Creativity: A multi-faceted phenomenon. In J. Roslanksy (Ed.), *Creativity* (pp. 19–32). Amsterdam: North-Holland.

Mervis, C. B., & Rosch, E. (1981). Categorization of natural objects. *Annual Review of Psychology, 32,* 89–115.

Miller, B. L., Cummings, J., Mishkin, F., Boone, K., Prince, F., Ponton, M., & Cotman, C. (1998). Emergence of artistic talent in frontotemporal dementia. *Neurology, 51,* 978–982.

Miller, G. F. (2000). *The mating mind: How sexual choice shaped the evolution of human nature*. New York: Doubleday.

Mithen, S. (1996). *The prehistory of the mind: The cognitive origins of art and science*. London: Thames & Hudson.

Mithen, S. (1998). Introduction to Part II. In S. Mithen (Ed.), *Creativity in human evolution and prehistory* (pp. 93–109). London: Routledge.

Morelock, M. J., & Feldman, D. H. (1999). Prodigies. In M. A. Runco & S. R. Pritzker (Eds.), *Encyclopedia of creativity* (Vol. 2, pp. 449–456). San Diego, CA: Academic Press.

Moulin, L. (1955). The Nobel prizes for the sciences from 1901–1950: An essay in sociological analysis. *British Journal of Sociology, 6*, 246–263.

Ochse, R. (1990). *Before the gates of excellence: The determinants of creative genius*. New York: Cambridge University Press.

Orians, G. (2001). An evolutionary perspective on aesthetics. *Bulletin of Psychology and the Arts, 2*, 25–29.

Orians, G. H., & Heerwagen, J. H. (1992). Evolved responses to landscapes. In J. H. Barkow, L. Cosmides, & J. Tooby (Eds.), *The adapted mind* (pp. 555–579). New York: Oxford University Press.

Pariser, D. (1995). Lautrec—Gifted child artist and artistic monument: Connections between juvenile and mature work. In C. Golomb (Ed.), *The development of artistically gifted children* (pp. 31–70). Hillsdale, NJ: Erlbaum.

Parker, S. T., & McKinney, M. L. (1999). *Origins of intelligence*. Baltimore: Johns Hopkins University Press.

Pincus, J. H. (1999). Aggression, criminality, and the frontal lobes. In B. L. Miller & J. L. Cummings (Eds.), *The human frontal lobes: Functions and disorders* (pp. 547–556). New York: Guilford Press.

Pinker, S. (1997). *How the mind works*. New York: Norton.

Pinker, S. (2002). *The blank slate: The modern denial of human nature*. New York: Viking Press.

Porath, M., & Arlin, P. K. (1997). Developmental approaches to artistic giftedness. *Creativity Research Journal, 10*, 241–250.

Ramachandran, V. S., & Hirstein, W. (1999). The science of art: A neurological theory of aesthetic experience. *Journal of Consciousness Studies, 6*, 15–51.

Renner, M. J., & Rosenzweig, M. R. (1987). *Enriched and impoverished environments: Effects on brain and behavior*. New York: Springer-Verlag.

Richards, R. L. (1994). Creativity and bipolar mood swings: Why the association? In M. P. Shaw & M. A. Runco (Eds.), *Creativity and affect* (pp. 44–72). Norwood, NJ: Ablex.

Rimland, B., & Fein, D. (1988). Special talents of autistic savants. In L. K. Obler & D. Fein (Eds.), *The exceptional brain: Neuropsychology of talent and special abilities* (pp. 474–492). New York: Guilford Press.

Robinson, N. M., Dale, P. S., & Landesman, S. (1990). Validity of Stanford-Binet IV with linguistically precocious toddlers. *Intelligence, 14*, 173–186.

Rosch, E. (1975). Universals and cultural specifics in human categorization. In R. W. Brislin, S. Bochner, & W. J. Lonner (Eds.), *Cross-cultural perspectives on learning* (pp. 177–206). New York: Wiley.

Rosch, E., Mervis, C. B., Gray, W. D., Johnson, D. M., & Boyes-Braem, P. (1976). Basic objects in natural categories. *Cognitive Psychology, 8*, 382–439.

Rossman, B. B., & Horn, J. L. (1972). Cognitive, motivational and temperamental indicants of creativity and intelligence. *Journal of Educational Measurement, 9*, 265–286.

Rostan, S. M. (1997). A study of young artists: The development of artistic talent and creativity. *Creativity Research Journal, 10*, 175–192.

Russ, S. (1993). *Affect and creativity: The role of affect and play in the creative process.* Hillsdale, NJ: Erlbaum.

Salovey, P., & Mayer, J. D. (1990). Emotional intelligence. *Imagination, Cognition, and Personality, 9*, 185–211.

Schaefer, C. E. (1969). The self-concept of creative adolescents. *The Journal of Psychology, 72*, 233–242.

Schmitt, A., & Grammar, K. (1997). Social intelligence and success: Don't be too clever in order to be smart. In A. Whiten & R. W. Byrne (Eds.), *Machiavellian intelligence II: Extensions and evaluations* (pp. 86–111). Cambridge, England: Cambridge University Press.

Selfe, L. (1995). Nadia reconsidered. In C. Golomb (Ed.), *The development of artistically gifted children: Selected case studies* (pp. 197–236). Hillsdale, NJ: Erlbaum.

Simonton, D. K. (1975). Age and literary creativity: A cross-cultural and transhistorical survey. *Journal of Cross-Cultural Psychology, 6*, 259–277.

Simonton, D. K. (1988a). Age and outstanding achievement: What do we know after a century of research? *Psychological Bulletin, 104*, 251–267.

Simonton, D. K. (1988b). *Scientific genius: A psychology of science.* Cambridge, England: Cambridge University Press.

Simonton, D. K. (1999). *Origins of genius.* New York: Oxford University Press.

Simonton, D. K. (2000). Talent and its development: An emergenic and epigenetic model. *Psychological Review, 106*, 435–457.

Sosniak, L. A. (1990). The tortoise, the hare, and the development of talent. In M. J. A. Howe (Ed.), *Encouraging the development of exceptional abilities and talents* (pp. 149–164). Leicester, England: British Psychological Society.

Sperber, D. (1994). The modularity of thought and epidemiology of representations. In L. A. Hirschfeld & S. A. Gelman (Eds.), *Mapping the mind: Domain specificity in cognition and culture* (pp. 39–67). Cambridge, England: Cambridge University Press.

Stanley, J. C. (1988). Some characteristics of SMPY's "700–800 on SAT-M before age 13 group": Youths who reason *extremely* well mathematically. *Gifted Child Quarterly, 32*, 205–209.

Stanley, J. C., Keating, D. P., & Fox, L. H. (Eds.). (1974). *Mathematical talent: Discovery, description, and development.* Baltimore: Johns Hopkins University Press.

Sternberg, R. J. (1988). A three-facet model of creativity. In R. J. Sternberg (Ed.), *The nature of creativity* (pp. 125–147). Cambridge, England: Cambridge University Press.

Stone, V., Baron-Cohen, S., & Knight, R. T. (1998). Frontal lobe contributions to theory of mind. *Journal of Cognitive Neuroscience, 10,* 640–656.

Stuss, D. T., Gallup, G. G., & Alexander, M. P. (2001). The frontal lobes are necessary for "theory of mind." *Brain, 124,* 279–286.

Terman, L. M. (1925). *Genetic studies of genius: Vol. 1. Mental and physical traits of a thousand gifted children.* Palo Alto, CA: Stanford University Press.

Thorndike, E. L. (1920). Intelligence and its uses. *Harper's Magazine, 140,* 227–235.

Tooby, J., & Cosmides, L. (1992). The psychological foundations of culture. In J. Barkow, L. Cosmides, & J. Tooby (Eds.), *The adapted mind: Evolutionary psychology and the generation of culture* (pp. 19–136). Oxford, England: Oxford University Press.

Tramo, M. J. (2001, January 5). Enhanced: Music of the hemispheres. *Science, 291,* 54–56.

Walberg, H. J, Strykowski, B. F., Rovai, E., & Hung, S. S. (1984). Exceptional performance. *Review of Educational Research, 54,* 87–112.

Walters, J., & Gardner, H. (1986). The crystallizing experience: Discovering an intellectual gift. In R. J. Sternberg & J. E. Davidson (Eds.), *Conceptions of giftedness* (pp. 306–330). New York: Cambridge University Press.

Wiener, N. (1953). *Ex-prodigy: My childhood and youth.* Cambridge, MA: MIT Press.

Wilson, G. D., & Jackson, C. (1994). The personality of physicists. *Personality and Individual Differences, 16,* 187–189.

Wise, L. L., Steel, L., & MacDonald, C. (1979). *Origins and career consequences of sex differences in high school mathematics achievement.* Washington, DC: American Institute for Research.

Zeldow, P. B. (1973). Replication and extension of the personality profile of "artists in the making." *Psychological Reports, 33,* 541–542.

6

CREATIVITY AS A CONSTRAINED STOCHASTIC PROCESS

DEAN KEITH SIMONTON

Creativity was originally viewed as something mysterious. According to the ancient Greeks, creativity was literally the gift of the Muses, the goddesses who presided over all major forms of human creativity. This basic idea persisted in various forms well into the Italian Renaissance. For example, Giorgio Vasari (1550/1968), author of the *Lives of the Painters, Sculptors, and Architects,* claimed that Michelangelo was a genius sent by God to produce wondrous art on earth. Yet after the advent of the Enlightenment, and especially after the emergence of the behavioral sciences, creativity began to be seen as a more naturalistic phenomenon. Creativity represented a capacity possessed by the individual rather than a gift bestowed by some supernatural agent. For instance, Francis Galton (1869) considered creative genius the consequence of natural ability, the latter consisting of a specific combination of intellect, energy, and motivation.

Eventually, in fact, creativity would become treated not just as a natural phenomenon, but as a rational phenomenon besides. That is, the creative person was someone who applied a logic, method, or set of techniques to a given domain of expertise. This notion first appeared in the area of scientific creativity, whether in the form of the inductive method of Francis Bacon or the deductive method of René Descartes. Yet it was only a matter of time before this concept of creativity made its way into the arts. For instance, Sir Joshua Reynolds (1769–1790/1966) made it clear to his students at the Royal Academy of Art that the assiduous mastery of a set of techniques was all that was required to demonstrate artistic creativity, even genius. This view found explicit scientific proponents among cognitive psychologists who saw creativity as a form of problem solving (e.g., Newell & Simon, 1972; Simon, 1986). All that was necessary to exhibit creativity in either the arts or sciences was the acquisition of the knowledge and techniques appropriate to a particular discipline (e.g., Hayes, 1989; Perkins, 2000; Weisberg, 1992). So straightforward has creativity become, from this viewpoint, that anyone can become a creative genius if they are merely willing to put in the necessary hard work. Indeed, computer programs have even been written that purport to make major scientific discoveries by the same step-by-step, logical procedures divulged in the experimental research on human problem solving (e.g., Langley, Simon, Bradshaw, & Zythow, 1987; Shrager & Langley, 1990).

Although these analyses have performed the important function of demystifying creativity, the rationalizing of creativity may have gone too far. It now seems too easy, too logical. As a result, this perspective tends to overlook a very important feature of creative behavior, namely, that it appears to be *stochastic* (Simonton, 2003). According to the dictionary definition, something is stochastic if it is "characterized by conjecture; conjectural," "involving or containing a random variable or variables," or "involving chance or probability" (*American Heritage Electronic Dictionary*, 1992). In other words, to claim that creativity is stochastic is to assert that it entails much more uncertainty and unpredictability than would be expected from a forthright, rational process. At the same time, to hold that creativity is stochastic is not tantamount to the assertion that it is totally random, and therefore capricious and illogical. On the contrary, I argue that creativity has the characteristics of *constrained* stochastic behavior. Creativity is to a certain degree predictable, but far from deterministic.

I will make my case by examining two phenomena that make it unquestionable that creative behavior has clear stochastic features. After offering explanations for these phenomena I will turn to the constraints on the degree to which creativity is stochastic.

TWO CHARACTERISTIC PHENOMENA

Admittedly, few researchers maintain that chance plays no role whatsoever in creativity. At least many are willing to accept the existence of serendipitous events in science and technology. These are occasions when someone supposedly discovered or invented something by complete accident (Austin, 1978; Cannon, 1940; Roberts, 1989). Nonetheless, serendipitous discoveries are usually considered the exception rather than the rule. Science normally proceeds by its inexorable logic, which chance intermittently interrupts (Simon, 1973). Therefore, it is necessary to turn to phenomena in which the stochastic nature of creativity appears as a regularity rather than as an anomaly. The two phenomena that satisfy this requirement are multiple discovery and creative productivity.

Multiple Discovery

I begin with the phenomenon in which two or more individuals independently make the same discovery. Classic examples include the calculus originated by Newton and Leibnitz, the theory of evolution by natural selection proposed by Darwin and Wallace, the laws of genetic inheritance discovered by Mendel, De Vries, Correns, and Tschermak, and the theory of emotion put forward by James and Lange. A particularly striking aspect of these independent discoveries is the fact that they often occur nearly simultaneously, sometimes even on the same day. Sociologists and anthropologists have argued that these multiples can only be explained as the consequence of sociocultural determinism (Lamb & Easton, 1984). At a particular moment in the historical development of any given scientific discipline, a given discovery becomes absolutely inevitable (Kroeber, 1917; Merton, 1961; Ogburn & Thomas, 1922). So high is the discovery's likelihood that it is often made by more than one scientist. The discovery is "in the air" and thus "ripe for picking" by anyone. It is the work of the zeitgeist rather than genius.

Yet this interpretation does not survive close logical and empirical scrutiny (Patinkin, 1983; Schmookler, 1966; Simonton, 2003). It is well documented that human beings often discern patterns in what are bona fide random events, and multiple discovery is no exception (Simonton, 2002b). The true nature of the phenomenon is demonstrated by the fact that stochastic models—mathematical models with random variables—can reproduce all of its key empirical features (Brannigan & Wanner, 1983a, 1983b; Price, 1963; Simonton, 1979, 1986a, 2003). For instance, multiples vary according to the number of individuals who are independently involved in the discovery, a count known as the *multiple's grade* (Merton, 1961). Moreover, the higher the grade of the multiple, the lower is the probability of its occurrence (Merton, 1961; Simonton, 1979). Speaking more precisely, the probabilities are accurately described by the Poisson distribution (Price, 1963; Simonton, 1978).[1]

---

[1]Like the normal distribution, the Poisson distribution can be derived from the binomial distribution with the parameters p (the probability of an event) and n (the number of trials). However, unlike the normal distribution, the derivation of the Poisson assumes that p is extremely small and n is extremely large. One final distinction is that unlike the equation for the normal distribution, which has two parameters (the mean μ and the variance σ^2), the equation describing the Poisson has only one because the mean equals the variance (i.e., $\mu = \sigma^2$, where $\mu = np$ as $n \to \infty$). In particular, the probability of i events occurring within a given unit is given by $P(i) = \mu^i e^{-\mu} / i!$ (where e is the exponential constant $2.718...$ and $i! = 1 \times 2 \times 3 \times ... \times i$).

Yet this distribution is generated by a stochastic process that applies to events that have a very low probability of occurrence. As a result, the events can only happen at all because there are so many trials. In terms of the binomial distribution (from which the Poisson can be derived; Molina, 1942), we can infer that p is very, very small and n is very, very large. These certainly are not inevitable events (Schmookler, 1966).

With a little elaboration, the stochastic model can account for other features of multiples, such as the degree of simultaneity of the independent discoveries and the distribution of multiple discoveries across scientists (Brannigan & Wanner, 1983a, 1983b; Simonton, 1986a, 1999b, 2003). For instance, the temporal separation of duplicated discoveries can be accommodated by introducing a "contagion" mechanism into the stochastic process (Brannigan & Wanner, 1983b; Simonton, 1986a). In fact, there is not one single empirical characteristic of multiples that cannot be predicted and explained using a stochastic model. Those who insist on attributing these events to sociocultural determinism are violating the law of parsimony because such an attribution evokes a causal principle that is unnecessary to explain the observed effects. Even worse, some predictions of traditional interpretation are flatly contradicted by the data. For instance, the probability distribution of multiple grades has a form inconsistent with the claim that discoveries and inventions are inevitable (Schmookler, 1966; Simonton, 1979).

In short, multiples represent coincidental rather than inevitable events.

Creative Productivity

One unfortunate feature of the multiples phenomenon is its exclusive relevance to scientific creativity. Although there are reasons why artistic creativity does not display the same phenomenon, these need not concern us here (see Simonton, 1988b; Stent, 1972). From our current perspective another task is more urgent: to provide an example of a stochastic phenomenon that applies just as well to artistic creativity as it does to scientific creativity. Not only does such a phenomenon exist, but also it is germane to the very essence of the creative enterprise. Ultimately the highest levels of creativity must result in a creative product. Inventors who invent nothing, or poets who write no poems, can hardly be considered creative no matter how they might score on some so-called "creativity test" (Simonton, 2000b). Indeed, the definition of creative genius that enjoys the greatest prima facie validity is predicated on creative output (Albert, 1975; Galton, 1869; Simonton, 2002b).

Given this connection, it becomes important to ask how creative products are distributed over the course of a career. The answer is striking: Products are more or less randomly scattered across the career course (Huber, 1998a, 2000; Huber & Wagner-Döbler, 2001). They do not tend to be clumped toward the beginning, middle, or end of the career. For the most part, "runs" are no greater than would be expected by chance alone. Basically, the production of works follows the pattern seen in flipping a coin. Sometimes there will appear a string of heads, and other times a string of tails, but not to an extent exceeding what would be normally expected from an unbiased coin. Instead, heads are interspersed among tails in a totally unpredictable fashion.

Just as curious is the fact that the number of products produced in a particular unit of time is described by the same distribution that describes multiple grades, namely the Poisson (Huber, 1998b, 2000; Huber & Wagner-Döbler, 2001). In fact, the key parameter of the Poisson is virtually identical for both situations (viz. the mean-variance $\mu \approx 1$, where $\mu = np$; Simonton, 2003). This again suggests that the creative product is a low-probability event (i.e., p is extremely small). The only reason why they occur at all is that there are so many trials both within and across creators (i.e., n is extremely large).

The foregoing conclusions were based on analyses of total output. Yet it could be argued that quantity is less important than quality. Perhaps only quality products should count—works that had and continue to have an impact. Nevertheless, this stipulation does not get us around the inference that creative productivity is fundamentally stochastic. Indeed, the stochastic nature of the phenomenon becomes all the more pronounced. The reason is that quality is itself a probabilistic function of quantity. In particular, the quality ratio of "hits" to total attempts randomly varies both across and within careers (Simonton, 1997, 1999b, 2002a). Those creators with the most hits are those with the most attempts, with a hit rate no different, on the average, than their less prolific colleagues (see, e.g., Davis, 1987; Feist, 1993; Over, 1990; Platz & Blakelock, 1960; Simonton, 1985; White & White, 1978). Likewise, within the career of any one creator, those periods in which the most works are produced tend to be the periods in which the most successful works tend to be produced, the ratio of hits to attempts fluctuating randomly across the career course (Simonton, 1984b, 1988a, 1997; see, e.g., Over, 1988, 1989; Quételet, 1835/1968; Simonton, 1977a, 1985). The single best work, moreover, tends to appear when the total output maximizes (Simonton, 1991a, 1991b, 1992a). I have described this phenomenon as the *equal-odds* rule (Simonton, 1991a, 1997). Combined with the previous findings, the conclusion that creative productivity represents a stochastic phenomenon is inescapable.

EXPLANATIONS

All of the central aspects of multiple discovery and creative productivity can be explicated by treating creativity as a completely random combinatorial process (Simonton, 1988b, 1997, 2003). Take the equal-odds rule as a case in point. Let each creator obtain a random sample of ideas from a particular domain, and then generate random combinations from this ideational repetoire. A few combinations will be good (true, beautiful, etc.), but far more will be bad (false, ugly, etc.). Clearly, those who produce the most total combinations will also produce the most good combinations. Even so, the ratio of hits to attempts should not systematically vary across creators. Quality will be a probabilistic consequence of quantity. Moreover, the odds of a good combination at any time in the career will be a probabilistic function of the total number of combinations generated in that period. The quality ratio of hits to total attempts will exhibit no systematic trends across the career course, but rather will fluctuate randomly. Similar arguments will account for the random distribution of career output, the Poisson distribution of output per unit of time, and the Poisson distribution of multiple grades.

From a psychological perspective, however, the combinatorial model seems unsatisfactory. Why should creativity be stochastic? Why *must* it be so? To address these questions I will look at three aspects of creativity: the process, the person, and the product.

Creative Process

At the beginning of this chapter I mentioned how cognitive psychologists have attempted to prove—via both laboratory experiments and computer simulations—that creativity was merely a guise of logical problem solving. All the creator needs to do is to (a) acquire the requisite expertise in a particular domain and (b) apply a set of problem solving techniques, some domain specific (algorithms) and others more general (heuristics). If true, it would be difficult to explain why creativity should appear so stochastic in actual operation. Solution should follow solution in an almost inevitable fashion. Something must be amiss.

Researchers adopting this position may have been led astray by the fact that this research tradition relies heavily on close-ended problems with solutions that are known a priori (Simonton, 2003). Participants and computers are accordingly asked to obtain the preordained "correct answer." This situation departs appreciably from real-world creativity in which no one knows what the answer is, or even whether the answer exists. Indeed, often no one even knows how best to express the problem in the first place, which is sometimes the key to the solution (Einstein & Infeld, 1938).

In contrast, if participants must cope with open-problems more similar to what is encountered in the real world of creative behavior, problem solving becomes far more unreliable and capricious (Simonton, 1999b, 2003). The individual must then rely on a host of diverse heuristics that may not necessarily work. In fact, the first step in creative problem solving may then involve the discovery of a workable heuristic. Moreover, the whole problem-solving process becomes more susceptible to random priming effects. Significantly, these effects are more than mere distractions: They actually facilitate successful solution (see, e.g., Seifert, Meyer, Davidson, Patalano, & Yaniv,

1995). Exposure to random or incongruous stimuli has actually been shown to enhance creativity in a wide range of problem-solving situations (Finke, Ward, & Smith, 1992; Proctor, 1993; Rothenberg, 1986; Sobel & Rothenberg, 1980).

But what about the computer programs that claim to make scientific discoveries? Why can these "simulations" not be taken as sufficient proof of the nonstochastic nature of creativity, at least in the sciences? It is impossible here to discuss all of the objections to this inference, so may it suffice just to mention one (cf. Simonton, 1999b; Sternberg, 1989; Tweney, 1990). These programs are actually *rediscovery* programs. That is, they solve problems that have already been solved, using procedures that have been hypothesized to lead to the solution based on a retrospective analysis of the discovery. This is cheating. Hindsight is always 100% correct. The programs are inadvertent tautologies. In contrast, if we turn to computer programs that actually manage to create rather than merely reproduce, we learn that a stochastic mechanism is always an integral part of the program (Boden, 1991). Probably the most striking examples are genetic algorithms and genetic programming techniques (Goldberg, 1989; Koza, 1992, 1994). These not only make rediscoveries, but also make new discoveries, via an explicitly stochastic process, frequently in the guise of a random number generator.

It is worth pointing out that some creators have left introspective reports about the mental processes that led to their creations (e.g., Hadamard, 1945; Helmholtz, 1898; Poincaré, 1921). These reports corroborate the conclusion that creative thought is essentially stochastic (Simonton, 1999b, 2003). The introspections are replete with references to free association, trial and error, vague hunches, analogical and metaphorical thinking, playful exploration, diversive thinking, and other unpredictable and logically unjustifiable activities (see also James, 1880; Mach, 1896). Naturally, such reports cannot be considered hard, scientific data (Nisbett & Wilson, 1977). But at least they show that the claim that creativity is stochastic is not inconsistent with what creators themselves say about their thought processes.

Creative Person

Rather than concentrate on the creative process, some researchers prefer to focus on the creative person. Research findings suggest that highly creative individuals have personal characteristics and developmental antecedents that set them apart from noncreative individuals (Martindale, 1989; Simonton, 1999a). Moreover, these distinctive features function so as to generate distinctively stochastic behavior.

Personal Characteristics

Many tests that purport to assess individual differences in creativity are based on the assumption that people vary in their capacity to engage in certain cognitive processes (Guilford, 1967). It is also apparent that the operation of these mental processes suggests that creativity must function in a stochastic manner (Simonton, 2003). The best example is Mednick's (1962) well-known Remote Associates Test. This test was based on the premise that creativity involves the ability to make remote associations between separate ideas. Highly creative individuals are said to have a flat hierarchy of associations in comparison to the steep hierarchy of associations of those with low creativity. A flat associative hierarchy means that for any given stimulus, the creative person has many associations available, all with roughly equal probabilities of retrieval. Persons who are very low in creativity, by comparison, have steep associative hierarchies in which any given stimulus elicits only one or two responses in a highly predictable fashion. Clearly, the thought processes of individuals with flat associative hierarchies should be more effectively stochastic than the thinking of persons with steep hierarchies. Besides the almost equiprobable—and hence largely unpredictable—nature of the associations, flat associative hierarchies are necessarily more susceptible to priming effects (Simonton, 1999b). Unexpected input of an external stimulus or an internal train of thought can easily change the relative probabilities of the associations making up the hierarchy.

Apart from the cognitive capacity for remote association, highly creative individuals feature dispositional traits that would render their thoughts and behavior less predictable and hence more stochastic (Simonton, 1999b). In the first place, creativity is positively associated with openness to experience (King, McKee Walker, & Broyles, 1996; McCrae, 1987), a disposition that includes a diversity of interests and hobbies, a preference for complexity and novelty, and a tolerance of ambiguity (Barron, 1963; Davis, 1975; Gough, 1979). A necessary repercussion of this characteristic is that the intellect of a highly creative individual is more frequently exposed to a tremendous variety of extraneous influences. Such diverse input can deflect the associative process toward more unanticipated directions. Indeed, such priming effects become all the more unpredictable if coupled with the flat associative hierarchies just mentioned (Simonton, 1999b). If a large number of associates have nearly equal probabilities, then the relative order of those associates will be highly unstable from one moment to the next.

A second trait of highly creative individuals operates in a more complicated manner: The creative person has some inclinations toward psychopathology (Juda, 1949; Ludwig, 1995; Post, 1994). This propensity is revealed by higher than average scores on the clinical scales of the Minnesota Multiphasic Personality Inventory (Barron, 1969) as well as elevated scores on the Psychoticism Scale of the Eysenck Personality Questionnaire (Eysenck, 1995; Rushton, 1990). These empirical results may partly reflect the creator's need for independence or autonomy to avoid the constraints of conventional views. Yet another portion of these findings may be more directly connected to the cognitive process behind creativity. Eysenck (1994) has shown, for example, that psychoticism is positively correlated with the capacity for un-usual associations and with appreciation for highly complex stimuli. Both of these outcomes would have the consequence of making the thought process more unpredictable, and hence more stochastic. Interestingly, Eysenck (1995) has also shown that psychoticism is positively associated with a relative in-ability to filter out extraneous information (i.e., weakened "latent inhibi-tion" and "negative priming"). Because of such attention failures, the cre-ative mind is more likely to be bombarded by stimuli that will influence the outcome in unexpected ways (see also Wuthrich & Bates, 2001). Not sur-prisingly, reduced latent inhibition also has a strong association with open-ness to experience (Peterson & Carson, 2000).

Developmental Experiences

The personal characteristics that support stochastic thinking and be-havior must come from somewhere. To some as yet undetermined extent, these cognitive and dispositional attributes may have a genetic foundation (Eysenck, 1995). In support of this assertion is the finding that highly cre-ative individuals tend to come from family lines that feature higher than average incidences of psychopathology (Jamison, 1993; Juda, 1949; Karlson, 1970). However, it is likely that the genetics of creativity is highly complex. Besides being polygenic, creativity may be emergenic (Simonton, 1999c). That is, the capacity for creativity may require the fortuitous confluence of a large number of separate genetically endowed traits, all of which are essential for the full manifestation of the behavior (Waller, Bouchard, Lykken, Tellegen, & Blacker, 1993). In addition, it is clear that early developmental experiences must also play a role in the acquisition of creative potential. Creativity is a product of both nurture and nature. What are these environ-mental influences?

Certainly one crucial factor is sufficient domain mastery. No one can expect to make contributions to a domain without acquiring the necessary knowledge and skill (Ericsson, 1996). This requirement is often expressed as the "10-year rule" (e.g., Hayes, 1989). To attain world-class mastery of a domain demands around a full decade of deliberate study and practice. Al-though this principle no doubt applies to some degree to creativity, its appli-cation includes a critical complication: Someone can acquire so much do-main-specific expertise that it militates against being creative (Simonton, 1976, 1984b, 2000a). For instance, one study of 120 classical composers found that the most famous composers actually spent *less* time in domain mastery prior to producing their first masterworks (Simonton, 1991b). Excessive do-main mastery can greatly restrict the originality and flexibility of thought that would be expected if creativity truly contains a stochastic component. Notice that this qualification fits what was said earlier about the wide inter-ests and diverse hobbies of highly creative people. By constantly maintaining exposure to a diverse range of experiences, the creator can preserve the cognitive unpredictability so essential to stochastic creativity (Simonton, 2003). It is no accident that many serendipitous events occur when creators are engaged in some recreational activity seemingly unrelated to the creative problems at hand (Simonton, 1999b).

This argument can be extended to other developmental factors as well. Creative development should be fostered by events and circumstances that encourage nonconformity, independence, appreciation of diverse perspectives, a variety of interests, and other favorable qualities. That indeed appears to be the case. For instance, eminent creators are more likely to have come from unconventional family backgrounds and enriched environments (Simonton, 1987), to have been subjected to multiple and diverse role models and mentors (Simonton, 1977b, 1984a, 1992a, 1992b), and to have had diversifying and atypical educational experiences and professional training (Simonton, 1976, 1984b, 1984c). It is difficult for highly original thinkers to emerge from highly conventional, stable, and homogeneous family and educational environments. These conditions would certainly function to limit an individual's ability to engage in the stochastic processes considered characteristic of creativity.

Creative Product

Thus far it looks like both the creative process and the creative person harbor characteristics that should support stochastic creativity. Yet one must still wonder why creators are not able to learn how to reduce the amount of chance or risk involved in generating creative products. Why can they not learn from past mistakes, refine their methods or criteria, and improve their hit rates over time? Why can the most prolific creators not attain higher quality ratios simply according to the principle that "practice makes perfect"? The answer comes from the following four considerations:

1. Creative products in most domains are by no means simple in conception or construction. Rather, they tend to be multidimensional in nature. Therefore, any one feature of a work of art or science will only account for a minuscule proportion of the work's aesthetic or scientific success (Martindale et al., 1988; Shadish, 1989; Simonton, 1980, 1986b). Making matters even more complicated, the numerous components must combine in just the right fashion to maximize the impact (Simonton, 1980, 1990). That is, creative products tend to be configurational in the sense that interaction effects dominate main effects. What may be the right technique for one problem may be the wrong technique for another. The multidimensional and configurational nature of

creative products makes it extremely difficult for the creator to learn what reliably works. Creativity is an incessant guessing game.

2. Creators cannot judge the value of their works in isolation from the rest of the world. Thus, scientists must depend on the feedback of their colleagues, poets on the responses of their readers, filmmakers on the reactions of moviegoers, and so forth. Unfortunately, this information tends to be inconsistent, ambiguous, global, and unstable, rendering it almost useless as meaningful feedback about what works and what does not (Simonton, 1999b, 2002a). Even in the sciences, peer evaluations of journal and grant submissions are so unreliable that the judgments can be considered little better than a dice roll (Cicchetti, 1991; Cole, Cole, & Simon, 1981; Lindsey, 1988; Scott, 1974).

3. Human information processing suffers from several limits and biases that make it very difficult to draw valid inferences under the best of circumstances (Faust, 1984; Fiske & Taylor, 1991). Especially problematic are judgments of multidimensional and configurational phenomena under conditions of ambiguous and inconsistent feedback—precisely the situation faced by the creator throughout the career course.

4. The generation of creative products must always confront an inescapable dilemma. To be considered creative, a product must be considered both original and adaptive or functional (Simonton, 2000b). If a creator conceives a work that satisfies both of these criteria, he or she cannot simply do more of the same thing and still satisfy the first criterion, that of originality. A mere replication, remake, or revision will not count as something really new. Instead, the next work must be somehow different; the more different the succeeding product, the more original it will be, thus satisfying the first criterion. Yet the more original that next product, the less the creator can be assured that it will meet the second criterion. The new idea might be original, but it also might be invalid, ugly, or unworkable rather than true, beautiful, or functional. Hence, the creator is fated to generate a mishmash of products, some satisfying the first criterion but not the second, some the second but not the first, and some, more rarely, satisfying both criteria. The odds of maximally satisfying both standards simultaneously are extremely small.

Given these four realities, it should not surprise us that (a) products are randomly distributed across the career course; (b) quality is a probabilistic function of quantity, following the equal-odds rule; and (c) the products appearing in any career period and the multiples appearing in any given scientific domain are described by the Poisson distribution.

CONSTRAINTS

Now the astute reader will have noticed a crucial omission. At the beginning I proclaimed that creativity was a constrained stochastic behavior or process. Yet I have said nothing about constraints. Instead, I have devoted most of this chapter to presenting the reasons why creativity should be stochastic. Yet the existence of constraints is critical to understanding a key fact: Creators are not interchangeable no matter what their domain of creativity may be. For example, creative scientists are not equivalent to creative artists (Simonton, 1999a, 1999b). The main contrast between scientific and artistic creativity is that scientists generally operate under more severe constraints than do artists. For the most part, a creative product in the sciences must satisfy more severe and precise evaluative criteria than does a creative product in the arts. This disparity should then be reflected in the characteristics expected of creative persons in the two broad domains.

The last inference is amply documented in the empirical literature. In particular, creative scientists tend to display personal attributes that place them somewhere between the creative artists and the general population (Feist, 1998; Schaefer & Anastasi, 1968). For example, the associations of scientists tend to be less remote (Gough, 1976) and their inclinations toward psychopathology much less pronounced (Ludwig, 1992; Post, 1994; Raskin, 1936). Their biographical backgrounds tend to be more stable and conventional as well (Goertzel, Goertzel, & Goertzel, 1978; Raskin, 1936; Schaefer & Anastasi, 1968). For instance, outstanding scientists are less likely than exceptional artists to have experienced traumatic experiences in childhood (Berry, 1981).

These contrasts operate at even a more refined level. For instance, not all forms of artistic creativity are equally unrestrained. On the contrary, some art forms or genres require more stringent criteria than others. In the visual arts, for example, highly formal painting, sculpture, and architecture are far more constrained than are comparable creative products in a highly expressive style. The developmental and dispositional profiles of the creators should vary accordingly. In line with this expectation, the incidence rate of mental illness corresponds to the magnitude of constraint imposed on a given form of artistic creativity (Ludwig, 1998). Finally, within any given aesthetic style the amount of constraint tends to diminish over time (Martindale, 1990). As these constraints break down, the creativity must become increasingly more stochastic, with corresponding changes in the creators who conceive products in that style. This stylistic trend is reflected in the amount of primary and secondary thematic content exhibited in the works produced at a given time (Martindale, 1990).

To sum up, not only is creativity a stochastic process, but additionally various forms of creativity can be placed along a dimension indicating the degree to which that process is constrained. The relative proportion of chance and constraint then dictates the characteristics that creators working within a domain are most likely to display. There are accordingly many different kinds of creators.

CONCLUSION

I have argued that creativity necessarily involves a heavy dose of chance. The probabilistic nature of creativity was first illustrated in the two phenomena of multiple discovery and creative productivity. I then explicated the stochastic feature of creativity in terms of the creative process, person, and product. Finally, I observed that constraints are usually imposed on this stochastic behavior, constraints that are largely defined by the creative domain. These contrasts in the relative importance of stochastic processes then determine the optimal personal characteristics and backgrounds of creators for various domains. The domain-specific nature of these profiles implies that the identification of creative individuals cannot operate on a "one size fits all" principle. Instead, identification must be carefully tailored to the particular needs of each domain—especially the extent to which creativity in a given domain is highly constrained. Yet in even the most constrained creative discipline the need for stochastic creativity is not totally obliterated. A domain in which achievement left nothing to chance would not be considered a creative domain.

REFERENCES

Albert, R. S. (1975). Toward a behavioral definition of genius. *American Psychologist, 30,* 140–151.

American Heritage Electronic Dictionary (3rd ed.). (1992). Boston: Houghton Mifflin.

Austin, J. H. (1978). *Chase, chance, and creativity: The lucky art of novelty.* New York: Columbia University Press.

Barron, F. X. (1963). The needs for order and for disorder as motives in creative activity. In C. W. Taylor & F. X. Barron (Eds.), *Scientific creativity: Its recognition and development* (pp. 153–160). New York: Wiley.

Barron, F. X. (1969). *Creative person and creative process.* New York: Holt, Rinehart & Winston.

Berry, C. (1981). The Nobel scientists and the origins of scientific achievement. *British Journal of Sociology, 32,* 381–391.

Boden, M. A. (1991). *The creative mind: Myths & mechanisms*. New York: Basic Books.

Brannigan, A., & Wanner, R. A. (1983a). Historical distributions of multiple discoveries and theories of scientific change. *Social Studies of Science, 13*, 417–435.

Brannigan, A., & Wanner, R. A. (1983b). Multiple discoveries in science: A test of the communication theory. *Canadian Journal of Sociology, 8*, 135–151.

Cannon, W. B. (1940). The role of chance in discovery. *Scientific Monthly, 50*, 204–209.

Cicchetti, D. V. (1991). The reliability of peer review for manuscript and grant submissions: A cross-disciplinary investigation. *Behavioral and Brain Sciences, 14*, 119–186.

Cole, S., Cole, J. R., & Simon, G. A. (1981). Chance and consensus in peer review. *Science, 214*, 881–886.

Davis, G. A. (1975). In frumious pursuit of the creative person. *Journal of Creative Behavior, 9*, 75–87.

Davis, R. A. (1987). Creativity in neurological publications. *Neurosurgery, 20*, 652–663.

Einstein, A., & Infeld, L. (1938). *The evolution of physics: The growth of ideas from early concepts to relativity and quanta*. New York: Simon & Schuster.

Ericsson, K. A. (Ed.). (1996). *The road to expert performance: Empirical evidence from the arts and sciences, sports, and games*. Mahwah, NJ: Erlbaum.

Eysenck, H. J. (1994). Creativity and personality: Word association, origence, and psychoticism. *Creativity Research Journal, 7*, 209–216.

Eysenck, H. J. (1995). *Genius: The natural history of creativity*. Cambridge, England: Cambridge University Press.

Faust, D. (1984). *Limits of scientific reasoning*. Minneapolis: University of Minnesota Press.

Feist, G. J. (1993). A structural model of scientific eminence. *Psychological Science, 4*, 366–371.

Feist, G. J. (1998). A meta-analysis of personality in scientific and artistic creativity. *Personality and Social Psychology Review, 2*, 290–309.

Finke, R. A., Ward, T. B., & Smith, S. M. (1992). *Creative cognition: Theory, research, applications*. Cambridge, MA: MIT Press.

Fiske, S. T., & Taylor, S. E. (1991). *Social cognition* (2nd ed.). New York: McGraw-Hill.

Galton, F. (1869). *Hereditary genius: An inquiry into its laws and consequences*. London: Macmillan.

Goertzel, M. G., Goertzel, V., & Goertzel, T. G. (1978). *300 eminent personalities: A psychosocial analysis of the famous*. San Francisco: Jossey-Bass.

Goldberg, D. E. (1989). *Genetic algorithms in search, optimization, and machine learning*. Reading, MA: Addison Wesley.

Gough, H. G. (1976). Studying creativity by means of word association tests. *Journal of Applied Psychology, 61*, 348–353.

Gough, H. G. (1979). A creative personality scale for the adjective check list. *Journal of Personality and Social Psychology, 37*, 1398–1405.

Guilford, J. P. (1967). *The nature of human intelligence.* New York: McGraw-Hill.

Hadamard, J. (1945). *The psychology of invention in the mathematical field.* Princeton, NJ: Princeton University Press.

Hayes, J. R. (1989). *The complete problem solver* (2nd ed.). Hillsdale, NJ: Erlbaum.

Helmholtz, H. von. (1898). An autobiographical sketch. In *Popular lectures on scientific subjects, second series* (E. Atkinson, Trans., pp. 266–291). New York: Longmans, Green.

Huber, J. C. (1998a). Invention and inventivity as a special kind of creativity, with implications for general creativity. *Journal of Creative Behavior, 32*, 58–72.

Huber, J. C. (1998b). Invention and inventivity is a random, Poisson process: A potential guide to analysis of general creativity. *Creativity Research Journal, 11*, 231–241.

Huber, J. C. (2000). A statistical analysis of special cases of creativity. *Journal of Creative Behavior, 34*, 203–225.

Huber, J. C., & Wagner-Döbler, R. (2001). Scientific production: A statistical analysis of authors in mathematical logic. *Scientometrics, 50*, 323–337.

James, W. (1880, October). Great men, great thoughts, and the environment. *Atlantic Monthly, 46*, 441–459.

Jamison, K. R. (1993). *Touched with fire: Manic-depressive illness and the artistic temperament.* New York: Free Press.

Juda, A. (1949). The relationship between highest mental capacity and psychic abnormalities. *American Journal of Psychiatry, 106*, 296–307.

Karlson, J. I. (1970). Genetic association of giftedness and creativity with schizophrenia. *Hereditas, 66*, 177–182.

King, L. A., McKee Walker, L., & Broyles, S. J. (1996). Creativity and the five-factor model. *Journal of Research in Personality, 30*, 189–203.

Koza, J. R. (1992). *Genetic programming: On the programming of computers by means of natural selection.* Cambridge, MA: MIT Press.

Koza, J. R. (1994). *Genetic programming II: Automatic discovery of reusable programs.* Cambridge: MIT Press.

Kroeber, A. L. (1917). The superorganic. *American Anthropologist, 19*, 163–214.

Lamb, D., & Easton, S. M. (1984). *Multiple discovery.* Avebury, England: Avebury.

Langley, P., Simon, H. A., Bradshaw, G. L., & Zythow, J. M. (1987). *Scientific discovery.* Cambridge, MA: MIT Press.

Lindsey, D. (1988). Assessing precision in the manuscript review process: A little better than a dice roll. *Scientometrics, 14*, 75–82.

Ludwig, A. M. (1992). Creative achievement and psychopathology: Comparison among professions. *American Journal of Psychotherapy, 46*, 330–356.

Ludwig, A. M. (1995). *The price of greatness: Resolving the creativity and madness controversy.* New York: Guilford Press.

Ludwig, A. M. (1998). Method and madness in the arts and sciences. *Creativity Research Journal, 11*, 93–101.

Mach, E. (1896, January). On the part played by accident in invention and discovery. *Monist, 6*, 161–175.

Martindale, C. (1989). Personality, situation, and creativity. In J. A. Glover, R. R. Ronning, & C. R. Reynolds (Eds.), *Handbook of creativity* (pp. 211–232). New York: Plenum Press.

Martindale, C. (1990). *The clockwork muse: The predictability of artistic styles.* New York: Basic Books.

Martindale, C., Brewer, W. F., Helson, R., Rosenberg, S., Simonton, D. K., Keeley, A., et al. (1988). Structure, theme, style, and reader response in Hungarian and American short stories. In C. Martindale (Ed.), *Psychological approaches to the study of literary narratives* (pp. 267–289). Hamburg: Buske.

McCrae, R. R. (1987). Creativity, divergent thinking, and openness to experience. *Journal of Personality and Social Psychology, 52*, 1258–1265.

Mednick, S. A. (1962). The associative basis of the creative process. *Psychological Review, 69*, 220–232.

Merton, R. K. (1961). Singletons and multiples in scientific discovery: A chapter in the sociology of science. *Proceedings of the American Philosophical Society, 105*, 470–486.

Molina, E. C. (1942). *Poisson's exponential binomial limit.* Princeton, NJ: Van Nostrand.

Newell, A., & Simon, H. A. (1972). *Human problem solving.* Englewood Cliffs, NJ: Prentice-Hall.

Nisbett, R. E., & Wilson, T. D. (1977). Telling more than we can know: Verbal reports on mental processes. *Psychological Review, 84*, 231–259.

Ogburn, W. K., & Thomas, D. (1922). Are inventions inevitable? A note on social evolution. *Political Science Quarterly, 37*, 83–93.

Over, R. (1988). Does scholarly impact decline with age? *Scientometrics, 13*, 215–223.

Over, R. (1989). Age and scholarly impact. *Psychology and Aging, 4*, 222–225.

Over, R. (1990). The scholarly impact of articles published by men and women in psychology journals. *Scientometrics, 18*, 71–80.

Patinkin, D. (1983). Multiple discoveries and the central message. *American Journal of Sociology, 89*, 306–323.

Perkins, D. N. (2000). *The eureka effect: The art and logic of breakthrough thinking.* New York: Norton.

Peterson, J. B., & Carson, S. (2000). Latent inhibition and openness to experience in a high-achieving student population. *Personality and Individual Differences, 28*, 323–332.

Platz, A., & Blakelock, E. (1960). Productivity of American psychologists: Quantity versus quality. *American Psychologist, 15*, 310–312.

Poincaré, H. (1921). *The foundations of science: Science and hypothesis, the value of science, science and method* (G. B. Halstead, Trans.). New York: Science Press.

Post, F. (1994). Creativity and psychopathology: A study of 291 world-famous men. *British Journal of Psychiatry, 165*, 22–34.

Price, D. (1963). *Little science, big science*. New York: Columbia University Press.

Proctor, R. A. (1993). Computer stimulated associations. *Creativity Research Journal, 6*, 391–400.

Quételet, A. (1968). *A treatise on man and the development of his faculties*. New York: Franklin. (Reprint of 1842 Edinburgh translation of 1835 French original)

Raskin, E. A. (1936). Comparison of scientific and literary ability: A biographical study of eminent scientists and men of letters of the nineteenth century. *Journal of Abnormal and Social Psychology, 31*, 20–35.

Reynolds, J. (1966). *Discourses on art*. New York: Collier. (Original work published 1769–1790)

Roberts, R. M. (1989). *Serendipity: Accidental discoveries in science*. New York: Wiley.

Rothenberg, A. (1986). Artistic creation as stimulated by superimposed versus combined-composite visual images. *Journal of Personality and Social Psychology, 50*, 370–381.

Rushton, J. P. (1990). Creativity, intelligence, and psychoticism. *Personality and Individual Differences, 11*, 1291–1298.

Schaefer, C. E., & Anastasi, A. (1968). A biographical inventory for identifying creativity in adolescent boys. *Journal of Applied Psychology, 58*, 42–48.

Schmookler, J. (1966). *Invention and economic growth*. Cambridge, MA: Harvard University Press.

Scott, W. A. (1974). Interreferee agreement on some characteristics of manuscripts submitted to the *Journal of Personality and Social Psychology*. *American Psychologist, 29*, 698–702.

Seifert, C. M., Meyer, D. E., Davidson, N., Patalano, A. L., & Yaniv, I. (1995). Demystification of cognitive insight: Opportunistic assimilation and the prepared-mind perspective. In R. J. Sternberg & J. E. Davidson (Eds.), *The nature of insight* (pp. 65–124). Cambridge, MA: MIT Press.

Shadish, W. R., Jr. (1989). The perception and evaluation of quality in science. In B. Gholson, W. R. Shadish, Jr., R. A. Neimeyer, & A. C. Houts (Eds.), *The psychology of science: Contributions to metascience* (pp. 383–426). Cambridge: Cambridge University Press.

Shrager, J., & Langley, P. (Eds.). (1990). *Computational models of scientific discovery and theory formation*. San Mateo, CA: Kaufmann.

Simon, H. A. (1973). Does scientific discovery have a logic? *Philosophy of Science, 40*, 471–480.

Simon, H. A. (1986). What we know about the creative process. In R. L. Kuhn (Ed.), *Frontiers in creative and innovative management* (pp. 3–20). Cambridge, MA: Ballinger.

Simonton, D. K. (1976). Biographical determinants of achieved eminence: A multivariate approach to the Cox data. *Journal of Personality and Social Psychology, 33*, 218–226.

Simonton, D. K. (1977a). Creative productivity, age, and stress: A biographical time-series analysis of 10 classical composers. *Journal of Personality and Social Psychology, 35*, 791–804.

Simonton, D. K. (1977b). Eminence, creativity, and geographic marginality: A recursive structural equation model. *Journal of Personality and Social Psychology, 35*, 805–816.

Simonton, D. K. (1978). Independent discovery in science and technology: A closer look at the Poisson distribution. *Social Studies of Science, 8*, 521–532.

Simonton, D. K. (1979). Multiple discovery and invention: Zeitgeist, genius, or chance? *Journal of Personality and Social Psychology, 37*, 1603–1616.

Simonton, D. K. (1980). Thematic fame, melodic originality, and musical zeitgeist: A biographical and transhistorical content analysis. *Journal of Personality and Social Psychology, 38*, 972–983.

Simonton, D. K. (1984a). Artistic creativity and interpersonal relationships across and within generations. *Journal of Personality and Social Psychology, 46*, 1273–1286.

Simonton, D. K. (1984b). *Genius, creativity, and leadership: Historiometric inquiries.* Cambridge, MA.: Harvard University Press.

Simonton, D. K. (1984c). Is the marginality effect all that marginal? *Social Studies of Science, 14*, 621–622.

Simonton, D. K. (1985). Quality, quantity, and age: The careers of 10 distinguished psychologists. *International Journal of Aging and Human Development, 21*, 241–254.

Simonton, D. K. (1986a). Multiple discovery: Some Monte Carlo simulations and Gedanken experiments. *Scientometrics, 9*, 269–280.

Simonton, D. K. (1986b). Popularity, content, and context in 37 Shakespeare plays. *Poetics, 15*, 493–510.

Simonton, D. K. (1987). Developmental antecedents of achieved eminence. *Annals of Child Development, 5*, 131–169.

Simonton, D. K. (1988a). Age and outstanding achievement: What do we know after a century of research? *Psychological Bulletin, 104*, 251–267.

Simonton, D. K. (1988b). *Scientific genius: A psychology of science.* New York: Cambridge University Press.

Simonton, D. K. (1990). Lexical choices and aesthetic success: A computer content analysis of 154 Shakespeare sonnets. *Computers and the Humanities, 24*, 251–264.

Simonton, D. K. (1991a). Career landmarks in science: Individual differences and interdisciplinary contrasts. *Developmental Psychology, 27*, 119–130.

Simonton, D. K. (1991b). Emergence and realization of genius: The lives and works of 120 classical composers. *Journal of Personality and Social Psychology, 61*, 829–840.

Simonton, D. K. (1992a). Leaders of American psychology, 1879–1967: Career development, creative output, and professional achievement. *Journal of Personality and Social Psychology, 62*, 5–17.

Simonton, D. K. (1992b). The social context of career success and course for 2,026 scientists and inventors. *Personality and Social Psychology Bulletin, 18,* 452–463.

Simonton, D. K. (1997). Creative productivity: A predictive and explanatory model of career trajectories and landmarks. *Psychological Review, 104,* 66–89.

Simonton, D. K. (1999a). Creativity and genius. In L. A. Pervin & O. John (Eds.), *Handbook of personality theory and research* (2nd ed.). New York: Guilford Press.

Simonton, D. K. (1999b). *Origins of genius: Darwinian perspectives on creativity.* New York: Oxford University Press.

Simonton, D. K. (1999c). Talent and its development: An emergenic and epigenetic model. *Psychological Review, 106,* 435–457.

Simonton, D. K. (2000a). Creative development as acquired expertise: Theoretical issues and an empirical test. *Developmental Review, 20,* 283–318.

Simonton, D. K. (2000b). Creativity: Cognitive, developmental, personal, and social aspects. *American Psychologist, 55,* 151–158.

Simonton, D. K. (2002a). *Great psychologists and their times: Scientific insights into psychology's history.* Washington, DC: American Psychological Association.

Simonton, D. K. (2002b). Persistent myths, probabilities, and psychologists as human beings. *Dialogue, 17,* 24–25.

Simonton, D. K. (2003). Scientific creativity as constrained stochastic behavior: The integration of product, process, and person perspectives. *Psychological Bulletin, 129,* 475–494.

Sobel, R. S., & Rothenberg, A. (1980). Artistic creation as stimulated by superimposed versus separated visual images. *Journal of Personality and Social Psychology, 39,* 953–961.

Stent, G. S. (1972). Prematurity and uniqueness in scientific discovery. *Scientific American, 227,* 84–93.

Sternberg, R. J. (1989). Computational models of scientific discovery: Do they compute? [Review of the book *Scientific discovery: Computational explorations of the creative process*]. *Contemporary Psychology, 34,* 895–897.

Tweney, R. D. (1990). Five questions for computationalists. In J. Shrager & P. Langley (Eds.), *Computational models of scientific discovery and theory information* (pp. 471–484). San Mateo, CA: Kaufmann.

Vasari, G. (1968). *Lives of the painters, sculptors, and architects* (A. B. Hinds, Trans.; W. Gaunt, Rev. Ed.; E. Fuller, Ed.). New York: Dell. (Original work published ca. 1550)

Waller, N. G., Bouchard, T. J., Jr., Lykken, D. T., Tellegen, A., & Blacker, D. M. (1993). Creativity, heritability, familiality: Which word does not belong? *Psychological Inquiry, 4,* 235–237.

Weisberg, R. W. (1992). *Creativity: Beyond the myth of genius.* New York: Freeman.

White, K. G., & White, M. J. (1978). On the relation between productivity and impact. *Australian Psychologist, 13,* 369–374.

Wuthrich, V., & Bates, T. C. (2001). Schizotypy and latent inhibition: Non-linear linkage between psychometric and cognitive markers. *Personality and Individual Differences, 30,* 783–798.

7

INVENTORS: THE ORDINARY GENIUS NEXT DOOR

SHEILA J. HENDERSON

Psychologists and scholars have been studying the nature of creativity for more than a century. Countless empirical studies have focused on artists, writers, and musicians as the exemplars of the creative. Relatively few scholars have focused on inventors and their creative process. This is curious in light of the profound influence inventors have had on the Western lifestyle and standard of living. Biographies of famous inventors such as Alexander Graham Bell and Henry Ford are plentiful in bookstores and libraries. Psychological studies of inventors, especially those less famous, are harder to come by. It is the entrepreneurs (e.g., Lee Iacocca, Steve Jobs, Dave Packard, and Bill Hewlett) at the helm of inventive companies who have traditionally enjoyed more of the public eye.

Would psychological studies of inventors be useful to our general understanding of creative behavior? Is it possible to have a full understanding of creative people without a portrait of the inventors who have collectively influenced our society? To ponder this question, let's consider the story of how the Internet came to exist. Tim Berners-Lee proposed a global hypertext

---

The chapter title was inspired by the following two titles: the article on resiliency titled, "Ordinary Magic," by Anne Masten, PhD, (2001), and the book title, *The Millionaire Next Door*, by Stanley and Danko (1996).

project in 1989 to facilitate technical collaboration at CERN, a particle physics laboratory in Geneva, Switzerland. Berners-Lee's project proposal initiated what later became the World Wide Web technology (Berners-Lee, 1999; Wright, 1997). Though Tim Berners-Lee can be credited for creating the initial technology and inspiring its extraordinary development, the World Wide Web and the Internet were built steadily over time through both the independent and collective work of thousands of inventors. We know about the life and work of Tim Lee, but what do we know about the high-tech inventors that brought his vision to reality?

Public interest has begun to shift toward the work of inventors, perhaps spurred by the bull market of the 1990s and the rise in high technology. Inventors are now being celebrated on center stage as the very individuals who have quietly built the technologies fueling a marketplace revolution. For example, the *New Yorker* (MacFarquhar, 1999) and *Fortune* magazine (Stipp, 1999) offered close-up profiles of one MIT trained inventor, David Levy. Hewlett Packard Company adopted "HP Invent" as their central marketing logo ("HP Invent," 1999). Some corporate Web sites now feature photographic stories of their staff inventors and associated innovation successes ("IBM Research News," 2003). The Lemelson-MIT program Web site now features "Inventor of the Week" (2003). As a critical complement to Rossman's (1935, 1964) study of early 19th century inventors, comparative studies of inventors have begun to emerge (see Brown, 1988; Henderson, 2003, 2004; Huber, 1998; Weber & Perkins, 1992).

INVENTION DEFINED

Invention and its ultimate influence on society is a complex interaction among human creativity, the current state of technology and knowledge, and ultimately the needs of the market consumer. The current state of science and technology reflects both incremental and dramatic leaps in human discovery. The variety of terms used to characterize an invention may distract from an accurate understanding of the creativity and market potential of an invention. Pick up a prominent business magazine, and one is sure to encounter terms such as, *create, innovate, develop, discover, improve,* and *disrupt* alongside or in place of the term *invent.* This proliferation of terms perhaps reflects the struggle within the English language to capture the nuance of creativity behind technical invention. The crux of the issue is that whereas some inventions leapfrog existing technology (e.g., the light bulb versus the candle lantern), most inventions improve on existing technology (e.g., amoxicillin versus penicillin). Innovation in its purest definition may more accurately refer to technology improvements, yet it is pervasively used in technology circles to characterize products that verifiably alter technology. For simplicity, the term *invention* is used exclusively through this chapter.

There are five critical dimensions that distinguish invention from other forms of creativity: (a) novelty, (b) utility, (c) cost-effectiveness, (d) impact on the marketplace, and (e) the opportunity for patent acquisition. The following broad definition of an invention, therefore, will guide the discussion in this chapter:

> An invention is created through the production of novel ideas, processes, or products that solve a problem, fit a situation, or accomplish a goal in a way that is novel, implementable, useful, and cost-effective and alters or otherwise disrupts an aspect of technology.

This conceptualization was derived from previous definitions offered by prominent scholars in creativity (see Amabile, 1983; Becker, 1994; MacKinnon, 1962; Rossman, 1964; Torrance, 1974; Vosburg & Kaufmann, 1999).

The above definition of invention carves out some important questions about what defines the creativity of inventing work. What does it mean for a product, process, or idea to be novel, implementable, useful, and cost-effective and to alter or disrupt existing technology? How is invention different from other products of creative behavior, such as fine art and sculpture? Do patents define an invention's merit to society?

Novelty

Consider novelty as it relates to fine art versus inventing work. Novelty in a painting or sculpture is an attribute that will catch the eye of art critics and collectors. Similarly, novelty in invention distinguishes a product or process from other existing technology. Novelty in art, however, is an end in itself. That is to say, novelty in art can be both *necessary* and *sufficient* to its function in the world. In the arena of invention, novelty is necessary but rarely sufficient. An invention must not only be novel but it must also "solve a problem, fit a situation, or accomplish a goal," as stated in the above definition. That is, an invention must meet a societal need and be adopted in the marketplace to be deemed successful and relevant. The novelty of artistic expression may define its aesthetic merit to society, whereas the novelty of invention will only partially determine its value to the market consumer.

Utility

The utility of an invention is defined by its implementability, cost-effectiveness, and its match with what is needed in current society. This concept is perhaps best illustrated by the story of one recent invention that has been the subject of much political controversy. Cities struggle with finding efficient ways to manage the transportation needs of the public in the face of road congestion. In response, Dean Kamen, a highly successful modern inventor, introduced the "Segway" to the market in 2002. The Segway is an electric scooter designed for use on sidewalks as an alternative to car commuting. It features a unique gyroscopic technology that facilitates maneuverability at speeds up to 15 miles per hour. However the Segway, which may indeed eventually revolutionize city transportation, has recently encountered some resistance to its implementation. The San Francisco city government, concerned about safety risks to the young, senior, and disabled people walking along sidewalks, recently outlawed the invention (Watercutter, 2003). Whereas novelty has been the Segway's advantage, concerns about its implementability are slowing its market adoption. Note, however, that an invention's utility often evolves well after the initial offering of a novel invention. For example, Henry Ford successfully introduced the Model T years after Nicholas August Otto invented the gas motor engine in 1876 (Bellis, 2003a).

Cost-Effectiveness

Consider inventions designed to keep city sidewalks clean and clear of debris. Many novel inventions out-price the market pocketbook. Consider the "Steamin' Gum Gun" designed to remove unsightly chewing gum from city sidewalks. This invention may be novel and useful yet too costly for many city governments. The "Steamin' Gum Gun" is now priced on the Internet at more than $4,000 per unit. Compare this to the leaf blower, which was and remains a controversial solution to dead leaves on the sidewalk. Despite the associated noise pollution, the leaf blower has succeeded in gaining significant market acceptance perhaps due to the efficiency and cost savings associated with the solution (unit price less than $100).

Impact

How many, how often, and how long people use an invention may indeed signal the novelty, utility, cost-effectiveness, and implementability of the invention. These dimensions will influence the *rate of the adoption* of any given invention. The *impact* of an invention also depends on the degree to which the invention alters and disrupts the way people think, feel, or act in the world. When considering the merit of an invention therefore, it is the resulting change in technology that becomes a central defining feature.

Patents

One last unique feature of inventions, something that has no analogue in art, is the patent award. Fine art may be appraised and insured, but to date paintings and sculptures have not been patented. This may be a distinguishing feature but not always a meaningful one when evaluating the creative merit of an invention. The U.S. Patent and Trademark office began protecting invention to track the development of technology but also to provide financial incentive for continued invention by allowing patentees to collect royalty income from their invention successes.

Although potentially lucrative, many inventors are nevertheless skeptical about the ability of a patent award to reflect accurately the importance of inventions and the expertise of inventors (Henderson, 1999). Inventions vary in technical complexity and in time required for development (i.e., time-to-market). Patent acquisition is expensive, and in practice more influenced by corporate priorities, incentives, and legal support (not to mention the changes in patent law) than novelty or impact on the marketplace. Furthermore, many an invention has been awarded a patent but has not endured well in the marketplace (e.g., 8-track cassettes). Ultimately it is the marketplace rather than the U.S. Federal Patent Office that awards an invention its creative merit.

INVENTORS AND CREATIVITY

The attribute that probably most distinguishes inventors from other creative people is their orientation toward problem solving. Although accidents have inspired many an invention (e.g., Silly Putty, Post-it Notes, the pacemaker, and the microwave), most inventions are deliberate solutions to problems in the current state of technology ("Inventor of the week archive," 1998; "Microwave oven," 2002). The process of inventing new products involves identifying unmet needs in society, zeroing in on the underlying technological conundrums, and then discovering novel solutions; inventors therefore can be deemed expert problem solvers in the physical world.

Problem solving is so central to the process of inventing, that graduate programs in engineering and product design teach the art of problem finding (Adams, 1972; Faste, 1972; MacFarquhar, 1999). Some product design programs require beginning students to create a list of problems in daily life, such as the annoyance of losing keys (Henderson, 2000a). Out of this list, students are then asked to solve a selection of these problems through invention.

Is it not true, one might ask, that artists solve technical problems to create what is in their mind's eye? Nearly all forms of creativity, in fact, involve problem-solving effort. Musicians are challenged by how to create novel sound with traditional instruments, filmmakers with how to create a mood behind a common scene, and writers with how to create a vivid scene in the mind's eye of readers, with mere words on a page. Scholars have found problem finding to be a critical cognitive process (Getz & Lubart, 1999) among all people and central to the process of successful artists. Getzels and Csikszentmihalyi (1976) found that novelty in fine art depended on delay of problem foreclosure by students in their artistic process.

Where the act of problem finding is common to both the artistic and the inventive process, the *motivation* behind problem solving is unique to inventors. Whereas artists solve problems in service of fulfilling a particular vision for their art, inventors solve problems in service of market need. For this reason, an inventor's process of invention will seldom bring notoriety, as is the case in an artist's technique and style (i.e., Seurat's and Lichtenstein's pointillism, Matisse's continuous line, Picasso's cubism, and Magritte's play on what is actually real). Writers have addressed key aspects of the inventing process, such as brainstorming, idea generation, and the management of corporate innovation (Kelley, 2001). The ideas are most commonly discussed in general rather than associated with the personal inventing styles of a particular individual. The point here is that inventors become known for their solutions to the needs of the marketplace (if they become known at all) rather than for the features of their artistic process.

PROFILES OF THE 21ST-CENTURY INVENTOR

Results from two recent interview- and survey-based studies on inventors (Henderson, 2003, 2004) inform the following discussion about the profile of the 21st-century corporate inventor and the underlying psychology of how and why they do the inventing work that they do.

Method of the Studies

Study 1 (Henderson, 2004) was qualitative in design, involving in-depth interviews of four product inventors and two similarly trained noninventing professionals as control based in Silicon Valley, California. These individuals were interviewed in three consecutive individual face-to-face or phone meetings. Three face-to-face focus group meetings were also held. The interviews were guided by semistructured, open-ended questions inquiring about the intrapersonal, interpersonal, environmental, social, and cultural factors that might have influenced the creative achievement of the participants. These inventors were employed at a technology incubator firm and the other inventors work at a start-up company advancing robotics technology.

Study 2 was a one-time, cross-sectional survey of corporate inventors with no control group. From a convenience sample of 1,070 employed inventors, 247 participants completed a 90-question on-line survey requiring a mean time of 20 minutes to complete. This survey evaluated inventor motivation, role identity, inventing skill, and their reports on early formative experiences. The survey's 23% response rate is lower than what would be expected for mail surveys but on par with the lower response rates found in on-line surveys (Dillman, 2000).

Almost all participants (96%) of Study 2 were employed by one of three multinational companies dedicated to the research, design, and creation of new scientific processes and products in the area of consumer products (household, electronic, or mechanical), computer and Internet solutions, and high technology. The other participants were recruited via a graduate engineering alumni e-mail list of a major university. The three participating companies were headquartered in Silicon Valley, California, and had offices worldwide. The size of these development labs ranged from 200 to 450 nonmanagerial individuals making a living by inventing.

Results

Role Identity as an "Inventor"

Individuals doing inventing work hold many different professional titles within the workplace, such as designer, developer, scientist, physicist, technician, and engineer. Because role identity is believed to have a strong influence on motivation (Petkus, 1996), the concept was evaluated in Study 2 using Erickson's concept of psychosocial identity (1968). To accomplish this, survey participants were asked the following two questions (Henderson, 2003) (a) How central is being an inventor to how you perceive yourself? and (b) How central is being an inventor to how others perceive you? The 6-item Likert scale was worded as follows: (a) completely central, (b) very central, (c) somewhat central, (d) not very central, (e) not at all central, and (f) N/A.

The majority (85%) of participants of Study 2 reported that "being an inventor" was "somewhat," "very," or "completely" central to the way they perceived themselves and the way others perceived them. Interestingly, the participating companies varied considerably in how much they promoted "inventor" as a professional identity. Whatever emphasis there was seemed to vary across managers within the organizations, and as expected, there were no significant differences in inventor identity across the recruiting sources of this study. It may be that individual role identity of people doing inventing emerges because of a long series of personal, educational, and professional experiences in different environments much the same as psychosocial identity. Thus, the role identity of "inventor" may have much more to do with an individual's present and historical work activities than it does the corporate job title.

There were no significant differences in role identity across ethnicity and education. There were differences, however, found within gender. The female participants in Study 2 were almost three times less likely to report that being an inventor was "very" or "completely" central to their role identity as an inventor than male participants. At the same time, the male participants were more likely to disclaim completely their inventor identity than their female counterparts. In this case, men in the study were two times more likely than women to report that being an inventor was "not at all" or "not very" central to their role identity.

Demographics of Inventors

Inventors of the Past. In the early 1900s, Rossman sent a psychology survey to successful inventors through the U.S. Patent Office. Through this method, he recruited the participation of 710 inventors. Given the proliferation of invention that began in the early 1900s, the Rossman study (1935, 1964) has offered important baseline information for all future research on inventors. Rossman's 710 participants were all male individuals who had obtained their first patent between the ages of 15–30, with 20,859 patents in total. Nearly two-thirds of the participants (59%) were college-educated individuals and had been awarded an average of 47.3 patents each, holding 95% of the total patents. The inventors without formal education (41%) averaged 3.6 patents per person.

Inventors Today. Since the days of Rossman's study, technology has advanced exponentially as has the technical complexity of inventing work. In this respect, the demand for technically agile and creative minds has spurred the availability of higher education in math, science, and engineering. Perhaps entertainment media have produced the most comical depictions of inventors. Often in movies, cartoons, and in comic books, inventors are characterized as zany eccentrics, like "Doc Brown" played by Christopher Lloyd in the mid-80s movie, *Back to the Future*. The truth is, though, that most inventors are little known and seldom stand out in a crowd (MacFarquhar, 1999; Rogers, 1986; Rossman, 1964). It is clear that the impact of an invention does not necessarily lead to fame. For example, though Vladimir Kosma Zworykin and Philo Farnsworth are credited with inventing the television (Postman, 2003), they may not hold much name recognition among the public. The same phenomenon applies to Jack Kilby and Robert Noyce, who invented the microchip (Bellis, 2003b; Weiss, 1999); it is Intel and other computer companies that have received the fame.

In Study 2, 247 inventors comprised a select sample of older, more experienced, and more highly educated inventors that included women and people of color. Of those participants willing to disclose their gender (96%, *n* = 238), approximately 81% were men and 19% women. Compared with U.S. national statistics on engineers and scientists in 1997, women in this study were slightly underrepresented (National Science Foundation, 1997: 77% men, 23% women). The mean age of participants in this study was 37.6 years (ranging from 19–74 years), with significant differences among men (38.4 years) and women (34.2 years). The average age of the study participants was on par with the national statistics collected in 1997. *Science and Engineering Indicators 2000* reported: "With the exception of new fields such as computer sciences (where 70 percent of degree holders are under age 40), the greatest population density of individuals with S&E [science and engineering] degrees [in science and engineering occupations] occurs between ages 40 and 49" (National Science Board, 2000, p. 22). This same report also explained that, "Because large numbers of women and minorities have entered S&E fields only relatively recently, women and minority men are generally younger and have fewer years of experience" (National Science Board, 2000, p. 10).

In terms of education level, approximately 31% of the participants had PhDs, 31% had Master's degrees, 6% had professional school training, 29% had college degrees, 2% had high school degrees, and 1% declined to answer. The participants together acquired an average of 6 patents each, 1,498 patents in total. Compared to national statistics (National Science Foundation, 1997), the participants in this study were more highly trained than engineers and scientists across the nation in 1997, 28% then holding MAs and 13% holding PhDs.

Of those willing to disclose ethnicity (92%, $n = 227$), 80% were White, 9% were of multi-heritage, 2% Korean, 2% Japanese, and the remaining 7% were Latino, Vietnamese, or "other." There were significant differences in education by ethnicity when grouped as White versus non-White ($x^2 (4,225) = 9.52, p < .05$) but not by gender. The 20% of non-White participants in this study compared favorably in terms of diversity to the 1997 nationwide National Science Foundation statistics, which indicated a presence of 16% non-White engineers and scientists. In this study, proportionally fewer non-White participants had education at the college, professional school, and Master's degree level of training, and proportionally more at the PhD level.

Caution is advised when generalizing the results of this study to inventors as a whole because the data were collected from a convenience sample without control group. Also, the proportion of White male inventors discussed above should by no means diminish the actual impact of women and people of color in the inventing world. Despite the well-known limits on social, political, educational, and economic opportunity available to people of color and to women over history, minorities have had an impact on the world as we now know it through invention. Diverse peoples, including young children, have contributed to the current technological revolution. Appendix 7.1 provides a list of Internet Web sites that discuss how diverse peoples have contributed to our technological progress.

THE PSYCHOLOGY OF THE MODERN INVENTOR

In the preceding sections, we examined invention and the creative properties of invention. We then discussed the role identity of people making a living by inventing in terms of whether or not they perceive themselves and are perceived by others as inventors. Then, we reviewed a snapshot of 21st-century inventors as compared with inventors of the early 1900s. Moving from a descriptive analysis of invention and the people who create them, we now move toward a more fundamental exploration of the internal attributes of inventors. The key question now is, what motivates inventors' creative achievement and how have they developed their interest in and talent and expertise at inventing? To provide context for this question, we start by outlining the overall framework and the measures of Study 2.

Framework

Martin Ford's living systems framework (1992) guided the studies. This framework addressed the psychological foundation for understanding human competence by outlining the internal and external determinants of achievement (see Figure 7.1) Four theoretical models served to elucidate further the components of Ford's framework. For example, the motivational systems theory (Ford, 1992) offered a structure for systematic study of three internal psychological functions that motivate goal-directed activity: *personal goals, emotion,* and *personal agency* (also known as self-efficacy). Whereas personal goals and personal agency were adequately addressed by the motivational systems theory, emotion needed further elaboration. Two models of creativity and affect offered by Sandra Russ (1993, 1999) and Melvin Shaw (1989, 1994) helped to expand concepts on the role of emotional arousal in inventing achievement. As a further complement to Ford's framework, *environment* and *skill* were addressed via John Krumboltz's social learning theory of career decision making (1979). The Krumboltz theory focused on how early home and school experiences of inventors might have contributed to later educational and professional endeavor in the inventing world.

Measures for Creative Achievement and Motivational Correlates

Inventing achievement was evaluated, both subjectively and objectively, through the use of five dependent variables. The first three measures involved subjective questions using a Likert scale: (a) place on a hypothesized ladder of recognition, (b) sense of accomplishment, and (c) personal rating of overall success as an inventor. The last two measures were objective using (d) numbers of publications and conference presentations made and (e) numbers of patents, both pending and awarded.

The independent measures were (a) skill, measured by years of inventing experience and level of education; (b) emotion, measured via a Likert scale with questions assessing subjective well-being in one's work life, with the type of work and in the current work situation; and (c) personal agency (also known as self-efficacy), which measured the participants' belief in their ability to invent with a Likert scale. The last two dimensions, personal goals and formative environment, were evaluated through open-ended questions soliciting a short written response.

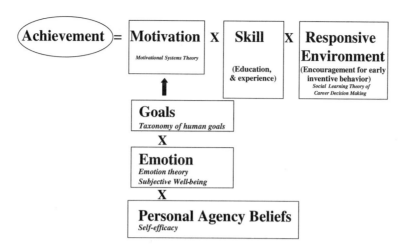

Figure 7.1. Key components influencing achievement. The living systems framework (Ford, 1992).

Linear regression was used to evaluate how skill and motivation (*emotion* and *personal agency*) might be associated with inventor achievement. The regression models for each of the five dimensions of achievement showed strong linear relationships (adjusted r^2 ranged from .19–.47) between achievement and the other components of Ford's motivational systems theory.

Because of the dearth of research scales relevant to inventors in the existing creativity literature, original scales were developed for subjective achievement and for personal agency. Although the scales were strong in theoretical grounding and in content validity by way of inventor review, the absence of existing well-validated scales made it difficult to establish concurrent or convergent validity. The use of original scales can be seen as a limitation of Study 2. It is hoped, however, that these new measures will spawn more research on subjective and objective measures of inventing achievement. Construct validity will come with time as these measures are tested in larger studies.

Internal Motivation

Personal Goals

Goal theory in psychology studies why people do what they do. This is an interesting question in the case of inventors because the process of inventing is often fraught with relentless hours of hard work, criticism, false starts, dead ends, setbacks, and frequent failures (Henderson, 2003). In Study 2, inventors were asked to provide three reasons for why they pursued the inventing work. The vignette responses were then coded according to the Taxonomy of Human Goals (Ford & Nichols, 1991). Figure 7.2 displays a

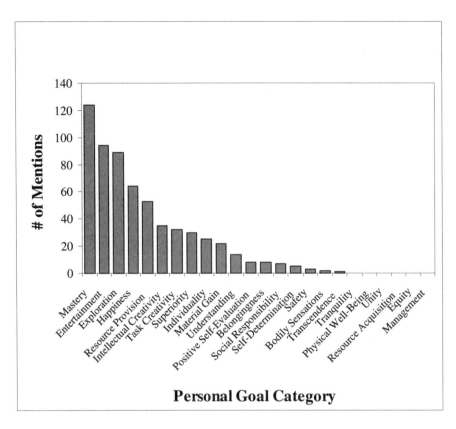

Figure 7.2. Reasons for doing inventing work sorted by frequency of mention. The survey question used was "What are your main reasons for inventing work? Reason 1, Reason 2, Reason 3." 616 reasons were provided by 247 inventors: 229 for Reason 1, 207 for Reason 2, 180 for Reason 3. Reasons were coded using Taxonomy of Personal Goals (Ford & Nichols, 1991).

chart of the personal goals reported by the participating inventors sorted by frequency of mention. In descending order of frequency, the most prominent personal goals were mastery, entertainment, exploration, happiness, resource provision, intellectual creativity, task creativity, superiority, individuality, and material gain.

The importance of these findings is threefold. First, seven out of the top ten goals mentioned suggest that inventors are intrinsically motivated in their work. That is, fame, financial remuneration, and competitive advantage were not dominant in their reason for pursuing inventing. Although two extrinsic goals, superiority and material gain, did rank in the top 10 goals for doing inventing work, they were ranked number 8 and 10. Second, mastery was ranked as the number one reason among the inventor participants to explain why they do the work they do. Indeed, the prominence of this personal goal is central to understanding how inventors can withstand the emotional and intellectual stress of inventing work and the constant threat of failure to their ideas. These data suggest that the more significant the challenge, the more fundamental the fulfillment derived from the ultimate accomplishment of invention. Thirdly, the vignettes suggested that entertainment, exploration, enjoyment, and resource provision (i.e., satisfaction and fun) were mentioned as the 2nd to 7th most frequent reasons.

Is intrinsic motivation unique to inventors? No, in fact, it appears that intrinsic motivation is something that inventors share with other types of creative people. Social psychology and other theories of creativity have long noted the importance of intrinsic motivation to creativity (Amabile, 1983; Deci & Ryan, 1985; Hennessey, 1999; Hennessey & Amabile, 1998; Urdan, 1997). When comparing intrinsic goal structures between inventors and artists, it is important to put intrinsic motivation in a context of financial remuneration. Though no salary data were requested in the survey, financial satisfaction data gathered from a subset of the participants (n = 92, 37% of total sample) indicated that they were "fairly satisfied" (5 on a 7-point Likert scale) with their financial compensation. Therefore, it is likely that the salaries of the participants amply covered their minimum financial needs (which may not be the case for all artists early in their career, nor, for that matter, all inventors).

It is also useful to put the intrinsic-motivation data into historical context. There was a flight of talent during the 1990s bull market, when many inventors left their corporate jobs and joined smaller start-up companies for greater financial payoff to their inventing work. This may have had an influence on what goal structures were evident for corporate inventor participants. Study 2 was conducted in February 2001. The inventors who stayed with larger corporations had less upside potential in their earnings than did their colleagues working in start-ups. One might wonder whether those inventors who joined start-up ventures had more extrinsic goal structures than the survey participants, who presumably had kept their more stable albeit less lucrative corporate inventing positions. What is clear and perhaps most significant is that the goal structures of the inventors in the survey did not mirror the media's emphasis on the extrinsic rewards of invention.

Personal Agency or Self-Efficacy

Participants were asked, via a self-efficacy survey, to rate on a 100-point scale (0–100%) how confident they were that they could accomplish 52 specific tasks. The 0% score indicated "not at all confident," and the 100% score indicated "completely confident." The factor analysis performed indicated that the 52 individual questions fell into the three distinct domains of self-efficacy. These were (a) *interpersonal ability*, (b) *hardiness*, and (c) *technical ability*.

On average, participants were 75% confident of their technical ability, 67% confident of their hardiness, and 75% confident of their interpersonal abilities. In the linear regressions, the participants' confidence in technical ability was most strongly associated with all measures. Participant belief in hardiness and interpersonal ability proved to be a significant correlate within the subjective dimensions. The findings are consistent with theories of self-efficacy, learned optimism, and learned resourcefulness, in which proven skill, positive methods of coping, and positive attribution styles for negative events are associated with emotional health and productive lifestyles (Bandura, 1997; Rosenbaum, 1990; Seligman, 1991).

Is a high level of personal agency unique to inventors? According to Bandura (1997) in his review of thousands of self-efficacy studies in a wide range of occupations, strong empirical evidence suggests that self-efficacy is a strong factor in individual and collective achievement. Bandura's well-validated theory clearly suggests, as does Martin Ford's motivational systems theory model (1992), that a high sense of personal agency would be instrumental in any creative endeavor.

Emotion

On average, the participants indicated that they were "very satisfied" at work (6 on a 7-point Likert scale). There were significant differences found in work satisfaction (subjective well-being) across gender but not ethnicity. Female participants were significantly less satisfied at work than their male counterparts, on average. Overall, these results on subjective well-being for inventors suggest that inventing can be a highly rewarding profession. The lower satisfaction among women inventors in a corporate setting may reflect the need for more progress in integrating women in a work environment traditionally dominated by male inventors.

Subjective well-being at work was found to be positively associated with inventing achievement in general, but specifically with only one measure of achievement: sense of accomplishment. The composite measure of subjective well-being was designed as an overall appraisal of happiness at work rather than a process-related measure of the ups and downs associated with inventing over time. More process-related measures of emotional arousal (yet to be developed in the literature) that evaluate the degree of positive emotion experienced at different points in the invention process may well have turned out to be stronger correlates with inventing achievement.

Scholars have long noted the joys of creating among inventors and other creative individuals (Adams, 1972; Bruch, 1988; Csikszentmihalyi, 1996; Henderson, 2003, 2004; Mace, 1997; Rossman, 1964); the role of positive emotion in creative endeavor (Henderson, 2004; Russ, 1993, 1999; Shaw & Runco, 1994); and the centrality of enjoyment, personal fulfillment, and contribution in attaining satisfying work and satisfying lives (Henderson, 1999/2000, 2000b; Krumboltz & Henderson, 2002). Paradoxically the social stereotypes attributed to engineers as depicted in Dilbert cartoons have suggested that the feeling world is out of reach to these technically trained individuals ("Dilbert," Adams, 2003). Conversations with inventors suggest entirely the contrary (Henderson, 2004) when it comes to inventing achievement. In fact, the emotional experience of inventors during the process of inventing was discussed as integral to the process.

Ford (1992) conceptualized emotional arousal as a critical component in mobilizing goal-directed effort. However, the role of emotional arousal in the creative process is highly complex because of the antecedent, concurrent, and consequential emotions that shift from one behavioral episode to another. Spontaneous feelings, such as excitement, frustration, confusion, and exhilaration, have a critical role in stimulating the actions needed to proceed through the arduous creative process (Shaw, 1989). Therefore, it is important to consider the way in which inventors enjoy their work in addition to their overall subjective well-being or the degree of emotional arousal experienced.

Russ (1993, 1999) outlined five affective dimensions found to be significant in the creative process, as derived from her research on children engaging in creative play. These categories were *access to affect laden thoughts*, *openness to affect states*, *affective pleasure in challenge*, *affective pleasure in problem solving*, and *cognitive integration and modulation of affect*. The interview discussions with inventors in Study 1 not only provided evidence to support the Russ model but also encouraged an elaboration and expansion of the model. One category (cognitive integration and modulation of affect) was expanded to include the role of intuition; four other categories were added (*affective pleasure in technical perspective-taking, in focus, in creating*, and *in self-expression*). These categories suggest that the way in which creativity in general, and the inventing process in particular, is experienced emotionally is highly individualized. How these categories of affect compare with the emotional experience of artists, musicians, and other creative people poses an interesting question for further research.

Skill

Over and above education, the participants in Study 2 had 14 mean years of experience, each with a spread of 9 years normally distributed. *Skill* proved to be significantly associated with all objective dimensions of achievement as well as in one subjective dimension, recognition. In a study of successful, highly creative people, Csikszentmihalyi (1996) asserted that it takes at least 10 years of focused effort, both in terms of education and applied experience, to achieve success in any intellectual domain. This assertion is consistent with the findings in this study.

Environment

Many researchers have investigated early school and home environments of artists and writers (Hébert, 1993; Rostan, 1997; Filippelli & Walberg, 1997) though none of this research has appeared in prominent literature.

Nevertheless, interest in environmental factors that are associated with creative talent is not new. As far back as 1935, Rossman published survey results that indicated that 87.5% of 695 male inventors responded positively to a question on whether they were interested in mechanical things as a boy.

A contemporary view among scholars is that the experiences that we craft for young people in schools and at home have a big influence on whether gifted talent can be actualized into the ability to achieve and contribute (Fetterman, 1990). The importance of classroom environments that support discovery learning for students interested in invention has been influential in engineering design programs (Adams, 1972; Faste, 1972; Henderson, 2000a). Stimulating environments and participatory learning have also been noted for their influence on student engagement and achievement (Astin, 1984; Pace, 1980; Sameroff, 1987).

The impact of the work environment on innovative achievement has also drawn substantial research interest. Several work-environment assessment scales have been developed for use in research and evaluation (see Amabile, 1995; Amabile, Conti, Coon, Lazenby, & Herron, 1996; Moos & Insel, 1974). The most prominent among these scales is the KEYS scale (Amabile, 1995), which evaluates work environment in terms of stimulants and obstacles to innovation.

Because the influence of work environment on creativity in the workplace is well understood, Study 2 focused on formative environments. It is clear that environmental factors shaping an individual's skills, career interests, and orientation toward achievement are complex interactions of person and environment over many behavior episodes. As mentioned above, this places the results of Study 2 on formative environments of inventors squarely within Ford's living systems framework (1992) and also within Krumboltz's social learning theory of career decision making (1979).

In Study 2, the inventor participants were asked in open-ended survey questions for recollections of formative experiences in and outside of school that may have contributed to their ability to invent. The resulting 616 vignettes provided anecdotal evidence for particular features of the environment that may foster inventive behavior. These vignettes were analyzed with the qualitative method of pattern coding (Miles & Huberman, 1994) for evidence of early inventive behavior and for aspects of the environment that supported and encouraged these inclinations.

Figure 7.3 illustrates the central themes evident in the vignettes submitted by the inventor participants. With notable frequency, the inventor participants mentioned having materials and resources that encouraged early inventive behavior. They had access to tools; toys for building things; toys, clocks, appliances and other equipment to take apart; and sometimes garage space, tool benches or tool shops in which to try out their inventive ideas. Both male and female participants had the opportunity to work with parents, extended family, neighbors, advisors, educators, and peers on inventive

Figure 7.3. Hypothesized features of a formative environment.

projects. The side-by-side collaboration was noted as instructive, inspiring, and enjoyable.

Many of the participants remembered having the opportunity to participate in activities based on active, problem-based discovery learning in early school years up through graduate education. Sometimes, these activities were built into the science and math curricula; other times, the inventors recalled these experiences as being associated with extra-credit projects, team projects for school events (e.g., such as designing the sets for a school play), special projects for the school (e.g., building a darkroom), science fairs, invention grants and competitions, product-design courses as well as graduate theses and dissertations. The participants remembered these forums as those that afforded freedom for their unique ideas to blossom and provided inspiration to express what they knew in terms of tangible discoveries, creations, and inventions.

The participants recalled the freedom they were given to explore their surrounding environments and the tolerance their parents and educators showed if they made a mess, broke something, or shorted out the electrical circuits as a result of their inventive endeavors. Some wrote about how living individuals and famous inventors of the past had inspired them to dream of inventive careers. Through these experiences, many remembered discovering a joy of inventing that endured through to adulthood. Perhaps most important, participants mentioned how, through these discovery forums at home and at school, they learned the value and importance of failure in discovery work and the dominant influence of early childhood successes in their later interest in inventing work.

The Development of Inventing Talent

One key question is whether inventing ability is innate or learned through a series of early life experiences. The express focus of both Study 1 and Study 2, as indicated by choice of underlying theoretical models, was to identify and explore personal attributes of adult inventors and their early environment that were malleable and therefore could be influenced by future initiatives in family, school, and higher education. Therefore, genetic predispositions to inventing were not directly evaluated. The survey questions that asked about influential childhood experiences were designed to elicit information about the inventor participants' early family, community, and school environments. Not surprisingly, the majority of the participants provided evidence for strong environmental influences on their ability to invent later in life. Two participants, despite the wording of the questions, did discuss their belief that their inventing talent was innate.

In the end, anecdotal evidence will not settle a debate as long-standing as that of nature versus nurture, neither in general nor in the study of creativity. Both genetic and environmental influences on creative behavior have been well elucidated in the creativity literature (Simonton, 1999; Sternberg, 1999). In human behavioral biology, Lewontin (1995) and Sapolsky (1998) have emphasized that the general debate of nature versus nurture goes well beyond an either–or debate but instead is a phenomenon of the interaction between genes and the environment.

In terms of limitations of the results on formative environments of inventors, Study 2 relies on participants' memory of their childhood experiences. Henry, Moffitt, Caspi, Langley, and Silva (1994) outlined the accuracy flaws inherent in study designs that rely on retrospective recall. Caution must be exercised when interpreting these results with causal inference. The vignette data from Study 2 on formative environments is best treated as information that can generate hypotheses for experimental and longitudinal studies in how educational, community, and family initiatives might influence future inventing talent.

CONCLUSION

How does one recognize an inventor living next door? One can spot an inventor neither through appearance, fame, role identity, patents, or individual success. One recognizes an inventor through his or her problem-finding vision and strong problem-solving focus. An inventor is likely to have a strong intrinsic motivation toward work, especially motivated by the most difficult of challenges. Good inventors learn to be tenacious, persistent, focused, and open to experience. Some will work exceptionally hard and are likely to deeply enjoy their creative work. Successful inventors are confident in their abilities, backed by a solid resume of educational and hands-on experience. They may even be able to spin an engaging story of childhood working side-by-side with their parents to solve a household need. They may not carry a camera, an easel, or a violin; even without traditional artistic tools, inventors are among the creative masters of the technical world.

APPENDIX 7.1
Inventive Contributions Among Diverse Peoples

The following Web sites recognize the contributions of inventors among

1) Children:
   http://www.inventors.about.com/science/inventors/
   msubmenuyounginventors.htm
2) African-American people:
   http://www.princeton.edu:80/~mcbrown/display/inventor_
   list.html
   http://www.si.edu/resource/faq/nmah/afinvent.htm
   http://inventors.about.com/cs/blackinventors/
3) Chinese, Latino, and other people of color:
   http://inventors.about.com/cs/chineseinventors/
   http://inventors.about.com/cs/hispanicinventors/
   http://www.uspto.gov/web/offices/ac/ahrpa/opa/pulse/epulse/
   pulse0103_4a.htm
4) Women:
   http://inventors.about.com/cs/womeninventors/

REFERENCES

Adams, J. L. (1972). Individual and small group creativity. *Engineering Education, 63*(2), 100–105, 131.

Adams, S. (2003). *Dilbert.* Retrieved on January 20, 2003 from http://www.dilbert.com/

Amabile, T. M. (1983). *The social psychology of creativity.* New York: Springer-Verlag.

Amabile, T. M. (1995). *KEYS: Assessing the climate for creativity.* Greensboro, NC: Center for Creative Leadership.

Amabile, T. M., Conti, R., Coon, H., Lazenby, J., & Herron, M. (1996). Assessing the work environment for creativity. *Academy of Management Journal, 39,* 1154–1184.

Astin, A. W. (1984). Student involvement: A developmental theory for higher education. *Journal of College Student Personnel, 25,* 297–308.

Bandura, A. (1997). *Self-efficacy: The exercise of control.* New York: W. H. Freeman.

Becker, G. M. (1994). Making it or finding it. In M. P. Shaw & M. A. Runco (Eds.), *Creativity and affect* (pp. 168–181). Norwood, NJ: Ablex Publishing.

Bellis, M. (2003a). Inventors of the modern computer. *What do you need to know about?* Retrieved January 20, 2003, from http://inventors.about.com/library/weekly/aa080498.htm

Bellis, M. (2003b). Automobile history. *What do you need to know about?* Retrieved January 20, 2003 from http://inventors.about.com/library/inventors/blcar.htm

Berners-Lee, T. (with Fischetti, M.). (1999). *Weaving the web: The original design and ultimate destiny of the World Wide Web, by its inventor.* San Francisco: Harper.

Brown, K. A. (1988). *Inventors at work.* Redmond, WA: Tempus Books of Microsoft Press.

Bruch, C. B. (1988). Metacreativity: Awareness of thoughts and feelings during creative experiences. *The Journal of Creative Behavior, 22*(2), 112–122.

Csikszentmihalyi, M. (1996). *Creativity.* New York: HarperCollins.

Deci, E., & Ryan, R. (1985). *Intrinsic motivation and self-determinism in human behavior.* New York: Academic Press.

Dillman, D. A. (2000). *Mail and internet surveys: The tailored design method.* New York: Wiley.

Erickson, E. H. (1968). *Identity, youth, and crisis.* New York: Norton.

Faste, R. (1972). The role of visualization in creative behavior. *Engineering Education, 63*(2), 124–127.

Fetterman, D. M. (1990, July 22). Wasted genius: How America is losing its next Einsteins. *San Jose Mercury News,* pp. 1C, 8C.

Filippelli, L. A., & Walberg, H. J. (1997). Childhood traits and conditions of eminent women scientists. *Gifted Child Quarterly, 41*(3), 95–104.

Ford, M. E. (1992). *Motivating humans: Goals, emotions, and personal agency beliefs.* Newbury Park, CA: Sage.

Ford, M. E., & Nichols, C. W. (1991). Using goal assessments to identify motivational patterns and facilitate behavioral regulation and achievement. In M. L. Maeher & P. Pintrich (Eds.), *Advances in motivation and achievement* (pp. 51–84). Greenwich, CT: JAI Press.

Getz, I., & Lubart, T. I. (1999). The emotional resonance model for generating associations. In S. W. Russ (Ed.), *Affect, creative experience and psychological adjustment* (pp. 41–56). Philadelphia: Brunner/Mazel.

Getzels, J. W., & Csikszentmihalyi, M. (1976). *The creative vision: A longitudinal study of problem finding in art.* New York: Wiley.

Hébert, T. P. (1993). Reflections at graduation: The long-term impact of elementary school experiences in creative productivity. *Roeper Review, 16* (1), 22–28.

Henderson, S. J. (1999). [Personal accounts and personality assessments of five product inventors.] Unpublished raw data.

Henderson, S. J. (1999/2000). Career happiness: More fundamental than job satisfaction. *Career Planning and Adult Development Journal, 15*(4), 5–10.

Henderson, S. J. (2000a). *Creative innovation courses: Forums for personal growth and career exploration.* Unpublished manuscript.

Henderson, S. J. (2000b). "Follow your bliss": A process for career happiness. *Journal of Counseling and Development, 78*(3), 305–315.

Henderson, S. J. (2003). Correlates of inventor motivation, creativity, and achievement. *Dissertation Abstracts International.*

Henderson, S. J. (2004). *Product inventors and creativity: The finer dimensions of enjoyment.* Manuscript submitted for publication.

Hennessey, B. A. (1999). Intrinsic motivation, affect, and creativity. In S. Russ (Ed.), *Affect, creative experience, and psychological adjustment* (pp. 77–90). Philadelphia: Taylor and Francis.

Hennessey, B. A., & Amabile, T. M. (1998). Reward, intrinsic motivation, and creativity. *American Psychologist, 53,* 674–675.

Henry, B., Moffitt, T. E., Caspi, A., Langley, J., & Silva, P. (1994). On the "remembrance of things past": A longitudinal evaluation of the retrospective method. *Psychological Assessment, 6, 2,* 92–101.

HP invent. (1999). *Hewlett Packard company annual report.* Palo Alto, CA: Hewlett Packard.

Huber, J. C. (1998). *Invention and inventivity is a random, Poisson process: A potential guide to analysis of general creativity, Creativity Research Journal, 11*(3), 231–241.

IBM research news. (2003). Retrieved on January 20, 2003, from http://www.research.ibm.com/resources/news/19980211_meyerson.shtml

Inventor of the week. (2003). Retrieved on January 20, 2003, from the Lemelson-MIT Program Web site: http://web.mit.edu/invent

Inventor of the week archive. (1998). Retrieved on January 20, 2003, from the Lemelson-MIT Program Web site: http://web.mit.edu/invent/iow/sherman.html

Kelley, T. (with Littman, J.). (2001). *The art of innovation.* New York: Doubleday.

Krumboltz, J. D. (1979). A social learning theory of career decision making. In A. M. Mitchell, G. B. Jones, & J. D. Krumboltz (Eds.), *Social learning and career decision making* (pp. 19–49). Cranston, RI: Carroll Press.

Krumboltz, J. D. & Henderson, S. J. (2002). A learning theory for career counselors. In S. Niles (Ed.), *Adult career development: Concepts, issues and practices* (3rd ed.). Alexandria, VA: National Career Development Association.

Lewontin, R. C. (1995). Genes, environment, and organisms. In R. B. Silvers (Ed.), *Hidden histories of science* (pp. 115–139). New York: New York Review.

Mace, M. (1997). Toward an understanding of creativity through a qualitative appraisal of contemporary art making. *Creativity Research Journal, 10*(2 & 3), 265–278.

MacFarquhar, L. (1999, December 6). Looking for trouble: How an inventor gets his best ideas. *The New Yorker,* pp. 78–93.

MacKinnon, D. W. (1962). The nature and nurture of creative talent. *American Psychologist, 17,* 484–495.

Masten, A. S. (2001). Ordinary magic: Resilience processes in development. *American Psychologist, 56,* 227–238.

Microwave oven. (2002). The great idea finder website. Retrieved on January 20, 2003, from http://www.ideafinder.com/history/inventions/story068.htm

Miles, M. B., & Huberman, A. M. (1994). *Qualitative data analysis*. Thousand Oaks, CA: Sage.

Moos, R. H., & Insel, P. N. (1974). *Work environment scale, Form R*. Palo Alto: Consulting Psychologist Press.

National Science Board. (2000). *Science and engineering indicators* (NSB-00-1). Retrieved on July 15, 2002, from the National Science Foundation Web site: http://www.nsf.gov/sbe/srs/seind00/pdfstart.htm

National Science Foundation. (1997). *Division of science resources studies, scientists and engineers statistical data system (SESTAT)*. Retrieved on July 15 2002 from the National Science Foundation Web site: http://srsstats.sbe.nsf.gov/

Pace, C. R. (1980). Measuring the quality of student effort. *Current Issues in Higher Education, 2*, 10–16.

Petkus, E., Jr. (1996). The creative identity: Creative behavior from the symbolic interactionist perspective. *Journal of Creative Behavior, 30*(3), pp. 188–196.

Postman, N. (2003). Philo Farnsworth. *Time 100*. Retrieved on January 20, 2003, from http://www.time.com/time/time100/scientist/profile/farnsworth.html

Rogers, E. M. (1986). *Silicon Valley fever: Growth of high-technology culture*. New York: Basic Books.

Rosenbaum, M. (1990). *Learned resourcefulness: On coping skills, self-control, and adaptive behavior*. New York: Springer.

Rossman, J. (1935). A study of childhood, education and age of 710 inventors. *Journal of the Patent Office Society, XVII*(5), 411–414.

Rossman, R. (1964). *Industrial creativity: The psychology of the inventor*. New Hyde Park, NY: University Books.

Rostan, S. M. (1997). A study of young artists: The development of artistic talent and creativity. *Creativity Research Journal, 10*(2 & 3), 175–192.

Russ, S. W. (1993). *Affect and creativity: The role of affect and play in the creative process*. Hillsdale, NJ: Lawrence Erlbaum Associates.

Russ, S. W. (1999). *Affect, creative experience and psychological adjustment*. Philadelphia: Brunner/Mazel.

Sameroff, A. (1987). The social context of development. In N. Eisenberg (Ed.), *Contemporary topics in developmental psychology* (pp. 167–189). New York: Wiley.

Sapolsky, R. M. (1998). *Why zebras don't get ulcers: An updated guide to stress, stress-related diseases, and coping*. New York: W. H. Freeman.

Seligman, M. (1991). *Learned optimism*. New York: Alfred A. Knopf.

Shaw, M. P. (1989). The eureka process: A structure for the creative experience in science and engineering. *Creativity Research Journal, 2*, 286–298.

Shaw, M. P. (1994). Affective components of scientific creativity. In M. P. Shaw & M. A. Runco, *Creativity and affect* (pp. 3–43). Norwood, NJ: Ablex Publishing.

Shaw, M. P., & Runco, M. A. (1994). *Creativity and affect*. Norwood, NJ: Ablex Publishing.

Simonton, D. K. (1999). *Origins of genius: Darwinian perspectives on creativity*. Cambridge: Oxford University Press.

Stanley, T. J., and Danko, W. D. (1996). *The millionaire next door: The surprising secrets of America's wealthy*. Atlanta, GA: Longstreet Press.

Sternberg, R. J. (1999). *The handbook of creativity*. Cambridge, MA: Cambridge University Press.

Stipp, D. (1999, March). Inventor on the verge of a nervous breakthrough. *Fortune*, 105–115.

Torrance, E. P. (1974). *Torrance test of creative thinking*. Lexington, MA: Ginn and Company (Xerox Corporation).

Urdan, T. (1997). Achievement goal theory: Past results, future directions. In M. L. Maehr & P. R. Pintrich (Eds.), *Advances in motivation and achievement* (Vol. 10, pp. 99–141). Greenwich, CT: JAI Press.

Vosburg, S., & Kaufmann, G. (1999). Mood and creativity research: The view from a conceptual organizing perspective. In S. W. Russ (Ed.), *Affect, creative experience and psychological adjustment* (pp. 19–39). Philadelphia, PA: Brunner/Mazel.

Watercutter, A. (2003, January 19). *Segway hits legal pothole in SF before scooters hit the streets*. Retrieved on January 20, 2003, from the SFGate Web site: http://www.sfgate.com/cgi-bin/article.cgi?file=/news/archive/2003/01/19/state1440EST0024.DTL

Weber, R. J., & Perkins, D. N. (1992). *Inventive minds: Creativity in technology*. New York: Oxford University Press.

Weiss, S. (1999). Robert Noyce (1927–1990). *Jones telecommunications and multimedia encyclopedia*. Retrieved on January 20, 2003 from http://www.digitalcentury.com/encyclo/update/noyce.html

Wright, R. (1997, May 19). The man who invented the World Wide Web. *Time Magazine*, 1619, pp. 64–68.

8

ARTISTIC SCIENTISTS AND SCIENTIFIC ARTISTS: THE LINK BETWEEN POLYMATHY AND CREATIVITY

ROBERT ROOT-BERNSTEIN AND MICHELE ROOT-BERNSTEIN

The literature comparing artistic and scientific creativity is sparse, perhaps because it is assumed that the arts and sciences are so different as to attract different types of minds, each working in very different ways. As C. P. Snow wrote in his famous essay "The Two Cultures," artists and intellectuals stand at one pole and scientists at the other: "Between the two a gulf of mutual incomprehension—sometimes . . . hostility and dislike, but most of all lack of understanding. . . . Their attitudes are so different that, even on the level of emotion, they can't find much common ground" (Snow, 1964, p. 4). Our purpose here is to argue that Snow's oft-repeated opinion has little substantive basis. Without denying that the *products* of the arts and sciences are different in both aspect and purpose, we nonetheless find that the *processes* used by artists and scientists to forge innovations are extremely similar. In fact, an unexpected proportion of scientists consists of amateur and sometimes even professional artists, and vice versa. Contrary to Snow's two-cultures thesis, the arts and sciences are part of one, common creative culture largely composed of polymathic individuals.

We base our argument on five types of evidence that correlate artistic and scientific creativity. First, successful artists and scientists tend to be polymaths with unusually broad interests and training that transcend disciplinary boundaries. Second, artists and scientists have similar psychological profiles as determined by widely used psychological tests. Third, arts proclivities predict scientific success just as intellectually challenging avocations predict success in all fields. Fourth, scientists and artists often describe their creative work habits in the same ways, using the same language, and draw on common, transdisciplinary mental toolkits that include observing, imaging, abstracting, patterning, body thinking, empathizing, and so forth. Fifth and finally, scientists often state that their art avocation fruitfully informs their vocation; artists often draw explicit sustenance from their scientific interests. The arts have often stimulated scientific discoveries and science has often influenced the nature of artistic creativity.

These observations have broad implications for our understanding of creativity, intelligence, and education. First, they establish a connection between personal or "little c" creativity, which most people experience, and "big C" domain-altering creativity, to which only a handful of people contribute. We contend that the individual producing "big C" creativity in one field more often than not exhibits a polymathic array of "smaller c" creativity in other fields. Learning how to manipulate the creative process in one discipline appears to train the mind to understand the creative process in any discipline. In other words, creative people tend to be generally creative, in the sense of being able to make personal contributions to disparate fields. For most people, these contributions vary widely in novelty and effectiveness. Such individuals may be unpublished amateur poets and Nobel Prize–winning chemists, or Sunday painters and paradigm-altering composers. In extreme cases, however, modern "Renaissance people" make relatively important contributions to several sciences, several arts, or to both. The very fact that individuals can participate in a range of creative vocations and avocations at various levels of novelty and effectiveness suggests to us a general creative intelligence independent of disciplinary or domain-specific boundaries.

Equally important, the five correlations we will explore suggest that the devaluation of the arts and the elimination of arts training from many schools may have significant detrimental effects on creativity across all disciplines. One of the few curricular areas in which students learn to make something of at least limited novelty is in the arts. If practice with the creative process through "little c" creative activities is essential to training people for "big C" creative activities, then limiting or eliminating arts programs must have a broad impact. In particular, because arts and crafts avocations are highly associated with scientific creativity, fostering arts education may be necessary to promote the highest forms of scientific creativity, an opinion expressed by many eminent scientists.

SCIENTISTS AS ARTISTS AND ARTISTS AS SCIENTISTS

Our interest in arts–sciences interactions began as graduate students when we serendipitously encountered a series of famous scientists who had also considered artistic careers or who had practiced the arts at a high level as adults (Root-Bernstein, 1987). One of us subsequently documented more than 400 instances (Root-Bernstein, 1989, pp. 318–327). Here we call attention to only a handful of examples. Louis Pasteur, Frederick Banting, and Santiago Ramon y Cajal were all excellent artists (Jackson, 1943; Ramon y Cajal, 1937; Vallery-Radot, 1987). Sir Humphrey Davy, the founder of modern atomic theory, wrote poetry that was praised by his friend and colleague Coleridge (Davy, 1840). Roald Hoffmann, the man who many chemists believe has brought more order to chemical theory than anyone since Mendeleev and his periodic table, is also a widely published poet and playwright (Djerassi & Hoffmann, 2001; Hoffmann, 1988). C. G. Jung, whose artistic output nearly rivaled his psychoanalytic work, described his art making as "a rite of entry" to his science (Jaffe, 1979, p. 205). Roger Guillemin, the Nobel laureate who isolated the first peptide hormones, is also a painter who has since made a reputation as a professional computer artist (Guillemin, 2002). Virologist and vaccine inventor Hilary Kaprowski, following in the footsteps of astronomer William Herschel and chemist Alexander Borodin, has taken time out from his scientific studies to record his musical compositions (Borodin, 1995; Herschel, 1995; Kaprowski, 1999).

We quickly determined that artists were also polymathic in the arts. Musical talent is so easily found among painters (e.g., Jean Ingres, Paul Klee, and Henri Matisse) that author Henry Miller once remarked, "Every artist worth his salt has his 'violin d'Ingres'" (Hjerter, 1986, frontispiece). In Miller's case, his metaphorical "violin" was painting—a typical avocation for writers (Miller, 1974). Many books have, in fact, illustrated the very strong connections that exist between visual talents and writing, most notably Kathleen Hjerter's *Doubly Gifted: The Author as Visual Artist* (1986) and Lola Szladits's and Harvey Simmonds's *Pen and Brush: The Author as Artist* (1969).

Indeed, if one goes to the Web site of the Nobel Foundation in Sweden, or biographical compendia concerning these laureates in literature, one finds that, although avocational interests are mentioned for only 55 of 98, at least a third had adult (a)vocations in at least one other art and that, most often, a visual art (Table 8.1). Some Nobel Prize–winning writers have also acted or directed theatrical productions, played musical instruments or composed. For many, these passions influenced their writing. For some, these multiple talents have been expressed as dual careers: Rabindranath Tagore composed the music for hundreds of his poems that he set as songs; Derek Walcott and Gao Xingjian have exhibited their paintings professionally; Gunter Grass was a professional sculptor and printmaker; Dario Fo has excelled not only as

TABLE 8.1
Arts Avocations and Vocations of Nobel Laureates in
Literature, 1901–2002

Noble prize		Visual arts and sculpture	Music	Drama* and dance
1903	Bjornstjerne Bjornson	/ X?		X
1912	Gerhart Hauptmann	X	X	X
1913	Rabindranath Tagore	X	X	
1915	Romain Rolland	X?	X	
1916	Verner Von Heidenstam	X		
1917	Karl Gjellerup	X	X?	
1922	Jacinto Benavente			X
1923	William Butler Yeats	X		X
1924	Wladyslaw Reymont	X		X
1925	George Bernard Shaw	X	X	
1929	Thomas Mann		X?	
1933	Ivan Bunin	X		
1936	Eugene O'Neill			X
1946	Hermann Hesse	X	X?	
1947	Andre Gide		X	
1948	Thomas Stearns Eliot		X	
1951	Par Lagerkvist	X?		
1953	Winston Churchill	X		
1956	Juan Ramon Jimenez	X		
1957	Albert Camus			X?
1958	Boris Pasternak		X	
1966	Nelly Sachs	X?	X?	/ X
1975	Eugenio Montale	X	X	
1979	Odysseus Elytis	X		
1983	William Golding		X	X
1985	Claude Simon	X		
1986	Wole Soyinka			X
1989	Camilo Jose Cela	X		X
1990	Octavio Paz	X?		
1991	Nadine Gordimer	X		
1992	Derek Walcott	X		
1997	Dario Fo	X	X	X
1998	Jose Saramago	X?		
1999	Gunter Grass	X / X		
2000	Gao Xingjian	X		X

Note. Between 31 and 35 literature laureates had at least one other art avocation or vocation out of a total 98 laureates. No information on nonwriting activities was found for 43 of the laureates. Sources include Pribic (1990); Nobel (2002); and Liukkonen (2002).
*Other than writing, as director, actor.

a dramatist, but also as an actor, director, and stage and costume designer (Nobel, 2002; Liukkonen, 1999).

Composers and choreographers tend to be equally multitalented. Arnold Schoenberg and George Gershwin were excellent amateur painters (Lebrecht, 1984); George Hindemith and Igor Stravinsky (who took lessons from Picasso) sketched; Iannes Xenakis composed architecture as well as music, often borrowing the visual line of his buildings from his scores (Matossian, 1986). The choreographer Merce Cunningham has published a book of drawings (Cunningham, 2001); Rod Rodgers, who often set his experimental dance to unusual music, was also a percussion player, a photographer, and graphics designer (Dunning, 2002). Successful artists of all kinds, like scientists, are often artistic polymaths.

Many artists have been amateur or even professional scientists as well. The French composer Olivier Messiaen, for example, was an amateur ornithologist who incorporated bird song into many of his compositions. George Antheil, whose "Ballet mechanique" revolutionized modern music, was an amateur endocrinologist and inventor who held key electronics patents with actress Hedy Lamarr (Antheil, 1945; Braun, 1997). Cesar Cui and Nicholas Rimsky-Korsakov were trained as engineers. Alexander Borodin earned his living as a chemist. Sir Edward Elgar took out several patents on chemical processes. Camille Saint-Saens was an amateur astronomer. Mikhail Balakirev, Ernest Ansermet, Diana Dabney, and Iannes Xenakis—among many other modern composers—earned advanced degrees in mathematics (Root-Bernstein, 2001). Susan Alexjander has drawn on the science of genetics to inform her latest compositions (Alexander, 1996).

Science avocations and vocations are also prevalent among writers. At least 20 of the 55 Nobel laureates in literature for whom nonwriting interests could be documented trained in, practiced, or otherwise immersed themselves in science, engineering, or mathematics (Table 8.2). Jose Echegaray and Salvatore Quasimodo practiced civil engineering, Echegaray for much of his literary life. Bertrand Russell, who won a Nobel for his philosophical writings, was also a mathematician. Alexander Solzhenitsyn taught math and physics for many years. Elias Canetti took a doctorate in chemistry (Pribic, 1990). Amongst writers outside the Nobel circle, science is also a common enterprise. August Strindberg dabbled in chemistry when he was not painting or taking photographs (Hjerter, 1986). Beatrix Potter, the author of the famous Peter Rabbit stories, was an expert on fungi who first suggested (correctly) that lichens were symbiotic plants (Linden, 1966). Novelist Vladimir Nabokov, employed at the Harvard museum of natural history as a lepidopterist, discovered a rare species of butterfly (Johnson & Coates, 1999). H. G. Wells also took his college degree in science, as has virtually every noteworthy science fiction writer since (Asimov, Greenberg, & Waugh, 1985; Clark, 1989). Similarly, a long list of writers that includes William Carlos Williams, Rabelais, Chekhov, John Keats, Sir Arthur Conan Doyle, A. J. Cronin, and Frank Slaughter have been trained in and have also practiced medicine (Coulehan, 1993; Stone, 1988).

In light of Snow's two-cultures thesis, these artist–scientists and scientist–artists are a surprising lot. And yet, perhaps, not as surprising as all that. The connection between polymath and creativity has certainly been described before, notably by Eliot Dole Hutchinson in 1959: "It is not by accident that

TABLE 8.2
Science and Engineering Training and Interests of Nobel Laureates in Literature, 1901–2002

Nobel prize		School* or university	Career, at some time	Self-study or avocation
1901	Sully Prudhomme	X		X
1904	Jose Echegaray	X	X	
1907	Rudyard Kipling			X?
1911	Maurice Maeterlinck			X
1913	Rabindranath Tagore			X?
1917	Karl Gjellerup			X
1917	Henrik Pontoppidan	X	X	
1927	Henri Bergson	X		X
1939	Frans Eemil Sillanpaa	X		X?
1944	Johannes V. Jensen	X		X
1950	Bertrand Russell	X	X	
1951	Par Lagerkvist	X		
1959	Salvatore Quasimodo	X	X	
1960	Saint-John Perse	X		
1962	John Steinbeck	X		X
1967	Miguel Angel Asturias	X		
1970	Alexander, Solzhenitsyn	X	X	
1976	Saul Bellow	X?		
1981	Elias Canetti	X		
1983	William Golding	X		

Note. Total sample is 18–20 out of 98 recipients, 1901–2002. No information on nonwriting interests found for 43 laureates. Sources include Pribic (1990); Nobel (2002); and Liukkonen (2002).

in the greatest minds professions disappear. . . . Such men are not scientists, artists, musicians when they might just as well have been something else. They are creators" (Hutchinson, 1959, pp. 150–152). Others have made similar remarks. So the question becomes what the polymathy–creativity connection means. In particular, what do sciences and arts, or scientists and artists, share of consequence? What might polymaths tell us about creative thinking?

SCIENTISTS AND ARTISTS SHARE SIMILAR PSYCHOLOGICAL PROFILES

One possible explanation for the correlation between creativity in the arts and sciences is that artists and scientists have similar psychological profiles that are not shared by other professionals. This explanation appears to have merit. The primary investigator of this phenomenon was Bernice Eiduson of the University of California, Los Angeles, who, between 1955 and 1980, explicitly compared a range of responses to psychological tests taken by groups of artists, businessmen, and scientists. Eiduson used four major instruments for investigating the participants' psychological profiles: (a) intensive and extensive interviews concerning themselves, their early development, and their personal history; (b) the Rorschach test; (c) the thematic apperception test; and (d) the Miller analogies test. Results were rated on a CA-L rating scale of 50 items by three independent clinical psychologists who did not know the nature of the study or the participants (Eiduson, 1962, 1966; Eiduson & Bechman, 1973; Root-Bernstein, Bernstein, & Garnier, 1993).

Eiduson found that both the artistic group and the scientific group could be clearly differentiated from the business group, but that the artists and scientists could not be distinguished. Artists for example, tended to have diverse intellectual interests and elaborate fantasies. They were highly responsive to sensory experiences as well, and motivated to find diverse ways to express these experiences. Scientists shared all of these characteristics, whereas business people were intellectually narrow, reality-centered, and uninterested in sensual experiences or ways to express them. Altogether, of the 50 cognitive, emotional, and motivational variables studied, only two statistically significant differences between artists and scientists appeared (scientists were more willing to work in structured situations and were less introspective about sex), whereas 20 statistically significant differences were found between the artists and businessmen and 15 between the scientists and businessmen.

Taking into account the interview material as well, Eiduson concluded as follows:

> On the basis of the clinical experimental data both artists and scientists seem to share the same ways of thinking about and perceiving problems and situations; seem to share many attitudes about what they do, respond to the same motivations, and display some of the same personality attributes. The experimental findings showed that artists and scientists were more alike in their cognitive characteristics than they were in personality features, but in both of these areas the persons who were in creative fields were significantly different from persons who had selected business vocations. Therefore, I feel that this material speaks for a general model of the person who goes into a creative vocation. (Eiduson, 1962, pp. x–xi)

Other investigators have also demonstrated cognitive overlaps between artists and scientists. For instance, numerous studies show that students of science perform significantly better on tests of visual thinking and visual memory than do students of the humanities, students of literature, and, surprisingly, students of the arts (Benbow, 1988; Casey, Winner, Brabeck, & Sulivan, 1990; Helson & Crutchfield, 1970; Hermelin & O'Connor, 1986; Winner & Casey, 1992). In fact, visual and spatial thinking tests are among the few reliable predictors of success in science and engineering (Humphreys, Lubinski, & Yao, 1993). And although Richard Mansfield and Thomas Busse (1981) claim that only a handful of psychological tests have ever shown documented correlations with demonstrated creativity in the sciences, the three that do are based on arts-related material: the Strong vocation interest blank test, the Barron-Welsh art scale, and the mosaic construction test.

On the Strong vocational interest blank test, choosing artist, musician, or author as alternative careers were all positively correlated with being ranked as a creative scientist or engineer. Similarly, creative architects chose physicist, chemist, or psychologist as alternative careers significantly more often than their average peers. As Eiduson's study suggested, choosing business-related preferences such as accountant, production manager, purchasing agent, office man, and salesman were negatively correlated with creativity for both scientists and architects. Similarly, most studies of scientists and mathematicians using the Barron-Welsh art scale and the Mosaic construction test have shown that those identified as creative are more likely to prefer, as artists do, complex and asymmetrical patterns as opposed to symmetrical ones (Mansfield & Busse, 1981). These findings also correlate with an extensive and growing literature on the importance of aesthetic considerations for creative work in science in which some scientists refer explicitly to developing their aesthetics through their artistic avocations (Root-Bernstein, 1996, 2002, 2003).

These observations suggest that scientists and artists may be being drawn from a single pool of talent, a suggestion we have found the great art historian and critic, Sir Kenneth Clark, made in 1981:

> Art and science . . . are not, as used to be supposed, two contrary activities, but in fact draw on many of the same capabilities of the human mind. . . . The development of science . . . has touched that part of the human spirit from which art springs, and has drained away a great deal of what once contributed to art. . . . We must . . . wait patiently for our faculties to be reunited. (Clark, 1981, pp. 25, 29)

Clark's observation is well worth further investigation, particularly as it has important sociological implications.

ARTS PROCLIVITIES PREDICT SCIENTIFIC SUCCESS

Given the fact that artistic psychological profiles and vocational and aesthetic preferences seem to be correlated with scientific creativity, one might reasonably expect that arts avocations predict scientific success. Many important scientists have conjectured as much. For example, Max Planck, the inventor of quantum physics and a pianist who considered a professional career, wrote in his autobiography that the "pioneering scientist must have an . . . *artistically* creative imagination" (Planck, 1949, p. 109). Similarly, J. H. Van't Hoff (1878/1967), who would become the first Nobel Prize winner in chemistry (1901) suggested that scientific imagination is always mirrored by evidence of nonscientific creativity. Studies of famous living mathematicians and physicists by P. J. Moebius (1900), Henri Fehr (1912), and Jacques Hadamard (1945) suggested he was right.

Subsequent studies by the Stanford University group led by Louis Terman confirmed the polymathy correlation. Terman's student R. K. White produced the first statistical studies of the versatility of geniuses across all disciplines during the 1930s. Analyzing hundreds of historical figures, he found that "the typical genius surpasses the typical college graduate in range of interests and . . . [h]e surpasses him in range of ability" (White, 1931, p. 482). During the 1950s, another Terman student, Catherine Cox, looked at high IQ individuals and found, in Terman's words, that, "there are few persons who achieved great eminence in one field without displaying more than average ability in one or more other fields" (Seagoe, 1975, p. 221). More recent studies by Roberta Milgram and her colleagues at Tel Aviv University following thousands of teenagers from military service through the subsequent 20 or so years of their civilian careers have validated Terman's conclusion. Milgram reports that school grades, IQ, standardized test scores, and psychological profiles do not predict career success reliably. The only reliable predictor of career success in any field is participation of an individual in an intellectually demanding avocation, such as one of the arts, poetry, music, chess, electronics, and so forth, over a long period of time (Milgram, Hong, Shavit, & Peled, 1997). Polymathy of any sort is highly correlated with vocational success.

We have found similar correlations among the forty scientists of the Eiduson study. Eiduson's group eventually included four Nobel laureates and eleven members of the National Academy of Sciences (United States), at one extreme, and several men who never achieved tenure or spent their careers in industry, at the other (Root-Bernstein, Bernstein, & Garnier, 1993). In 1988, Maurine Bernstein (who had taken over the study when Dr. Eiduson died), Robert Root-Bernstein, and Helen Garnier sent out a new questionnaire to the scientists and reviewed Dr. Eiduson's earlier interviews of her subjects. By analyzing publications, citations rates, and multiple interviews, they found that although none of the psychological parameters that Eiduson had investigated correlated with scientific success, statistically significant correlations existed between the number and type of hobbies that a scientist practiced as an adult and his success as a scientist (Table 8.3). In particular, scientists who made or collected art, who practiced photography, or who were active as musicians were much more likely than their colleagues to produce one or more papers cited 100 or more times within 15 years or papers cited 10 or more times in a single year (we called these groupings *citation clusters*). All of the Nobel laureates in the study were in the top citation cluster as were most of the members of the U.S. National Academy of Sciences. The more artistic hobbies a scientist engaged in as an adult, the greater their probability of achieving eminence within science (Root-Bernstein, Bernstein, & Garnier, 1995).

Equally interesting was the finding that the cognitive styles of the scientists were correlated to their avocations. Those who engaged in visual arts or music tended to use various modes of thinking, especially visual and kines-

TABLE 8.3
Hobbies × Citation Cluster for Scientists of the Eiduson Study

	A	B
Painting	.42***	7.64**
Collecting art	.42***	7.64**
Drawing	.29*	5.74*
Sculpting	.12	2.07
Sum of all arts	.38**	—
Poetry	.31**	3.16
Photography	.30**	1.89
Crafts	.31**	2.83
Singing	.25*	4.76
Collect records	.23	2.89
Play instrument	.19	2.07
Nonarts hobbies	−.22	2.95
Sum of all hobbies	.42**	—

Note. A = Pearson product-moment pairwise correlation coefficients. B = Chi-square statistics. Source: Root-Bernstein, et al. (1995).
*p < .10; **p < .05; ***p < .01.

thetic, at significantly higher rates than those who had primarily word-related hobbies. Writers tended to think in verbal patterns. Sculptors tended to be nonvisual and kinesthetic thinkers. Those who engaged in electronics-related hobbies used a wide range of mental tools (Root-Bernstein et al., 1995).

In addition, the study found that different modes of problem solving also correlated with scientific success. Scientists who reported solving problems using primarily visual forms of thinking tended to have higher impact and publication cluster rankings than did scientists who used primarily verbal and symbolic forms of thinking. The wider the range of thinking modes a scientist used, the more likely they were to be in the most successful group (Root-Bernstein et al., 1995).

These results raise various interesting possibilities. Do avocations build cognitive strengths or merely mirror them? Do hobbies represent artistic outlets for the scientists' existing mental strengths or do hobbies develop the cognitive bases on which creative science grows? These data obviously do not answer these important questions, but they do make them significant. Likely, future research will reveal that, as with all human traits, innate talents are strengthened by the practice of artistic avocations benefiting vocational skills, and vice versa.

As surprising as the finding that artistic avocations correlate with scientific success may be, it appears to be quite general. We are currently at work on a follow-up investigation of all Nobel Prize winners that is validating the results from the Eiduson study. So far, we have only completed studying the 134 chemists who have won Nobel prizes between 1901 and 2000. We were fortunate to find a control group with which to compare these ex-

TABLE 8.4
Frequency of Arts Avocations in Chemistry Nobel Prize Winners
Compared With Sigma Xi Members

Avocation	% Respond @	% Members ~	% Nobelists>
Photography	14.5	1.4	12.8
Music	12.5	1.2	24.6 **
Art +	1.8	0.2	11.9 **
Woodworking ^	1.5	0.1	4.4 **
Writing #	1.2	0.1	9.0 **
Poetry #	0.3	0.03	5.2 ***
Metalworking ^	0.3	0.03	1.5 **
Handicrafts ^	0.3	0.03	ni
Drawing +	0.3	0.03	3.7 ***
Theater or acting<	0.2	0.02	3.7 ***
Etching or printing*	0.2	0.02	1.5 **
Architecture	0.2	0.02	0.7 **
Stagecraft ^	0.1	0.01	0.7 **
Pottery ^	0.1	0.01	0
Weaving ^	0.1	0.01	0
Rugs^	0.1	0.01	0
Sculpture+	0.1	0.01	0.7***
Dancing <	0	0	1.4 +++
Performing (cum <)	0.2	0.02	5.2 ***
Arts (cum +)	2.3	0.2	17.2 ***
Crafts (cum ^)	2.4	0.2	10.4 **
Writing (cum #)	1.5	0.1	12.7 **

Note. Chi-squared analysis using respondents. ** $p < .01$;*** $p < .001$; +++ probability cannot be calculated. Cum = cumulative. ni = no information available. @ c. 4,000 respondents. ~ c. 42,500 members. > 134 chemistry Nobel Prize winners, 1901–2000. Sources include Farber (1961); James (1993); Nobel (2002); and Ward & Ellery (1936).

traordinary scientists in the form of a survey of avocations sent out in 1936 to the members of Sigma Xi, the National Research Society (Ward & Ellery, 1936). Of the approximately 42,500 members of Sigma Xi at that time, just over 4,000 responded to the survey indicating one or more avocations ranging from the arts to gardening and athletics, to stamp, coin, and fossil collecting, to reading. Using the Sigma Xi data as a baseline for calculating distribution and frequency of various hobbies, the same data were collected from biographical and autobiographical sources for the Nobel laureates. For almost all art-related avocations other than photography, Nobel laureates have statistically significantly greater participation in arts avocations as adults than do their peers (Table 8.4). Particularly noteworthy is the fact that Nobel Prize winners practice poetry and other forms of creative writing and the visual arts at rates many times those of average scientists. Although none of the thousands of Sigma Xi members reported dance as an avocation or recreation, two of the Nobel laureates did. Preliminary analysis of the results for Nobel laureates in medicine and in physics show the same strong trends. We therefore feel confident in saying that the most creative scientists not only have the psychological profiles of artists, but more often than not, *are* artists.

SCIENTISTS AND ARTISTS USE COMMON
TOOLS FOR THINKING

What benefit can there be for the scientist to be an artist or the artist a scientist? One possibility is that these apparently disparate professions share common ways of creative problem raising and problem solving. Our fourth correlation, therefore, concerns the common cognitive processes shared by artists and scientists. Many individuals, including Arthur Koestler (1964), Loren Eisely (1978), and Jacob Bronowski (1967) have already noted that the creative process as practiced by artists and scientists is virtually identical. One might expect to find, then, that particular cognitive modes used by scientists and artists will also be the same. We spent more than a decade reading hundreds of autobiographical, biographical, interview, and archival sources to determine what creative people in many disciplines say about how they actually think when solving disciplinary problems. Our book-length study, which appeared in 1999 as *Sparks of Genius*, proposed that individuals across the arts and sciences used a similar vocabulary to describe 13 intuitive, imaginative processes. These "tools for thinking" include observing, imaging, abstracting, pattern recognizing, pattern forming, analogizing, empathizing, body thinking, dimensional thinking, modeling, playing, transforming, and synthesizing—all categories that emerged clearly from the sources themselves. Whereas some of these mental tools are well known to psychologists (e.g., observing, imaging, and pattern recognizing), others are in need of much more study (e.g., analogizing, empathizing, and modeling).

Space does not permit a full description of all 13 tools here, but several examples will suffice to demonstrate how artists and scientists similarly define and use them. *Observing*, an essential skill, means paying attention to what is seen, but also what is heard, touched, smelled, tasted, and felt within the body (Berg, 1983). It involves actively seeing rather than passively looking, listening rather than hearing, thoughtfully being in motion rather than merely moving. Georgia O'Keeffe clarified the distinction when she recounted how a teacher "started me looking at things, looking very carefully at details. . . . Still—in a way—nobody sees a flower—really—it is so small—we haven't the time—and to see takes time, like to have a friend takes time" (Root-Bernstein & Root-Bernstein, 1999, p. 32). Nobel Prize–winning ethologist Konrad Lorenz said virtually the same thing: observing takes the "patience of a yogi. . . . To really understand animals and their behavior you must have . . . the patience to look at them long enough to see something" (Root-Bernstein & Root-Bernstein, 1999, p. 36).

Imaging is another mental tool shared by artists and scientists. It is the ability to recall or imagine, in the absence of external stimulation, the sensations and feelings we have observed. We can image visually and also aurally, as well as with smells, tastes, and tactile and muscular feelings (Barlow, Blakemore, & Weston-Smith, 1990; Ferguson, 1992; Roe, 1951). Sir James Black, pharmacologist and Nobel Prize winner, says that the focus of his thinking "is an imaginative sense, entirely open-ended and entirely pictorial. That is a vital part of my life. I daydream like mad . . . you can have all these 'chemical' structures in your head, turning and tumbling and moving" (Root-Bernstein & Root-Bernstein, 1999, p. 53). Composer Henry Cowell said similarly that,

> The most perfect [musical] instrument in the world is the composer's mind. Every conceivable tone-quality and beauty of nuance, every harmony and disharmony, of any number of simultaneous melodies can be heard at will by the trained composer; he can hear not only the sound of any instrument or combination of instruments, but also an almost infinite number of sounds which cannot yet be produced on any instrument. (Root-Bernstein & Root-Bernstein, 1999, p. 59)

Scientists and artists share an ability to create imaginary worlds within their minds.

Observing and imaging produce data that are too complicated to understand in unmodified form. *Abstracting,* whether in science or art, means focusing on a single property of a thing or process in order to simplify it and grasp its essence. Physicist Werner Heisenberg, for example, defined abstracting as "the possibility of considering an object or group of objects under one viewpoint while disregarding all other properties of the object. The essence of abstraction consists in singling out one feature, which, in contrast to other properties, is considered to be particularly important" (Root-Bernstein & Root-Bernstein, 1999, pp. 72–73). This process of eliminating unnecessary information while retaining the integrity of an idea or thing is a "step toward greater generality." Picasso agreed:

> To arrive at abstraction it is always necessary to begin with a concrete reality. . . . you must always start with something. Afterward you can remove all traces of reality. There's no danger then, anyway, because the idea of the object will have left an indelible mark. It is what started the artist off, excited his ideas, and stirred his emotions. (Root-Bernstein & Root-Bernstein, 1999, pp. 71–72)

Once an artist or scientist has found a powerful abstraction, he or she naturally wants to know how generally it can be applied. This process involves *pattern recognizing,* the ability to organize the random events we see, hear, or feel by grouping them. Virginia Woolf, for one, consciously explored pattern recognition in her work. As she developed scenes and characters she felt that she

> put the severed parts together . . . in writing I seem to be discovering what belongs to what. . . . From this I reach what I might call a philosophy; at any rate it is a constant idea of mine; that behind the cotton wool [of daily events lived unconsciously] is a hidden pattern. (Root-Bernstein & Root-Bernstein, 1999, p. 128)

Her purpose in writing was to make that pattern manifest. Many scientists similarly view their purpose as finding the patterns within apparently unrelated data. Nobel laureate Christiane Nusslein-Volhard not only designs her own complex puzzles as an avocation, but likens her embryological work to assembling "pieces of a jigsaw puzzle": "The most important thing is not any one particular piece, but finding enough pieces and enough connections between them to recognize the whole picture"—and to recognize the pattern of the whole picture *before* you have all the pieces (Root-Bernstein & Root-Bernstein, 1999, pp. 104–105, 111).

For many creative people, abstractions and patterns are literally felt within the body rather than seen or heard. Such *body thinking* relies on emotions and proprioceptive sensations of body movement, body tension, and body balance. Sculptor Auguste Rodin wrote that his "Thinker," meant to represent creative individuals of every kind, thought "not only with his brain, with his knitted brow, his distended nostrils, and compressed lips, but with every muscle of his arms, back and legs, with his clenched fist and gripping toes" (Root-Bernstein & Root-Bernstein, 1999, pp. 168–169). Thinking, Rodin tells us, integrally involves how we feel. MIT professor Cyril Stanley Smith, who was considered by many people to be the greatest metallurgist of the past century, certainly found it so:

> In the long gone days when I was developing alloys . . . I certainly came to have a very strong feeling of natural understanding, a feeling of how I would behave if I were a certain alloy, a sense of hardness and softness and conductivity and fusibility and deformability and brittleness—all in a curiously internal and quite literally sensual way even before I had touched the metal. (Root-Bernstein & Root-Bernstein, 1999, p. 171)

Some scientists and artists go even further, not only feeling bodily a thing or idea, but *empathizing* with it, feeling as it would feel. Like an actor, novelist, or playwright, Nobel Prize–winning chemist Peter Debye confessed to solving his problems by thinking about what the characters in his scenario felt—because these were molecules he asked himself, "what does the carbon atom want to do?" Jonas Salk said that he solved the polio vaccine problem by "imagining how the virus would behave" (Root-Bernstein, 1989, pp. 96–97). Philosopher Karl Popper even argued that

> the most helpful suggestion that can be made . . . as to how one may get new ideas in general [is] . . . 'sympathetic intuition' or 'empathy.'. . . You should enter into your problem situation in such a way that you almost become part of it. (Root-Bernstein & Root-Bernstein, 1999, p. 187)

The result of using these mental tools is what chemist–philosopher Michael Polanyi has called "personal knowledge"—an intuitive, sensual, emotional, organic understanding of how things behave or what they mean (Polanyi, 1958). Polanyi's emphasis on "personal knowledge" is particularly noteworthy, because so many philosophers and cognitive scientists reject the possibility that thinking can occur in the absence of verbal or logical formulations. Yet a very large number of the people we have studied describe knowing something intuitively without initially being able to express their understanding.

The rub of intuitive understanding, of course, is that such knowledge is necessarily private. Consequently, many artists and scientists recognize as a key step in their creative process the difficult one of *transforming* imagistic, corporal, empathic ideas into the public language of words, numbers, images, sounds, or movement. They *translate* subjective observations, images, patterns, and body feelings into cogent, disciplinary products that can be reproduced and described objectively. Poet Gary Snyder says that it is a three-step process for him: "The first step is the rhythmic measure, the second step is a set of preverbal visual images which move to the rhythmic measure, and the third step is embodying it in words" (Root-Bernstein & Root-Bernstein, 1999, pp. 8–9). Einstein, who confessed to solving his physics problems in images and muscular feelings, wrote similarly that "[c]onventional words or other signs [presumably mathematical] have to be sought for laboriously only in a secondary stage, when the associative play [of images and feelings] . . . is sufficiently established and can be reproduced at will" (Root-Bernstein & Root-Bernstein, 1999, p. 5). A scientist does not think in mathematical formula, Einstein observed; nor does a poet imagine in words—a point to which we return below in our conclusion. Suffice it to say here that the admonition to "think before we speak" is more insightful than first appears.

Once it is recognized that creative thinking takes place in intuitive, imagistic and private forms before symbolic communication to others, the value of polymathy to the inventive individual begins to clarify. The individual's choice of public discourse determines the domain to which his or her ideas contribute, rather than the way in which the ideas are initially conceived. Polymaths express their personal insights in several domains in order to maximize the process of communication. Moreover, each expression captures different elements of a single insight. In the end, the polymathic, creative individual not only feels that she knows, but knows what she feels in several communicable ways, thereby combining subjective and objective forms of understanding synthetically. We call this *synthetic* form of understanding *synosia* from the Greek roots of the words *synaesthesia* (a combining of the senses) and *gnosis* (knowledge). We believe, along with philosopher John Dewey and historian of science Howard Gruber, that the ability to form integrated networks of enterprise among many avocations and many ways of understanding things is what forms the basis of creative thinking (Dewey, 1934; Gruber, 1988).

SCIENCE FOSTERS ART AND ART FOSTERS SCIENCE

If scientists and artists really think the same way, then it should follow that they can also benefit from insights obtained in the complementary discipline. Art, in short, should foster better science, for, as historian of technology David Pye has written, "One who is capable of invention as an artist is commonly capable also of useful invention" in general (Ferguson, 1992, pp. 23–26). And so we come to our fifth creative correlation between the arts and sciences, which is that artists and scientists often recognize and use arts–sciences interactions in their work.

Roughly one fifth of Nobel laureates in literature have found rich harvest in the study of natural history generally and Darwinian evolution specifically. Sully Prudhomme, whose taste for mathematics and the natural sciences dictated the content of many literary meditations, was known for his "scientific poetry" and philosophical essays on scientific inquiry. Maurice Maeterlinck, best known for his symbolist stories and plays, not only kept bees in his garden but he wrote about them—and termites, ants, and flowers as well—in scientifically accurate essays meant to probe natural analogies to human behavior. At one time or another in their careers, Karl Gjellerup, Frans Eemil Sillanpää, Johannes Jensen, and John Steinbeck all parlayed an intense interest in Darwinian evolution and other scientific theories into thematic materials driving their novels, poetry, plays, and essays (Liukkonen, 1999; Nobel, 2002; Pribic, 1990). Jensen explicitly recognized the connection between his scientific avocation and his literary recreations of large sweeps of human history. He wrote in his Nobel autobiography: "The grounding in natural sciences which I obtained in the course of my medical studies, including preliminary examinations in botany, zoology, physics, and chemistry was to become decisive in determining the trend of my literary work" (Nobel, 2002). In the six-volume epic cycle that earned him the Nobel, this trend involved a personal interpretation of evolutionary theory and its moral implications as it applied to the cultural past and present. John Steinbeck similarly meshed scientific and literary interests. In his collaboration with the ecologist Ed Ricketts on *The Sea of Cortez* (1941/1971), Steinbeck not only returned to the marine biology he had studied in college, he determined that the shaping of science writing was as creative an act as the shaping of his fiction. Moreover, he used Ricketts' conceptual insights into the interrelated ecology of all life in *To A God Unknown* and other novels (Liukkonen, 1999; Pribic, 1990).

Science has also had a tremendous impact on the arts through studies of perception, color theory, perspective, and other novel geometries and the development of new techniques and instruments. A vast literature exists on this topic, so we will not describe it here (e.g., Kemp, 1990; Strosberg, 1999; Vitz & Glimcher, 1984; Waddington, 1969). Suffice it to say, art is permeated with scientific and technological know-how transferred there both by scientific artists and artistic scientists. A phenomenon that is less well known is that science is also permeated with art. Historian Brooke Hindle has spent a lifetime documenting art-to-science creativity for a wide range of artists-turned-inventors. His most famous case study involves two of America's greatest inventors, Samuel Morse and Robert Fulton, both of whom established themselves among the very best American painters before turning, in middle age, to careers as inventors (Hindle, 1981). More to the point, for both men, artistic training made possible and informed the nature of their inventions. Just to give one example, Morse's first working model of a telegraph was made out of a canvas stretcher adapted from his painting days.

Hindle suggests in this and many other cases that technical and manipulative skills developed in art were essential to industrial invention. In addition, a great many eminent anatomists of the 19th and early 20th centuries—Francis Seymour Hayden and Nobel laureates Santiago Ramon y Cajal and Emilio Golgi among them—formally trained themselves in visual arts because, as Hayden put it, "How much sooner would the eye [trained to draw] . . . learn to gauge the aberrations which make up the facies of the disease; how much better the hand, trained to portray them accurately, be able to direct with precision and safety the course of the knife!" (Zigrosser, 1976, p. 148; see also Berg, 1983). In other sciences, as well, artists have used their highly honed observational skills to discover what others overlooked. The protective coloration and patterning of animals that we call camouflage was discovered not by a biologist but by a late 19th century portraitist and painter of angels, Abbott Thayer, whose hobby was evolutionary theory (Root-Bernstein, 2000).

Artists also invent new structures that scientists then discover in nature. Virologists attempting to understand the structure of the protein shells that surround spherical viruses such as polio during the 1950s were directed by knowledge of architect–writer Buckminster Fuller's geodesic domes. Fuller's architecture also became the model for 60-unit carbon spheres aptly named buckminsterfullerenes, which are the most stable chemicals in the universe. Their inventor, Nobel laureate Hans Kroto, is himself an amateur artist who was aware of Fuller's concepts (Root-Bernstein, 2003). Cambridge physicist and artist Roger Penrose has also invented a new fundamental structure by playing around with variations of Escher-style tilings called aperiodic, or nonrepeating, tilings. He soon turned his recreation into a professional asset by working out the mathematical properties of such aperiodic tilings and giving the field its first complete theory. Martin Gardner's mathematical recreations column in *Scientific American* brought Penrose's avocation to the attention of a broad array of scientists, some of whom recognized that aperiodic tilings explain anomalous crystal structures in metal alloys called *quasicrystals* (Root-Bernstein, 2000). In this manner, artistic exploration has led to multiple scientific insights. Indeed, we would argue, artistic and scientific thinking are not two different kinds of cognitive activity, but two aspects of the same creative impulse.

CONCLUSIONS: CREATIVITY AS
CONCEPTUAL COMPLEMENTARITY

To summarize, we have found that artists and scientists, and also artistic and scientific thinking, are more similar than they are different. Many scientists pursue artistic avocations throughout their lives. Many artists reciprocate. Psychologically, scientists and artists appear to be very similar to each other in cognitive and personality factors and quite different from people who choose business- and humanities-related vocations, suggesting that scientists and artists may be drawn from a single, discrete pool of talent. Scientists and artists use a common set of intuitive and personal "thinking tools" for recognizing and solving their problems; practicing these mental tools in one field may foster their use in other fields. The pursuit of artistic activities by scientists correlates significantly with success as a scientist. We presume, but currently lack appropriate control groups, that the same correlation exists between polymathy and success in the arts. We hypothesize further that polymathy correlates with success in any discipline, as Roberta Milgram's data suggest. Certainly, many scientists, artists, and writers are explicitly aware that they have benefited from integrating disparate disciplinary interests. Thus, arts foster scientific creativity and conversely science fosters artistic creativity.

Should we recommend, then, that all students, regardless of vocational goals or personal preferences, take classes in painting, printing, sculpting, music composition and performance, dance, theater, creative writing, mathematics, and the sciences, as a way of fostering creative potential? If only it were so simple. No; what our research shows is something more subtle and difficult to achieve, and that is that creative people *integrate* apparently disparate skills, talents, and activities into a synergistic whole. A *functional interaction* must exist between intellectual and aesthetic activities to make avocations of value to vocational goals. Dewey has called this polymathic interrelatedness "integrated activity sets" (Dewey, 1934), Gruber dubbed it "networks of enterprise" (Gruber, 1988), and we have used the term "correlative talents" (Root-Bernstein, 1989). All three terms refer to an ability to recognize *useful* points of contact and *analogous skills* among an apparently diverse set of interests. Merely requiring a "distribution requirement" of "creative" activities will not, therefore, achieve synthetic talent integration.

The phenomenon of correlative talents does, however, have immediate implications for cognitive studies. Howard Gardner (1999) and Mihalyi Csikszentmihalyi (1996) have made it fashionable to argue that creativity occurs only within recognized domains of cognitive activity such as the visual–spatial or musical or kinesthetic or logico–mathematical. Gardner has gone so far as to doubt the possibility of "horizontal faculties" that would allow transdisciplinary or transdomain creativity (Gardner, 1999, p. 104).

Yet the pervasiveness of polymathy among innovators in both the sciences and arts argues strongly for the existence of horizontal faculties of some sort.

We suggest that one of the primary reasons that Gardner and Csikszentmihalyi ignore these horizontal faculties is that they have focused their research on the unique types of *products* that characterize disciplines or domains rather than on common creative *processes* that transcend them. This focus on product is built into their work from the outset. Gardner's "frames of mind," for example, are defined by the existence of unique, domain-specific languages and artifacts by which they can be identified (Gardner, 1999). His mistake, from our point of view, has been to confuse the formal mode of communication chosen by individual creators with the mode in which they do their creative thinking. As we have pointed out above and documented elsewhere (Root-Bernstein, 2001, 2002, 2003; Root-Bernstein & Root-Bernstein, 1999), creative people use personal and intuitive tools for thinking to achieve their insights, resorting *only in an explicitly secondary step* to translating their personal knowledge into a formal language in order to communicate with other people. Although we have no doubt that Gardner and Csikszentmihalyi are correct to contend that most (but not all) people have a *preferred mode of communication,* we strongly object to their assumption that people *think* in the same terms that they use to communicate. Our research suggests that thinking and communicating require very different skills. Creative artifacts and expressive products are transformations of thought and therefore unreliable guides to the processes by which those thoughts are generated. Languages are certainly based in cognition but cognition is not based in language (Barlow, Blakemore, & Weston-Smith, 1990; Root-Bernstein & Root-Bernstein, 1999).

One consequence of our view that cognition and communication are separate skills is that we find the concepts of domains, disciplines, and even vocations and avocations problematic. Hutchinson, whom we quoted above, hit the nail on the head when he said that for the most creative people, disciplines disappear. Creative people tend to have multiple forms of training, several kinds of jobs, and many ways of expressing themselves that ignore accepted categories and expectations (Root-Bernstein & Root-Bernstein, 1999, chaps. 15 & 16). How, for example, shall we describe Sophya Kovalevskaya, who attained international recognition as both a poet–playwright and also as one of the greatest mathematicians of the 20th century? Each activity fed the other in her mind:

> You are surprised at my working simultaneously in literature and in mathematics. Many people who have never had occasion to learn what mathematics is confuse it with arithmetic and consider it a dry and arid science. In actual fact, it is the science which demands the utmost imagination. . . . The poet must see what others do not see, must see more deeply than other people. And the mathematician must do the same. (Kovalevskaya, 1978, pp. 102–103)

Getting a grasp on polymaths is difficult because the very categories embedded in our language militate against a satisfactory description of transdisciplinary activity. Is Desmond Morris a scientist because he spent much of his life as a professor of zoology at Oxford University; or is he a writer because he has written dozens of best-selling books; or is he a film-maker because he has created art films and dozens of documentaries on animal and human behavior for the BBC, The Learning Channel, and other stations; or is he an artist because he has spent more time creating and showing his Surrealist paintings than doing anything else? Morris, whose passport labels him as a zoologist, identifies himself as none of these things. "I never thought of myself as a zoologist who painted or as a painter who was interested in zoology. They are both equally important to me because they both involve visual exploration" (Morris, 1987, p. 9). He goes on to say that

> If my paintings do nothing else, they will serve to demonstrate that such titles are misleading. In reality, people today are not scientists or artists ... they are explorers or non-explorers, and the context of their explorations is of secondary importance. Painting is no longer merely a craft, it is a form of personal research. ... So, in the end, I do not think of myself as being part scientist and part artist, but simply as being an explorer, part objective and part subjective. (Morris, 1971, p. 25)

Elsewhere Morris calls for the abolition of categorical thinking in a manner that strikes us as a fitting summary of our own argument as well: "Perhaps the time will come when we will give up the folly of separating subadults into the imaginative and the analytical—artists and scientists—and encourage them to be both at once" (Remy, 1991, p. 18).

So many innovative people are anomalously "both at once" that those who study creativity must pay attention. We conclude by suggesting that it is the very fact that polymaths cannot be pigeonholed into one discipline or domain that accounts for their extraordinary creativity. Innovations, by definition, are effective surprises that bring together problems, concepts, techniques, and materials that were previously unrelated (Root-Bernstein, 1989). By exploring many different ways of being "small c" creative, polymaths master an unusually wide range of imaginative and technical skills that reveal unexpected analogies between weakly related fields. Their innovations create formal bridges where none existed before, opening the way for "big C" creativity that redefines disciplinary boundaries and cognitive domains.

We further suggest that the fact that creative polymaths straddle domains explains why "genius" is so often associated with a struggle for recognition, whereas "normal" activities (in the Kuhnian sense) are often highly rewarded, but rarely remembered by posterity. Creativity is revealed through the intellectual and social redefining of boundaries, of which the creative product is simply a physical manifestation. The reason that the mimic or forger is not considered creative, though his or her product may be indistinguishable from the original, is because creativity lies not in the product, but in the *process of bridging and linking* domains. For Creative people, C. P. Snow's "two cultures" have never existed (Root-Bernstein et al., 1995; Root-Bernstein & Root-Bernstein, 1999). If there *is* a divide in creative culture that withstands scrutiny, it is between those who alter disciplines and their boundaries and those who do not. The first are likely to cultivate highly correlative, polymathic talents. The second are more likely to be highly specialized individuals and less likely to combine relevant avocations with vocation. Only when the imaginative processes that enable polymaths to link knowledge in new and extraordinary ways and the correlative talents that allow them to transcend the public discourse of disciplines are more fully understood will creative thinking yield up its secrets to cognitive science.

REFERENCES

Alexander, S. (1996). *Sequencia. Logos series CD.* Berkeley, CA: Science and the Arts.

Antheil, G. (1945). *Bad boy of music.* Garden City, NY: Doubleday.

Asimov, I., Greenberg, M., & Waugh, C. (1985). *Great science fiction stories by the world's great scientists.* New York: Primus.

Barlow, H., Blakemore, C., & Weston-Smith, M. (1990). *Images and understanding.* Cambridge, England: Cambridge University Press.

Benbow, C. (1988). Neuropsychological perspectives on mathematical talent. In L. Obler & D. Fein (Eds.), *The exceptional brain: Neuropsychology of talent and special abilities* (pp. 48–69). New York: Guilford.

Berg, G. (Ed.). (1983). *The visual arts and medical education.* Carbondale, IL: Southern Illinois University Press.

Borodin, A. (1995). String quartets nos. 1 & 2. On *The lark quartet* [CD]. New York: Arabesque Recordings.

Braun, H. -J. (1997). Advanced weaponry of the stars. *Invention & Technology, 12,* 10–17.

Bronowski, J. (1967). *Scientific genius and creativity.* New York: W. H. Freeman.

Casey, M. B., Winner, E., Brabeck, M., & Sulivan, K. (1990). Visual-spatial abilities in art, maths and science majors: Effects of sex, family, handedness and spatial experience. In K. Gihooly, M. Keane, R. Logie, & G. Erdo (Eds.), *Lines of thinking: Reflections on the psychology of thought* (pp. 275–294). New York: Wiley.

Clark, K. (1981). *Moments of vision.* London: Murray.

Clarke, A. C. (1989). *Astounding days.* London: Gollancz.

Coulehan, J. (1993, March/April). Physician as poet, poem as patient. *Poets & Writers Magazine,* pp. 57–59.

Csikszentmihalyi, M. (1996). *Creativity.* New York: Harper.

Cunningham, M. (2001). *Other animals: Drawings and journals*. New York: Aperture.

Davy, H. (1840). Parallels between art and science. In J. Davy (Ed.), *The collected works of Sir Humphrey Davy* (Vol. 8, pp. 306–308). London: Smith and Cornhill.

Dewey, J. (1934). *Art as experience*. New York: Minton, Balch.

Djerassi, C., & Hoffmann, R. (2001). *Oxygen*. Weinheim: Willey-VCH.

Dunning, J. (2002, March 29). Rod Rodgers, choreographer of modern dance, dies at 64. *The New York Times*, p. A22.

Eiduson, B. (1962). *Scientists: Their psychological world*. New York: Basic Books.

Eiduson, B. (1966). Productivity rate in research scientists. *American Scientist, 54*, 57–63.

Eiduson, B., & Bechman, L. (Eds.). (1973). *Science as a career choice*. New York: Russell Sage.

Eisely, L. (1978). *The star thrower*. New York: Times Books.

Farber, E. (Ed.). (1961). *Great chemists*. New York: Interscience.

Fehr, H. (1912). *Enquete de l'enseignmement mathematique et sur la methode de travail des mathematicians* [Study of the teaching of mathematics and on the working method of mathematicians]. Paris: Gauthier-Villars.

Ferguson, E. S. (1992). *Engineering and the mind's eye*. Cambridge, MA: MIT Press.

Gardner, H. (1999). Intelligence reframed. New York: Basic Books.

Gruber, H. (1988). The evolving systems approach to creative work. *Creativity Research Journal, 1*, 27–51.

Guillemin, R. (2002). [Electronic art]. Available from www.duganne.com/gallery.html

Hadamard, J. (1945). *The psychology of invention in the mathematical field*. Princeton, NJ: Princeton University Press.

Helson, R., & Crutchfield, R. (1970). Creative types in mathematics. *Journal of Personality, 38*, 177–197.

Hermelin, B., & O'Connor, N. (1986). Spatial representations in mathematically and in artistically gifted children. *British Journal of Educational Psychology, 56*, 150–157.

Herschel, W. (1995). Music by the father of modern astronomy. On *The Mozart orchestra* [CD]. Providence, RI: Newport Classic.

Hindle, B. (1981). Emulation and invention. New York: New York University Press.

Hjerter, K. (1986). *Doubly gifted. The author as visual artist*. New York: Abrams.

Hoffmann, R. (1988, March 21). How I work as poet and scientist. *The Scientist*, p. 10.

Humphreys, L. G., Lubinski, D., & Yao, G. (1993). Utility of predicting group membership in the role of spatial visualization in becoming an engineer, physical scientist, or artist. *Journal of Applied Psychology, 78*, 250–261.

Hutchinson, E. D. (1959). *How to think creatively*. New York: Abingdon-Cokesbury.

Jackson, A. Y. (1943). *Banting as an artist*. Toronto: Ryerson.

Jaffe, A. (Ed.). (1979). *C. G. Jung: Word and image*. Princeton, NJ: Princeton University Press.

James, L. K. (Ed.). (1993). *Nobel laureates in chemistry, 1901–1992*. Washington, DC: American Chemical Society and Chemical Heritage Foundation.

Johnson, K., & Coates, S. (1999). *Nabokov's blues: The scientific odyssey of a literary genius*. Cambridge, MA: Zoland.

Kaprowski, H. (1999). Fleeting thoughts. On *Songs and chamber music* [CD]. Woburn, MA: MMC Recordings.

Kemp, M. (1990). *The science of art*. New Haven: Yale University Press.

Koestler, A. (1964). *The act of creation*. London: Hutchinson.

Kovalevskaya, S. (1978). *A Russian childhood* (B. Stillman, Trans.). New York: Springer-Verlag.

Lebrecht, N. (1984, March 11). Schoenberg's other compositions. *Sunday Times Magazine* (London), pp. 36–43.

Linden, L. (1966). *The journal of Beatrix Potter from 1881–1897*. London: Frederick Warne.

Liukkonen. P. (1999). Biographies prepared by Petri Liukkonen. *Pegasos*. Retrieved November 30, 2002 from www.kirjasto.sci.fi

Mansfield, R. S., & Busse, T. V. (1981). *The psychology of creativity and discovery: Scientists and their work*. Chicago: Nelson-Hall.

Matossian, N. (1986). *Xenakis*. London: Kahn & Averill.

Milgram, R. M., Hong, E., Shavit, Y. W., & Peled, R. W. (1997). Out of school activities in gifted adolescents as a predictor of vocational choice and work accomplishment in young adults. *Journal of Secondary Gifted Education, 8*, 111–120.

Miller, H. (1974). *Insomnia or the devil at large*. Garden City, NY: Doubleday.

Moebius, P. J. (1900). *Ueber die Anlage zur Mathetmatik* [On the predisposition to mathematics]. Leipzig: Johan Umbrosius Barth.

Morris, D. (1971, October 10). The naked artist. *The Observer Magazine*, pp. 22–25.

Morris, D. (1987). *The secret surrealist: The paintings of Desmond Morris*. Oxford: Phaidon.

Nobel E-Museum. (2002). Available from the Nobel Foundation Web site: www.nobel.se

Planck, M. (1949). *Scientific autobiography and other papers* (F. Gaynor, Trans.). New York: Philosophical Library.

Polanyi, M. (1958). Personal knowledge: Towards a post-critical philosophy. Chicago: Chicago University Press.

Pribic, R. (Ed.). (1990). *Nobel laureates in literature: A biographical dictionary*. New York: Garland Publishing.

Ramon y Cajal, S. (1937). *Recollections of my life* (E. H. Craigie & J. Cano, Trans.). Cambridge, MA: MIT Press.

Remy, M. (1991). *The surrealist world of Desmond Morris* (L. Sagaru, Trans.). London: Jonathan Cape.

Roe, A. (1951). A study of imagery in research scientists. *Journal of Personality, 19*, 459–470.

Root-Bernstein, R. S. (1987). Harmony and beauty in biomedical research. *Journal of Molecular and Cellular Cardiology, 19,* 1–9.

Root-Bernstein, R. S. (1989). *Discovering.* Cambridge, MA: Harvard University Press.

Root-Bernstein, R. S. (1996). The sciences and arts share a common creative aesthetic. In A. I. Tauber (Ed.), *The elusive synthesis: Aesthetics and science* (pp. 49–82). Netherlands: Kluwer.

Root-Bernstein, R. S. (2000). Art advances science. *Nature, 407,* 134.

Root-Bernstein, R. S. (2001). Music, science, and creativity. *Leonardo, 34,* 63–68.

Root-Bernstein, R. S. (2002). Aesthetic cognition. *International Journal of the Philosophy of Science, 16,* 61–77.

Root-Bernstein, R. S. (2003). The art of innovation: Polymaths and the universality of the creative process. In L. Shavanina (Ed.), *International handbook of innovation,* pp. 267–278. Amsterdam: Elsevier.

Root-Bernstein, R. S., Bernstein, M., & Garnier, H. (1993). Identification of scientists making long-term high-impact contributions, with notes on their methods of working. *Creativity Research Journal, 6,* 329–343.

Root-Bernstein, R. S., Bernstein, M., & Garnier, H. (1995). Correlations between avocations, ascientific style, work habits, and professional impact of scientists. *Creativity Research Journal, 8,* 115–137.

Root-Bernstein, R. S., & Root-Bernstein, M. M. (1999). *Sparks of genius: The thirteen thinking tools of the world's most creative people.* Boston: Houghton Mifflin.

Seagoe, M. (1975). *Terman and the gifted.* Los Altos, CA: W. Kaufmann.

Snow, C. P. (1964). *The two cultures: And a second look.* Cambridge, England: Cambridge University Press.

Steinbeck, J., & Ricketts, E. F. (1971). *Sea of Cortez.* Mamaroneck, NY: Paul P. Appel. (Original work published 1941)

Stone, J. (1988, June 12). Listening to the patient. *New York Times Magazine,* pp. 108–109.

Strosberg, E. (1999). *Art and science.* Paris: UNESCO.

Szladits, L., & Simmonds, H. (1969). *Pen & brush: The author as artist.* New York: The New York Public Library.

Van't Hoff, J. H. (1967). *Imagination in science* (G. F. Springer, Trans.). *Molecular Biology, Biochemistry and Biophysics, 1,* 1–18. (Original work published 1878)

Vitz, P. C., & Glimcher, A. B. (1984). *Modern art and modern science. The parallel analysis of vision.* New York: Praeger.

Vallery-Radot, M. (1987). *Pasteur dessins et pastels* [Pasteur drawings and pastels]. Paris: Hervas.

Waddington, C. H. (1969). *Behind appearance. A study of the relations between painting and the natural sciences in this century.* Cambridge, MA: MIT Press.

Ward, H. B., & Ellery, E. (Eds.). (1936). *Sigma Xi half century record and history.* Schenectady, NY: Union College.

White, R. K. (1931). The versatility of genius. *Journal of Social Psychology, 2,* 482.

Winner, E., & Casey, M. B. (1992). Cognitive profiles of artists. In G. C. Cupchick & J. Laszlo (Eds.), *Emerging visions of the aesthetic process: Psychology, semiology, and philosophy* (pp. 154–170). Cambridge: Cambridge University Press.

Zigrosser, C. (Ed.). (1976). Ars *medica: A collection of medical prints*. Philadelphia: Philadelphia Museum of Art.

9

WHY CREATIVITY IS DOMAIN GENERAL, WHY IT LOOKS DOMAIN SPECIFIC, AND WHY THE DISTINCTION DOES NOT MATTER

JONATHAN A. PLUCKER AND RONALD A. BEGHETTO

The question of whether creativity is domain general or domain specific is one of the most enduring controversies in the field. Strong opinions are regularly shared in support of both positions (e.g., Brown, 1989; Runco, 1987), which has led to a polarization of the debate. The dominant perspective currently appears to be that of domain specificity, probably due in large part to the pendulum swing toward situated cognition in the social sciences in general (Barab & Plucker, 2002). However, considerable evidence supports the idea that creativity has both specific and general components, and that the level of specificity–generality changes with the social context and as one develops through childhood into adulthood.

For example, consider the following chance encounter that happened to one of us during an international conference. While discussing creativity in a local coffeehouse, an elderly gentleman interrupted the first author (Plucker) and his wife and asked if he could join the conversation. He proceeded to describe his experiences as a young dental student in the United

153

States many decades earlier. During his studies, he became frustrated with the drills that dentists were being trained to use. He designed an alternate drill, despite his lack of any training or interest in electrical engineering or manufacturing. His professors shared his frustration with the available tools, but they encouraged him to focus on "things he knew" and not on "things he did not understand." Our new friend graduated from dental school and began his dental practice. After only a few years in private practice, his continued frustration with the drills led him to revisit his discredited idea. He worked with electrical engineers to refine his idea and eventually received a patent for his design. We asked him if his idea was successful, and he chuckled in reply. Yes, he shared, it was successful, and he quickly retired and has traveled the world for many years enjoying the fruits of his creativity. He concluded the conversation by noting that "People who don't know anything are more creative."

We do not agree with his conclusion, but we see his experience as a cautionary tale for those adopting either extreme position in the generality–specificity debate. Although the dentist's experiences are purely anecdotal, considerable examples from the history of ideas parallel his story. For example, Michelangelo's commission to paint the Sistine Chapel was surprising because he was known as an accomplished sculptor, not a painter. In addition, a wide range of empirical work informs this debate. For example, Baer (1991, 1994a, 1994b, 1998) has developed a line of research that strongly argues for specificity. Among his arguments are that domain-specific performance assessments correlate poorly with each other, and that task-specific training programs tend to show only task-specific benefits (Baer, 1998). Several authors have argued for similar, task-specific interpretations of creativity (Csikszentmihalyi, 1999; Diakidoy & Spanoudis, 2002; Gardner, 1993; Han & Marvin, 2002). In response, Plucker (1998) has argued that specificity research overlooks important theoretical and methodological issues, a position that also has its share of supporters (e.g., Cramond, 1994; Kogan, 1994; Plucker, 1999a, 1999b). Studies of implicit theories of creativity also provide support for domain-general conceptualizations (Kaufman & Baer, 2002; Lim & Plucker, 2001; Runco & Bahleda, 1986; Runco, Johnson, & Bear, 1993; Sternberg, 1985).

This debate closely mirrors controversies in related areas. For example, the idea of multipotentiality, one individual having the potential to make significant contributions in two or more domains, is highly controversial within the education and psychology literature. Many scholars believe that multipotentiality exists and can pose significant problems as students with numerous talents and interests begin to consider important educational, career, and personal decisions (Gagné, 1998; Kerr, 1991; Kerr & Erb, 1991; Pask-McCartney & Salomone, 1988; Rysiew, Shore, & Leeb, 1999). However, other researchers argue that evidence of multipotentiality is hard to find (Achter, Benbow, & Lubinski, 1997; Milgram & Hong, 1999; Robinson,

1997). Yet in spite of this research, gifted students and their parents believe multipotentiality is a problem (Emmett & Minor, 1993; Moon, Kelly, & Feldhusen, 1997).

Methodological issues (i.e., how one studies a construct) and conceptual issues (i.e., how one defines the construct of interest) raise the question of whether one is comparing apples and oranges in the multipotentiality debate. The same appears true in other domain-general versus domain-specific debates, such as that involving creativity or cognition in general (Kaufman & Baer, 2002; Sternberg, 1998). Significant methodological issues exist in the creativity generality–specificity debate (Plucker, 1998, in press), as do questions about the definition of creativity being used (Plucker, Beghetto, & Dow, in press).

For these reasons, we present our position that creativity is a developmental construct that can be viewed as exhibiting both domain-specific and domain-general characteristics. Furthermore, we argue that from an educational perspective, these distinctions simply are not very important. In the following sections, we present our conception of creativity, describe why creativity can (and should) be viewed as both context-free and context-dependent, and review the theoretical, empirical, and educational implications of this conceptualization using a preliminary model drawn from our analysis.

WHAT IS CREATIVITY?

The first step in our analysis is to consider what we mean by *creativity*, a term often mired in myth, misconception, and mystery (Sternberg & Lubart, 1995). It is often used to describe a process (e.g., "It will take some creativity to be an effective teacher"), desired outcome ("This office layout has been designed to increase the creativity of our employees"), or personality characteristic ("She is such a creative artist" or "He is a bit creative with his interpretation of the rules"). Above all, however, it is a term that is rarely explicitly defined in the literature. For example, Plucker and colleagues (in press) found that only 40% of a sample of articles drawn from *Creativity Research Journal* and the *Journal of Creative Behavior* explicitly defined creativity, only slightly better than the 33% of creativity articles published in other, out-of-field journals.

Explication of a definition of creativity is necessary for the study of creativity to continue to grow, thrive, and contribute meaningfully to our understanding of the processes and outcomes across and within various domains (e.g., the creative and performing arts, physical and social sciences, business, and education). A ready example is the debate about creativity's domain-general or domain-specific nature. In this section, we offer our definition of creativity and analyze its implications for this debate.

Creativity Defined

Plucker and colleagues (in press) offer an empirical definition of creativity that was systematically derived from an array of multidisciplinary, peer-reviewed studies and articles. The definition represents a synthesis of reoccurring themes and constituent elements present within and across publications principally concerned with creativity.

> Creativity is the interplay between ability and process by which an individual or group produces an outcome or product that is both novel and useful as defined within some social context.

Ability and Process

This definition stresses the interplay between ability and process. Creativity, much like intelligence, is sometimes conceptualized and discussed as an individual ability[1] (James & Asmus, 2001). Other times, creativity is described or studied as a process (Jung, 2001; Van Hook & Tagano, 2002). Although not always explicitly recognized, a discussion of creative ability involves (at some level) a discussion of process. Regardless of ability, there is a general method or process by which an individual enacts his or her creative ability. This is not to say that the process a highly skilled individual engages in is identical to that of an unskilled individual. Rather, a process or procedure serves as a vehicle for enacting individual ability. Similarly, a discussion of creative process involves (at some level) a discussion of individual ability. That is, the variation in creative products resulting from some particular process will vary as a function of the ability of the individual engaged in that process.

Recognizing the interplay between ability and process provides a rationale for examining efforts at enhancing the creativity of all individuals and also places realistic constraints on what can be expected by such enhancement efforts. Recognizing that ability alone is not sufficient for the generation of creative products provides the rationale for identifying and examining the processes and procedures of creative production from which everyone can benefit (e.g., the efficacy of the brainstorming process, creative problem-solving process, problem-finding process, etc.). At the same time, recognizing that a process or method for generating creative products is not sufficient prevents the overselling of technique (i.e., not all individuals will produce similar results regardless of the technique used). Rather, understanding that creativity results from the interaction between ability and process allows for a much more robust and complex conceptualization of creativity.

---

[1]The term *ability* is purposefully used instead of *trait*. Trait implies a static or "entity" view of creativity thereby rendering it resistant to change (i.e., creativity is present in a set quantity that does not change with experience, learning, or maturation). Alternatively, ability implies a more plastic nature of creativity—and thereby an assumption that creativity can be influenced by experience, instruction, and maturation.

Observable Outcome

Creativity, like most human functions, involves a combination of observable and unobservable abilities and processes. A robust line of scholarship is working toward eliciting the latent cognitive abilities and processes of creativity (Smith, Ward, & Finke, 1995; Ward, Smith, & Vaid, 1997). This work is important in developing a comprehensive understanding of the nature of creativity, but cognitive theories of creativity are not sufficient. Observable artifacts (i.e., products, behavior records) are also necessary for inferring, labeling, and evaluating creativity.

The observable processes and outcomes of an individual (or group of individuals) substantiate (or refute) what is theoretically posited. With respect to creativity, without the production of some observable process or product (outcome) there could be no determination whether an individual (or group of individuals) has been creative. For example, the question of whether Mozart was creative before he composed his first piece of music is an interesting question. However, without an observable artifact (e.g., a musical composition) this question is impossible to answer with any level of confidence and does little to advance what we know about creativity. However, we can answer the question of whether a particular composition of Mozart is creative. Answering this question requires an agreed-on definition of creativity, a heuristic for determining what is or is not creative, and agreement among key stakeholders. Although disagreement among key stakeholders is expected, such a question can be addressed and contributes to what is known about creativity. Evaluating whether an observable artifact is creative helps advance our understanding of creativity because it provides concrete exemplars of the attributes of creativity.

Novel and Useful

Two key elements in the definition of creativity are novelty (i.e., original, unique, new, fresh, different) and usefulness (i.e., specified, valuable, meaningful, relevant, appropriate, worthwhile). The combination of these two elements serves as the keystone in scholarly discussions and definitions of creativity (e.g., Cropley, 1999; Halpern, 1996; Parkhurst, 1999; Reis & Renzulli, 1991). As with ability and process, novelty and usefulness work in tandem. That which is novel but has no use, merit, or significance is simply novel, not creative. Likewise, that which is useful but is not novel, unique, or original is simply useful, not creative.

Social Context

The synthesis of novelty and usefulness speaks to the pragmatic nature of this definition. In particular, there is a contextually and socially determined element of usefulness in the definition (i.e., usefulness for whom, in what context, and at what cost to self and others). The definition explicitly recognizes the importance of the social context in defining creativity (see also Nuessel, Stewart, & Cedeño, 2001; Redmond, Mumford, & Teach, 1993; Richards, 2001). The recognition that creativity varies as a function of the social context in which it is situated is an acknowledgment that what is viewed as creative within one social context will not necessarily be seen as creative in another social context.

Creativity is often distinguished as being *Big C* (eminent creativity) or *Little c* creativity (pedestrian or everyday creativity). Recognizing that stakeholders within a particular social context determine what is or is not creative reframes the split between Big C and Little c creativity. In doing so, Big C and Little c creativity are no longer viewed as qualitatively different, but rather seen as different in scale. Little c creativity is determined within a narrower scope of a particular social context, whereas Big C creativity is determined by a much broader social context, such as society at large (Richards, 2001).

Social context also establishes a range in which the uniqueness and novelty will be acceptable. The norms of a social context establish boundaries of uniqueness and usefulness. As such, some things may be so unique that they are rejected, ignored, or dismissed as irrelevant (even though they have much potential usefulness). A historical example is Mendel's early work with genetics. Tales of the monk performing experiments in secret are largely apocryphal: Mendel circulated his paper to the major European scientific societies, who collectively ignored his work. A generation later, biology advanced to the point where Mendel's work was finally appreciated, and his creativity became the stuff of legend.

Why Creativity Is Domain General, and Why It Looks Domain Specific

Determining whether a person, process, or product is considered creative only within a particular domain or generalizes across domains is an interesting and important endeavor, but such a task is largely a question of definition. On the basis of our definition of creativity, we believe that the construct has both domain-general and domain-specific characteristics. As discussed earlier in this section, creativity has been notoriously elusive with respect to a common definition.

Empirically establishing the domain generality or specificity of creativity is a potentially fruitful line of inquiry. However, it is not the only approach for examining the nature of creativity, nor do we take that approach in this chapter. Moreover, the underlying assumptions of establishing domain specificity or domain generality force a (potentially false) dichotomy on how creativity is conceptualized and how empirical results will be interpreted. Rather than artificially split creativity, domain-specific *and* domain-general features of creativity can be examined. In doing so, a richer question can be addressed: What aspects of creativity are domain general and which aspects are domain specific?

We believe that sufficient evidence exists to conclude that each component of our definition (interplay between ability and process, observable outcome or product, novelty and usefulness, and social context) has both domain-general and domain-specific characteristics. For example, the interrelated nature of creative ability and creative process can certainly be conceptualized as having strong domain-specific components (Barab & Plucker, 2002), but a large body of research provides evidence that cognitive abilities and processes, both in general and those devoted to creativity and problem solving (Carroll, 1993; Runco, 1994; Runco & Okuda, 1988), apply across domains. Similarly, observable outcomes are possible across domains, although any given domain may generally prefer one type of product over others.

Novelty, usefulness, and social context need to be discussed collectively. Social context is a key factor in determining what is creative, regardless of domain. Within each domain, however, determinations of what is creative are constrained by the boundaries of the context and the relevant community of practice, which is often domain related. Plucker and colleagues (in press) describe an example of a fourth-grade science fair project and a Nobel Prize–winning discovery that illustrates this point. Within the domain of science, what is considered creative at the fourth-grade science fair is determined by a local community of practice populated by individuals who are seen as legitimate members of that community (e.g., science teachers, local scientists). The contextual boundary of the science fair and local community of practice will inform the criteria of what is sufficiently novel and useful when judging whether a science fair project is creative. If a student produces a project that, in the eyes of the judges, presents a model of how popcorn pops in a novel and useful way within the context of a science fair, it will probably be evaluated as creative.

Similarly, the contextual boundaries and community of practice making up the Nobel Prize Committee will inform the criteria for determining whether a particular scientific discovery or line of inquiry is sufficiently unique and useful to be called creative. It is unlikely that a project deemed creative at a fourth-grade science fair would obtain the same distinction by the Nobel Prize Committee. Conversely, the body of work that earns a scientist a Nobel Prize may not be appreciated at the science fair. Indeed, the science fair project judged to be the most creative may not be considered creative by the same community of practice if the student were older, if the project were produced by a teacher or other adult, or if the breaking news story the morning of the fair just happened to deal with the evils of popcorn. Social context matters, and it tends to matter in ways that manifest as domain specificity. Simply stated, the empirical definition of creativity we present in this chapter is domain general. However, features of the definition, primarily assessments of what or who is creative, are domain specific.

WHY THE DISTINCTION DOES NOT MATTER

In truth, the distinction does matter—but only a little, and far less than some proponents of the domain-general and domain-specific positions would have us believe. Indeed, Baer (1998) argued that the implications of the debate are critical. If creativity is indeed domain specific, attempts to enhance creativity must focus on task-specific strategies. Baer also reasoned that if the converse were true (i.e., creativity is domain general), than using task-specific strategies does no harm, but using general strategies if creativity is actually domain specific would prevent enhancement programs from being effective. As we have personally retreated from viewing this debate dichotomously, we have come to believe that this conceptualization, which is widely held, is incorrect. If the question is truly one of determining in what context a person is creative, then either view has misleading and unfortunate implications. To extend this point, in this section we discuss the theoretical, empirical, and educational implications of our hybrid position.

Theoretical and Empirical Implications

The primary implication of our position is that it is more important to describe how people have chosen to be creative or are viewed by others to be creative as opposed to whether they should be called creative at all. The "all or nothing" label simply does not reflect current theory and research on creativity, especially given our emphasis on creative production.

To elaborate on the implications of our perspective, we constructed a model of the development of creative domain specificity (Figure 9.1). The model attempts to depict the direct relationship between a person's (a) age and experience and (b) task commitment and motivation as they influence the level of domain specificity of a person's creative endeavors. As one ages or gains experience in a certain domain or with a specific task, she or he will become more domain specific in her or his focus. This reflects research on the development of expertise, which generally appears to result from an often enormous time commitment (Gardner, 1993; Lubinski & Benbow, 2000; Simonton, 1999), which forces the individual to focus his or her efforts. Sternberg (1999) has conceptualized intelligence as the development of expertise, and specificity of creativity appears to have a similar relationship with experience.

The second dimension of the model is the relationship of specificity to one's interest and commitment to a particular topic or problem. Although a

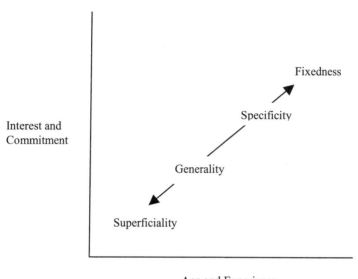

Figure 9.1. Conceptualization of domain specificity and generality of creativity.

commitment to be creative can be viewed as a common trait of creators across domains (Sternberg, 2002a, 2002b), Renzulli's body of work suggests that task commitment is a critical component of creative productivity (Renzulli, 1994). And as people become more interested in a topic or task, they have less time to devote to work in other areas. As has been well-documented in the psychological literature, people are usually cognitive misers, exhibiting a tendency to restrict and, therefore, preserve cognitive resources. In short, creativity may look task specific, but this is because, in part, people make choices in life that force specificity on them.

The model also strongly implies that too much of either position will hinder creativity: A person who continually deals with domain-general techniques and approaches to creativity may never scratch the surface of a problem, yet someone who focuses tightly for long periods of time in a domain or on a particular task is likely to experience functional fixedness or, if the unit of interest is a group, groupthink. The optimal condition for creative production is a flexible position somewhere between generality and specificity in Figure 9.1, with the individual or group moving between positions as the task or problem of the moment dictates. In this way, the model values diversity in all its forms more than either extreme position: Specificity downplays the importance of outside perspectives, generality overemphasizes the importance of all other information, and the hybrid position values perspectives from other domains but acknowledges the value of expertise and task commitment.

Educational Implications

Although the focus of this volume is not on educational matters, our conception does carry educational implications that we mention briefly. As noted previously, Baer (1998) offered a strong argument that the generality–specificity distinction matters, and as a result, educators should use task-specific methods to enhance creativity. But this perspective has an important flaw, both from our perspective and based on the literature on transfer. In fact, Baer noted that task-specific training does not transfer to other tasks, which the literature on situated cognition often cites as a major limitation: Transfer is often limited, if not prevented, by focusing only on one context (Anderson, Reder, & Simon, 1996). The distinction between general and specific approaches does not matter because the key issue is transfer, which is hindered by too much generality or too much specificity.

A better strategy is to expose students to a wide range of contexts in which they can apply their creativity in a search for an optimal interaction of ability and context (Barab & Plucker, 2002). Renzulli's (1994) schoolwide enrichment models attempt to walk this fine line between generality and specificity, and the research on the models' efficacy is promising.

Another advantage of the hybrid position is that it avoids two important effects of training based on the extreme positions. In our experience, the domain-specificity position is often used to discourage outside perspectives and "guard one's turf." Although this is an understandable reaction given human nature, is there really a danger in encouraging third graders, or for that matter, college students, to apply creativity to all aspects of their life without concerning them with the fact that the nature of creativity for each task or domain may be different? The task-specific approach would preclude such encouragement, which is overly pessimistic. People already use too little of their creativity, why further discourage them from applying it to life's problems?

A third implication of the hybrid position is that flexible thinking becomes a highly valued education outcome in order to promote transfer of knowledge to problems in different areas. The ability to apply information from a different area to a problem is often mentioned as a key component of insight (Sternberg & Davidson, 1995), and flexibility appears to be teachable (Chi, 1997; Runco & Okuda, 1991). This flexibility has the added benefit of encouraging novices to develop competence by openly testing their conceptions. Without open testing of ideas and behaviors, valid information regarding performance is hard to come by. Without valid information, individuals are much more likely to engage in ineffective, self-sealing behaviors (Argyris & Schon, 1974).

Individuals who engage in self-sealing behaviors buffer their awareness from valid information and thereby impede the development of competence. Kruger and Dunning (1999) found that individuals who were most incompetent were those who are least aware of their incompetence. They argued that "those with limited knowledge in a domain suffer a dual burden: Not only do they reach mistaken conclusions and make regrettable errors, but their incompetence robs them of the ability to realize it" (p. 1132). Flexible thinking, then, aids in the development of domain-specific competence because it encourages the open testing of knowledge within and across domains. In doing so, individuals become aware of limits to what they know within particular domains and are thereby in a better position to develop their competence than are those who remain blissfully unaware.

CONCLUSION

In conclusion, we share another anecdote about a well-known marine scientist. We observed one of his lectures and were intrigued when he digressed into a story about his entry into the field roughly 20 years earlier. He was pursuing graduate study in chemistry and stumbled on a solution to a problem that had perplexed marine chemists for years. He excitedly wrote a long letter to a leading marine scientist, sharing his solution to the problem in great detail. He soon received a dismissive letter from the senior scholar, in which he criticized the student for working in a field about which he knew nothing. Dejected but undeterred, the student pursued the line of work and eventually gained acceptance for his idea—and became a leading marine scientist himself. What made the story remarkable was the scientist's conclusion that his experience could not be repeated today because marine science had progressed to the point where outsiders could not make meaningful contributions. Unfortunately, we find this dismissive and discrediting attitude to be quite common and, for reasons outlined in this chapter, unnecessary.

A question we have asked ourselves during the preparation of this chapter is whether the development of "Renaissance people" like da Vinci is still possible today. After writing this chapter, we remain unsure. On the one hand, the rise of domain- and task-specific approaches appears to prevent the development of multicreative people. But on the other hand, history provides many examples of how creativity continually beats the odds and surfaces when we would least expect it.

REFERENCES

Achter, J. A., Benbow, C. P., & Lubinski, D. (1997). Rethinking multipotentiality among the intellectually gifted: A critical review and recommendations. *Gifted Child Quarterly, 41,* 5–15.

Anderson, J. R., Reder, L. M., & Simon, H. A. (1996). Situated learning and education. *Educational Researcher, 25*(4), 5–11.

Argyris, C., & Schon, D. A. (1974). *Theory in practice.* San Francisco: Jossey-Bass.

Baer, J. (1991). Review of creativity across performance domains. *Creativity Research Journal, 4,* 23–39.

Baer, J. (1994a). Divergent thinking is not a general trait: A multi-domain training experiment. *Creativity Research Journal, 7,* 35–36.

Baer, J. (1994b). Generality of creativity across performance domains: A replication. *Perceptual and Motor Skills, 79,* 1217–1218.

Baer, J. (1998). The case for domain specificity of creativity. *Creativity Research Journal, 11,* 173–177.

Barab, S. A., & Plucker, J. (2002). Smart people or smart contexts? Talent development in an age of situated approaches to learning and thinking. *Educational Psychologist, 37,* 165–182.

Brown, R. T. (1989). Creativity: What are we to measure? In J. A. Glover, R. R. Ronning, & C. R. Reynolds (Eds.), *Handbook of creativity* (pp. 3–32). New York: Plenum Press.

Carroll, J. B. (1993). *Human cognitive abilities: A survey of factor-analytic studies.* New York: Cambridge University Press.

Chi, M. T. H. (1997). Creativity: Shifting across ontological categories flexibly. In T. B. Ward, S. M. Smith, & J. Vaid (Eds.), *Creative thought: An investigation of conceptual structures and processes* (pp. 209–234). Washington, DC: American Psychological Association.

Cramond, B. (1994). We can trust creativity tests. *Educational Leadership, 52*(2), 70–71.

Cropley, A. J. (1999). Creativity and cognition: Producing effective novelty. *Roeper Review, 21,* 253–260.

Csikszentmihalyi, M. (1999). Implications of a systems perspective for the study of creativity. In R. J. Sternberg (Ed.), *Handbook of creativity* (pp. 313–335). New York: Cambridge University Press.

Diakidoy, I. N., & Spanoudis, G. (2002). Domain specificity in creativity testing: A comparison of performance on a general divergent-thinking test and a parallel, content-specific test. *Journal of Creative Behavior, 36,* 41–61.

Emmett, J. D., & Minor, C. W. (1993). Career decision-making factors in gifted young adults. *Career Development Quarterly, 41,* 350–366.

Gagné, F. (1998). The prevalence of gifted, talented, and multitalented individuals: Estimates from peer and teacher nominations. In R. C. Friedman & K. B. Rogers (Eds.), *Talent in context: Historical and social perspectives on giftedness* (pp. 101–126). Washington, DC: American Psychological Association.

Gardner, H. (1993). *Creating minds.* New York: Basic Books.

Halpern, D. F. (1996). *Thought and knowledge: An introduction to critical thinking* (3rd ed.). Mahwah, NJ: Erlbaum.

Han, K., & Marvin, C. (2002). Multiple creativeness? Investigating domain-specificity of creativity in young children. *Gifted Child Quarterly, 46,* 98–109.

James, K., & Asmus, C. (2001). Personality, cognitive skills, and creativity in different life domains. *Creativity Research Journal, 13,* 149–159.

Jung, D. I. (2001). Transformational and transactional leadership and their effects on creativity in groups. *Creativity Research Journal, 13,* 185–195.

Kaufman, J. C., & Baer, J. (2002). Could Steven Spielberg manage the Yankees? Creative thinking in different domains. *Korean Journal of Thinking & Problem Solving, 12*(2), 5–14.

Kerr, B. (1991). *A handbook for counseling the gifted and talented.* Alexandria, VA: American Association for Counseling and Development.

Kerr, B., & Erb, C. (1991). Career counseling with academically talented students: Effects of a value-based intervention. *Journal of Counseling Psychology, 38,* 309–314.

Kogan, N. (1994). Diverging from divergent thinking. *Contemporary Psychology, 39,* 291–292.

Kruger, J., & Dunning, D. (1999). Unskilled and unaware of it: How difficulties in recognizing one's own incompetence lead to inflated self-assessments. *Journal of Personality and Social Psychology, 77,* 1121–1134.

Lim, W., & Plucker, J. (2001). Creativity through a lens of social responsibility: Implicit theories of creativity with Korean samples. *Journal of Creative Behavior, 35,* 115–130.

Lubinski, D., & Benbow, C. P. (2000). States of excellence. *American Psychologist, 55,* 137–150.

Milgram, R. M., & Hong, E. (1999). Multipotential abilities and vocational interests in gifted adolescents: Fact or fiction? *International Journal of Psychology, 34,* 81–93.

Moon, S. M., Kelly, K. R., & Feldhusen, J. F. (1997). Specialized counseling services for gifted youth and their families: A needs assessment. *Gifted Child Quarterly, 41,* 16–25.

Nuessel, F. H., Stewart, A. V., & Cedeño, A. A. (2001). Course on humanistic creativity in later life: Literature review, case histories, and recommendations. *Educational Gerontology, 27,* 697–715.

Parkhurst, H. B. (1999). Confusion, lack of consensus, and the definition of creativity as a construct. *Journal of Creative Behavior, 33,* 1–21.

Pask-McCartney, C., & Salomone, P. R. (1988). Difficult cases in career counseling: III. The multipotentialed client. *Career Development Quarterly, 36,* 231–240.

Plucker, J. (1998). Beware of simple conclusions: The case for content generality of creativity. *Creativity Research Journal, 11,* 179–182.

Plucker, J. (1999a). Is the proof in the pudding? Reanalyses of Torrance's (1958 to present) longitudinal study data. *Creativity Research Journal, 12,* 103–114.

Plucker, J. (1999b). Reanalyses of student responses to creativity checklists: Evidence of content generality. *Journal of Creative Behavior, 33,* 126–137.

Plucker, J. (in press). Generalization of creativity across domains: Examination of the method effect hypothesis. *Journal of Creative Behavior.*

Plucker, J., Beghetto, R. A., & Dow, G. T. (in press). Why isn't creativity more important to educational psychologists? Potential, pitfalls, and future directions in creativity research. *Educational Psychologist*.

Redmond, M. R., Mumford, M. D., & Teach, R. (1993). Putting creativity to work: Effects of leader behavior on subordinate creativity. *Organizational Behavior & Human Decision Processes, 55*, 120–151.

Reis, S. M., & Renzulli, J. S. (1991). The assessment of creative products in programs for gifted and talented students. *Gifted Child Quarterly, 35*, 128–134.

Renzulli, J. S. (1994). *Schools for talent development: A practical plan for total school improvement*. Mansfield Center, CT: Creative Learning Press.

Richards, R. (2001). Creativity and the schizophrenia spectrum: More and more interesting. *Creativity Research Journal, 13*, 111–132.

Robinson, N. M. (1997). The role of universities and colleges in educating gifted undergraduates. *Peabody Journal of Education, 72*, 217–236.

Runco, M. A. (1987). The generality of creative performance in gifted and nongifted children. *Gifted Child Quarterly, 31*, 121–125.

Runco, M. A. (Ed.). (1994). *Problem finding, problem solving, and creativity*. Norwood, NJ: Ablex Publishing.

Runco, M. A., & Bahleda, M. D. (1986). Implicit theories of artistic, scientific, and everyday creativity. *Journal of Creative Behavior, 20*, 93–98.

Runco, M. A., Johnson, D. J., & Bear, P. K. (1993). Parents' and teachers' implicit theories of children's creativity. *Child Study Journal, 23*, 91–113.

Runco, M. A., & Okuda, S. M. (1988). Problem finding, divergent thinking, and the creative process. *Journal of Youth and Adolescence, 17*, 211–220.

Runco, M. A., & Okuda, S. M. (1991). The instructional enhancement of the flexibility and originality scores of divergent thinking tests. *Applied Cognitive Psychology, 5*, 435–441.

Rysiew, K. J., Shore, B. M., & Leeb, R. T. (1999). Multipotentiality, giftedness, and career choice: A review. *Journal of Counseling and Development, 77*, 423–430.

Simonton, D. K. (1999). Creativity from a historiometric perspective. In R. J. Sternberg (Ed.), *Handbook of creativity* (pp. 116–133). New York: Cambridge University Press.

Smith, S. M., Ward, T. B., & Finke, R. A. (Eds.). (1995). *The creative cognition approach*. Cambridge, MA: MIT Press.

Sternberg, R. J. (1985). Implicit theories of intelligence, creativity, and wisdom. *Journal of Personality and Social Psychology, 49*, 607–627.

Sternberg, R. J. (1998). Domain-generality versus domain-specificity: The life and impending death of a false dichotomy. *Merrill-Palmer Quarterly, 35*, 115–130.

Sternberg, R. J. (1999). Intelligence as developing expertise. *Contemporary Educational Psychology, 24*, 359–375.

Sternberg, R. J. (2002a). Creativity as a decision. *American Psychologist, 57*, 376.

Sternberg, R. J. (2002b). Encouraging students to decide for creativity. *Research in the Schools, 9*, 61–70.

Sternberg, R. J., & Davidson, J. E. (Eds.). (1995). *The nature of insight.* Cambridge, MA: MIT Press.

Sternberg, R. J., & Lubart, T. I. (1995). *Defying the crowd: Cultivating creativity in a culture of conformity.* New York: Free Press.

Van Hook, C. W., & Tagano, D. W. (2002). The relationship between creativity and conformity among preschool children. *Journal of Creative Behavior, 36,* 1–16.

Ward, T. B., Smith, S. M., & Vaid, J. (1997). *Creative thought: An investigation of conceptual structures and processes.* Washington, DC: American Psychological Association.

10

VERTICAL AND HORIZONTAL MENTORING FOR CREATIVITY

MIA KEINÄNEN AND HOWARD GARDNER

Many authorities have commented on the importance of mentoring relationships within the arts. Usually a mentor is described as a person of absolute authority and wisdom, an all-knowing guru who the mentee looks up to unconditionally. In Homer's epic poem "The Odyssey," Mentor was part human and part god: the personification of wisdom that the young mentee wished to become.

However, as John-Steiner (2000) pointed out, many different kinds of relationships can provide the benefits of a mentoring connection to the artist. Through a study of biographical, autobiographical, historical, and other published materials, John-Steiner concluded that the relationships among family members, lovers, and peers can be seen as mentorial. For example William and Dorothy Wordsworth, the great English poet and his sister, shared

We are indebted to the choreographers and dancers Trisha Brown, Jamie DiMare, Simone Forti, Sally Gross, Anna Halprin, K. J. Holmes, Pooh Kaye, Wendy Perron, Stephen Petronio, Leslie Satin, and Gabriela Simon for their thoughtful insights on mentoring in modern dance. Jacques d'Amboise provided us invaluable perspective on George Balanchine. We would also like to thank the Spencer Foundation and Thomas E. Lee for their generous support of this study.

a mentoring connection throughout their adult lives. Dorothy's journals provided William important material for his poetry, and William wholly trusted Dorothy's sensibility and judgment when giving feedback on his poems. Also well documented are the mentoring connections between romantic partners in the arts such as Georgia O'Keefe and Alfred Stieglitz. As an example of a mentorial relationship between peers, John-Steiner cited Picasso and Braque, whose work together brought about a new paradigm in visual art, namely cubism. Kealy and Mullen (1996) investigated mentoring among the Neo-Impressionist painters during the late 19th century. They found that, instead of the traditional one-on-one mentoring relationships, the painters actually had a network of mentors, each mentor embodying a slightly different role for the mentee. These authorities suggested that it might be difficult for one person to meet the multifarious needs of a developing artist. Instead, multiple mentors allow the artists a high degree of individual freedom to choose different sources of encouragement and growth and whom to influence and by whom to be influenced.

As part of our Good Work Project (Gardner, Csikszentmihaly, & Damon, 2001), we have recently conducted a study of mentoring relations within a lineage of modern dance choreographers in the United States. The lineage head for our study was Anna Halprin. In a number of respects, this study confirmed the situations described by John-Steiner and Kealy and Mullen.

First, the participants consciously wanted to distance themselves from the traditional model of mentoring described at the beginning of this chapter. They did not seek such mentoring figures and in turn did not want to be anybody's "guru." Instead, they looked for mentoring relationships that allowed for a high degree of autonomy and shied away from a direct instructional approach with their mentees. The goal was to be "transparent": to be as open as possible in one's thinking and working process.

Second, the artists in our sample talked about the importance of a network of mentors that included teachers, other artists, choreographers, and peers. The role of peers was pronounced; often the participants considered peers to be as important as the more "traditional" mentors they named. One of our participants, Pooh Kaye, explains the role of peers as mentors in her life and work:

> We were all influential to one another. I mean, I think that is a huge thing, that effect of one's own generation, because you are forming ideas at the same time. . . . But the thing with the peers, you know there was an ethic, which had to do with the idea that you could be an auteur, that you were responsible of making your own universe. So I feel that very strongly and I think that was one of the things that Simone [Forti] inspired [in] me. That she was so unique, she was such an individual. But all the people in my generation were just working really hard and intensely to define their own universes and it was such a lush atmosphere.

Thus, an alternative picture to the traditional hierarchical mentoring model emerged in our study, one that stressed equality over hierarchy and placed premium importance on mentoring network and peer mentoring.

Mentoring relationships may vary by domain and population. For example, apprenticeship relationships are a normative and central aspect of training in the natural sciences (Zuckerman, 1977), but less prevalent in the field of medicine (Duncan, 1996). Li (1997) distinguished between creativity in vertical and horizontal domains. Vertical domains, such as classical ballet and Chinese painting, are resistant to transformation and place more value on preserving the tradition. Thus the resultant works adhere to the traditional standards, and creativity is exhibited within certain highly specific constraints. In horizontal domains, such as modern visual art and modern dance, creativity can occur in an indefinite number of dimensions and novelty is encouraged. The resulting works deviate significantly and purposefully from the previously established practice.

Pertinent to Li's distinction we postulated that the process of mentoring in the arts is also shaped by domain-specific structure and needs. However, like any other domain, dance includes practices that are very different from one another, some of which could be categorized as vertical and some as horizontal. Indeed, even within modern dance styles differ from each other radically. For example, the so-called classical modern dance styles, like the Humphrey, Graham, and Cunningham styles, are each based on the work of their perspective originators, Doris Humphrey, Martha Graham, and Merce Cunningham. The dancers working within these traditions usually embody the style and pass it on to the next generations unchanged. The style of Anna Halprin, however, does not involve a codified dance technique. Rather it is based on improvisation and combination of many different influences. The dancers working within this tradition, although integrating in their work what they have learned from their respective mentors, focus on changing the tradition.

In what follows we do not connect the vertical–horizontal distinction to the domain level. Rather, we connect it to the particular characteristics of the practice. In other words, we term as vertical those practices in which the preservation of tradition is of outmost importance vertical. We term as horizontal those practices in which the focus is on innovation and individual expression.

We investigated two examples of mentoring in the arts: George Balanchine's neoclassical ballet tradition as an example of a vertical artistic practice, and Anna Halprin's modern dance tradition as an example of a horizontal artistic practice. Thus our focus is on two subdomains within the overarching domain of dance. We investigated Balanchine as a mentor by reviewing the literature; we investigated Halprin through empirical interview data attained from her and her students.

Our investigation revealed distinctive differences between mentoring in vertically and horizontally oriented artistic practices. We call these two styles *vertical* and *horizontal mentoring*. In this chapter, we first describe our research method and our sample. We then discuss the case of vertical mentoring as exemplified by Balanchine and the case of horizontal mentoring as exemplified by Halprin and her disciples. Finally, we contrast these different mentoring styles and offer an account of how the specific nature of the different artistic practices affects the process of mentoring in that practice.

RESEARCH METHOD

We investigated Balanchine's mentoring style by reviewing appropriate literature and videos (Ashley, 1984; Belle, 1995; Belle & Dickson, 1997; Bentley, 1983; Buckle, 1988; Caras, 1985; Farrell, 1990; Kent, 1997; Kirstein, 1984; Mason, 1991; McDonagh, 1983; Shearer, 1987; Tallchief, 1997; Taper, 1996; Tracy, 1983). The method of collection for our empirical data on Anna Halprin and her students was in-depth interviews. We conducted one or two focused interview sessions per participant. The interviews lasted from one to three hours. The form of the interviews was a semistructured, standardized interview format: Prefigured questions were asked of all participants in the same order (Rossman & Rallis, 1998).

The interview protocol was developed for the "Transmission of Excellence: A Study of Mentoring in Creative Work" project.[1] The purpose of this umbrella study is to gain a deeper understanding of the mentoring process as well as the manner in which individuals' goals, practices, and values are transmitted across generations. The general topics included in the protocol are (a) formative background (including role of mentors); (b) valued practices, beliefs, and goals; (c) significant factors (positive and negative) affecting the enactment of these values; (d) experiences as a mentor for others; (e) perspectives of the field. All interviews were recorded and transcribed. The transcribed interviews were then coded and examined for themes, patterns of themes, and relationships between themes (Maxwell, 1996; Miles & Huberman, 1994).

SAMPLE

Our sample included the written record about George Balanchine and in-depth interviews with Anna Halprin and her students. In this section we

---

[1]"Transmission of Excellence: A Study of Mentoring in Creative Work" is a component of the Good Work Project. The Good Work Project is a large-scale research study codirected by Mihaly Csikszentmihalyi, William Damon, and Howard Gardner. See Gardner et al. (2001) and goodworkproject.org

provide details about these samples, why we chose them, and how we gathered data from them.

George Balanchine

We chose Balanchine as an example of mentoring in a vertical artistic practice because his work and his relationship to his dancers have been well documented. To investigate his tradition we reviewed printed and video material pertaining to his influence as a mentor at different points in his career and also interviewed one of his principal dancers.

George Balanchine is regarded as one of the most important contemporary choreographers in the world of ballet. Born in Russia in 1904, Balanchine studied ballet and music in St. Petersburg. At the invitation of Lincoln Kirstein, who had a dream of establishing a ballet company and school in America, Balanchine came to the United States in late 1933. Together Balanchine and Kirstein founded the School of American Ballet in 1934 and the New York City Ballet in 1948. Both the school and the company are still operating today.

Throughout his career, Balanchine brought dance and music closer together by emphasizing the fact that ballets can consist of dance and music without any specific story to follow. His style has been called neoclassic because it moved ballet away from the theatrical storytelling toward abstract dance. Often working with modern music and simple themes, he created ballets that are known for their imagination and originality. In doing so, Balanchine has been credited with the successful fusion of modern concepts with older ideas of classical ballet.

Anna Halprin and Her Disciples

The participant selection in our empirical study is lineage based. We identified an individual who is widely recognized within her field: (a) she displays excellence in the domain and (b) she has a number of students who are active in the field. Two subsequent generations were then identified through nominations from the participants themselves—first the individual's students and then the students' students. One of the second generation (G2) participants, Sally Gross, requested that three of her mentees be interviewed— She did not want one of her close mentees to feel left out. Thus we included an extra person in the case of Gross. Selecting three students in the second generation and two (or three in one case) students per mentor in the third generation yielded a sample of eleven individuals in a lineage structure illustrated in Figure 10.1.

The lineage head, Anna Halprin, is regarded as one of the most important figures in American modern and postmodern dance. Born Anna Schumann in Winnetka, Illinois, in 1920, Anna was first struck by the beauty

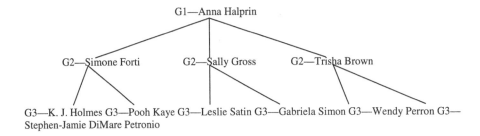

Figure 10.1. Lineage structure in the proposed study (*n* = 10). G1 = first generation. G2 = second generation. G3 = third generation.

of movement at the age of four through observing her grandfather, a Hassidic Jew, pray by singing and moving around vigorously. Her mother later took her to a ballet class, but Anna never felt comfortable there. To Halprin's delight, her mother took her out of the ballet classes and instead placed her in a modern dance class: first in an Isadora Duncan technique class, and then in a Denishawn dance technique class. Halprin immediately fell in love with the freer approach to dance. These classes mark the beginning of her lifelong exploration in dance.

Halprin adapts an analytical approach to improvisation and her work has been extremely influential for the development of postmodern dance in the United States. The term *postmodern dance* is used to describe various styles of dance that have emerged in the United States since the 1950s. The choreographers working within this tradition rebelled against the content and form of classical modern dance by integrating improvisation, spoken word, everyday movement, and silence (or any sound) as music in their works. Halprin is also an early pioneer in the expressive arts healing movement. Halprin is a founder of *Impulse Magazine*, San Francisco Dancer's Workshop, and the Tamalpa Institute. She holds honorary doctorates for her work as a dance innovator from several universities and arts institutes. She is a recipient of the National Endowment for the Arts Choreographer's Fellowship, the Guggenheim Fellowship, and the American Dance Guild Award, among many others.

VERTICAL MENTORING

Balanchine as a Guru

During his long creative career Balanchine was an extremely influential mentor and teacher for many generations of dancers. As the originator of a new style of ballet, he was a powerful man working relentlessly to establish his creative empire. For his dancers, Balanchine, or Mr. B., was the absolute authority, a figure close to a god who was idolized. As New York City Ballet dancer Toni Bentley describes, "Most women have two important men in their lives—their father and their lover. We have three. Mr. Balanchine is our leader, our president, our mother, our father, our friend, our guide, our mentor, our destiny" (Bentley, 1983, pp. 58–59). Balanchine dancer Gelsey Kirkland (1986), who questioned Balanchine's authority more than most of his ballerinas, nevertheless described her relationship to him as follows:

> In spite of my temperamental resistance, I internalized Balanchine's system with the fury of a fanatic, if not the devotion of a true believer. His place in the hierarchy was beyond question. I always hoped what I was doing would please him. I had to please him. I loved him more than my own father. (p. 50)

Thus Balanchine's style as a mentor closely resembles the historical view of a mentor based on the Greek myth. For his mentees, Balanchine was the unquestioned leader who held the destiny of his dancers in his hand. In vertical artistic practice the goal is to pass on a tradition or style unchanged: It may be therefore beneficial for the mentor to hold such authority in the eyes of his mentees. Idolization and unreachability of the mentor may fuel the mentees' dedication and willingness to absorb every little detail in their mentor's teachings, which in turn ensures that knowledge is passed on in its purest, unchanged form. Indeed, as a mentor, Balanchine strove to make sure that his students stayed faithful to his doctrine: He developed a training system that immersed his mentees in his style as fully as possible.

Passing on a Style

Most of Balanchine's dancers became indoctrinated into his style through their schooling at the School of American Ballet, where the dancers usually enter at the age of eight or nine. The goal for most students in the school is to win a place in the New York City Ballet. Thus, during Balanchine's leadership of the company, the goal of the dance training was to prepare the dancer for his or her possible working relationship with Balanchine, who personally picked the dancers in his company from the school. Such an arrangement accentuated Balanchine's position of power and ensured that the students would strive to learn his style and to please him in any possible way.

As a remarkably gifted, fluent, and, at the same time, disciplined choreographer, Balanchine ran a tight ship. He demanded perfection in everything that the dancers were doing. In class, he always asked for the utmost energy and precision that was humanly possible. Outside class he demanded his dancers to be respectful in their manner and dignified in their way of dressing (Ashley, 1984).

Further, once the dancers entered the company, Balanchine expected them to take his class daily so that they could perform his work as he intended it to be performed. Balanchine never indicated clearly that he expected his dancers to do this: Only when they failed to attend did the dancers realize the repercussions of their absence. For example Peter Martins, who was hired by the New York City Ballet from the Royal Danish Ballet, discovered this unwritten rule the hard way. Balanchine taught his ballet classes in an idiosyncratic way: He liked to make the exercises either extremely slow or quick, or to make shortcuts in the class such as moving straight from the bar work into big jumps. Not accustomed to Balanchine's style of teaching a class, Martins found the classes physically too taxing. Therefore he started to take classes with another teacher in the school.

Balanchine, however, immediately started to take roles away from Martins and literally ignored him in the corridors of the school and theater. Devastated by the cold shoulder he was receiving, Martins decided to ask Balanchine's reason for such behavior. Balanchine answered:

> You see dear, you don't seem to be interested. I never see you anywhere, not in class, maybe in O'Neals' restaurant. When people show interest, I use them. If they don't, I leave them alone. And you don't show interest. (Taper, 1984, p. 335)

Martins quickly reversed his ways, and ended up being one of the most important male dancers in Balanchine's company and indeed, his successor. Another Balanchine dancer, Merrill Ashley (1984), recalled similar experiences. She explained that for her to be considered in Balanchine's ballets, she needed to show her commitment by being in every single class Mr. B was giving. It was not enough to say she was committed to him. Regrettably, according to Ashley, many never understood this unspoken code of conduct, and thus never received important roles.

Indeed, Balanchine required absolute commitment from his dancers, in class, in rehearsal, in performance, and outside of theater. If they were to be Balanchine dancers, they had to surrender completely to his aesthetics and lifestyle. Although Balanchine invited guest teachers to teach his company, taking classes with teachers he had not chosen was not looked on favorably. For example, in her memoir, Gelsey Kirkland (1986) wrote that because of painful tendons and other physical problems, she started to take classes with the famed New York City ballet teacher Maggie Black. Kirkland felt that under Maggie's guidance her condition improved considerably and that the clarity and strength of her movement was greatly enhanced. According to Kirkland's reflection, regardless of the improvements Kirkland felt, Balanchine was not impressed. Rather he noted that she looked "constipated" and showed open hostility toward the competing teacher by naming her "Black Magic" (Kirkland, 1986, p. 71).

Thus, as is customary in vertical practices, Balanchine made sure his mentees received their information mainly from him. Balanchine preferred having control over the way his dancers were educated because ultimately they would perform his choreography. Further, although Balanchine tailor-made his ballets to suit the strengths of the particular dancers, when choreographing he did not expect his dancers to make up any steps or to contribute to his creative process in any way—another way to keep his tradition and style unchanged. Balanchine describes his intentions in the following manner: "I don't tell them what to express which could cause them to stray from the way in which their role has been conceived. I show each dancer exactly what he is to do and demand that he obeys me down to the smallest detail" (McDonagh, 1983, p. 171). In class he corrected his dancers with firm words and rarely offered praise. "A dancer is like an instrument. It must be played with full-bodied tone—and pitilessly," he once said to an interviewer (Taper, 1984, p. 331). Further, he compared his dancers to racehorses, who, according to Balanchine, were lazy by nature and would never race if you did not put a rider on them to make them race. Balanchine saw himself as that rider (Taper, 1984). He knew what his dancers needed to excel and he expected his dancers to be fully receptive of his guidance and give everything they had in classes and rehearsals.

However, as most of Balanchine's dancers understood, the purpose of such rigorous training was not to make the dancers into nonthinking machines, but rather to guide them to become vessels of great art. By shedding their ego, the dancers are able to reveal pure, timeless humanity that can speak to the audience directly (Homans, 2002). Indeed, most of Balanchine's dancers' first and foremost goal was to perfect their technical and performing skills rather than learn choreographic skills. Thus Balanchine's training and choreographing method suited their needs perfectly.

Setting an Example

Regardless of Balanchine's rather doctrinaire mentoring style, the manner in which he was working with his dancers and colleagues was always calm and collected. People who worked with him for thirty years reportedly never saw him angry (Taper, 1984). If he expected perfection from his dancers, he required no less from himself. He got up every morning at dawn, had his tea and collected his thoughts for an hour, then dressed in clean and ironed clothes and was ready to start working by seven o'clock. During the day he would teach a company class, choreograph new work, and rehearse the existing repertory. After taking a short break for a dinner, he stayed for the evening's performance, observing it from the wings.

Throughout the long day, his manner was always dignified and unfailingly respectful toward his dancers and other staff as well as the space within which they worked. For Balanchine the art of dance was sacred and he expected everybody to think and act in a similar manner (Ashley, 1984). Indeed, even though he preferred talking about ballet as a craft rather than art, and construed himself as a craftsman like a carpenter or a chef rather than a creative genius, there was no mistaking his own or his company's dedication to ballet. As one of the company members explained, "He doesn't do it by talking but he implies at every moment that there is great art of classical dancing that all of us, including him, are serving" (Taper, 1984, p. 7).

Although verbally he played down the idea of ballet as an important creative and artistic endeavor, Balanchine's actions spoke differently. Following his example, his dancers picked up habits that made them treat their own and Balanchine's work as serious art (Ashley, 1984). In class Balanchine would correct his dancers diligently and drive them toward better execution of the movement. However, as ballerina Merrill Ashley (1984) explained, dancers also learned a lot just by watching him:

> If he could correct verbally, he did, but if that did not work he demonstrated the step himself. Many of the subtleties that were so hard to comprehend from verbal instructions alone were plainly visible when he moved. You could learn much just by watching him. He always put us to shame with his grace and finesse. Never have I seen *any* dancer move as beautifully as Balanchine. (p. 34)

Indeed, there seems to be a disconnect between what Balanchine conveyed verbally and physically. Verbally Balanchine purposefully downplayed his and his dancers' work as "lowly" crafts rather than art. In fact he was strongly opposed to his dancers analyzing his ballets. "You have to be *vairy* careful when you use your mind or you will get into trouble" (Taper, 1984, p. 13) he used to tell his dancers. Yet, in his actions, by embodying the craft fully and skillfully and by showing respect in his mannerism, he projected just the opposite picture. Such disconnect between what Balanchine said and did was based on Balanchine's deep mistrust of the power of words to describe and analyze the art of dance. He preferred action rather than words. As he advised his dancers: "Don't talk, just do it, analyze later—when you cannot do it, you can talk about it" (J. d'Amboise, personal communication, February 3, 2003). Further, by limiting the dancers' input in the creative process, he ensured that the dancers did not add unnecessary or indulgent personal preferences or interpretations to the choreography. By cultivating a rigorous and respectful work ethic through his own example, he ensured that his dancers had the proper working mentality. With this combination, his dancers were primed to absorb Balanchine's tradition fully.

Mentoring Relationship Gone Awry

For some of his students, Balanchine's authoritarian approach to creating and teaching worked. Although often a bit scared of him, they nevertheless enjoyed Balanchine's presence and absorbed the wisdom he had to share. With Balanchine's guidance they developed into breathtakingly beautiful interpreters of his work. Merrill Ashley (1984) for example, felt that

Balanchine's style of teaching and demand for perfection matched completely her own aspirations for technically immaculate dancing. In fact, she mentioned that often in the class she felt as quick and strong as a racehorse, using the same metaphor that Balanchine used when talking about his dancers to a biographer (Ashley, 1984). It is easy to see why Balanchine and Ashley enjoyed working with each other.

But for other dancers, the demand of absolute immersion into Balanchine's world was more problematic. Gelsey Kirkland (1986) talked about these difficulties at length in her book *Dancing on My Grave*. For her, Balanchine's absolute authority and power was debilitating:

> We were spared any consideration of history. It was as if ballet were born with Balanchine. His official version of what was supposed to be the orthodox of ballet made him the living repository of all practical knowledge pertinent to the art. We thought he had all the answers. . . . With his ballets as the testing ground, he was the only judge of talent. He set the style. His monopoly on taste and creative control was absolute. If anyone dared mention the unusual fashion of the emperor's new clothes, the hapless soul was banished from Mr. B's little empire. (Kirkland, 1986, p. 48)

Further, Kirkland disliked the fact that Balanchine shied away from talking about ballet as art. For her, this habit fueled subtle reduction of the value of the work the dancers were putting in, forcing them to a lowly, powerless position. Balanchine in turn stood on a pedestal that was wholly unreachable.

> Balanchine assembled steps that were supposed to have been predetermined by God and humbly described himself as an instrument of divine will. His word was holy. To have a private audience with such an exalted being was inconceivable; we settled for brief encounters, moments of confession and supplication outside the elevator that led to his office, catching him on his way, terrified to invade the inner sanctum of his thoughts. (Kirkland, 1986, p. 49–50)

Mentoring relationships may have a negative, hindering effect on the development of the individual (Bishop, 1988; Blackburn, Chapman, & Cameron, 1981; Emenhiser, 1989; Gordon, 1983; Powell, 1999). Using the classic view of the mentor as wisdom personified, Powell (1999) pointed out some possible pitfalls of mentoring. First, there is a danger that if the mentor's power or knowledge is seen as divine, then it is never truly shared with the "mortal" mentee. Second, if the mentor is seen in such a divine light, the identity the mentee assumes in the world can be entirely determined by the mentor. The mentor knows what is best for the mentee. These paradigms may lead the mentee to overestimate the legitimacy and extent of his or her mentor's power, which may lead to unrealistic expectations of the mentoring relationship or even to psychological or physical abuse.

Because the mentoring connections in vertical practices can be extremely intense, they may be more prone to the negative aspects of mentoring. Ballerina Kirkland was uncomfortable with the fact that Balanchine had the keys to determine her identity and a place in the world. In fact, Kirkland (1986) felt psychologically and even physically abused by the situation and attributed her own struggle with drugs later in her life to this unhealthy relationship. However, sometimes an extremely close relationship between the mentor and the mentee can also be counterproductive for the mentor.

The Blurring of the Mentee–Mentor Line

An important aspect of Balanchine's choreography was to have a muse who, along with music, would inspire him for creating new ballets and personify his style and aspirations. For Balanchine, the muses were always women. He regarded ballet as "female," and thus the position of the ballerina in comparison to the male lead was always highlighted.

Indeed, Balanchine's relationship with women was complicated. He was infatuated by many of his leading ballerinas and was in fact married to four of them. His relationship with Suzanne Farrell was perhaps the most complex and difficult one. Farrell was Balanchine's last muse, a dancer of intense musicality, refinement, and unbounded speed who embodied everything Balanchine ever dreamed his dancers to be capable of. For many years, the relationship between Farrell and Balanchine was exceptionally close and charged; Balanchine was enamored by Farrell and gave Farrell nearly all the important roles in his ballets. They were regarded as a romantic couple for awhile (Belle & Dickson, 1997).

Nevertheless, when Balanchine made sexual advances to Farrell, he was refused. Perhaps this unreachability made Balanchine even more obsessed with Farrell, and he hoped that despite their 40-year age difference, Farrell would marry him. Instead, Farrell married a young company dancer, Paul Meija. As a consequence, Balanchine limited Meija's roles in the company repertory. Eventually, one night Farrell tried to pressure Balanchine by refusing to perform herself unless Meija was allowed to perform a soloist role he usually danced. Faced with such an ultimatum, Balanchine chose to let Farrell go (J. d'Amboise, personal communication, February 3, 2003). However, losing Farrell was difficult for Balanchine. He had idolized and adored Farrell to such an extent that he had become somewhat dependent on her. Once she was gone, Balanchine faced a difficult period creatively, although he ultimately composed many additional works of significance (Taper, 1984).

Although six years later Farrell and Balanchine were able to work again together, their story illustrates the overt dependency between the mentor and the mentee that Gordon (1983) warns against. Such dependence is counterproductive both for the mentor and the mentee; it can also lead to a very difficult separation.

In sum, the intensity and close mentoring relationships in vertical practices, such as Balanchine's mentoring relationship to his dancers, offer the
mentee a unique opportunity for phenomenal growth and complete com-
mand of an important artistic tradition. Yet the closeness has also a dark side,
one of oppression and dependency that might severely impair both the
mentor's and the mentee's future prospects as independent artists.

HORIZONTAL MENTORING

Democratic Mentoring Model

Contrary to the case of Balanchine, the artists in our modern dance
sample consciously avoided hierarchical mentoring relationships. Indeed, from
an early age the lineage head Anna Halprin looked for an alternative apprenticeship experience and found it with the teacher Margaret H'Doubler
at the dance program of Wisconsin University:

> At the time I was studying dance, there were three major modern danc-
> ers: Martha Graham, Doris Humphrey, and Hanya Holm. Their approach
> to teaching was idiosyncratic: each dancer taught her unique personal
> style. I was fortunate, however, to have a teacher, dance professor Mar-
> garet H'Doubler at the University of Wisconsin, who taught dance as a
> science, a philosophy, and an art. This approach was objective and broad
> which enabled each student to develop their own style, and provided a
> sound foundation to generate creativity for themselves and in their in-
> teraction with others.

H'Doubler's approach to movement through anatomy and physiology
allowed Halprin to explore her own movement rather than copy the teacher's
personal style as was the case with Balanchine and his students. Halprin explains that this method fitted her needs well because her upbringing had
emphasized the value of independent thinking and action:

> "Thou shalt not bow down to a Golden Image." This was instilled in me
> since early childhood and later translated into an approach to dance that
> was suspicious of authority figures or guru types. I was instead attracted
> to education of experiential learning. Since each person's experience is
> unique and personal, this can lead to a deep connection of life and art.
> [As I say] "As art expression expands, life experience deepens." Another
> aspect of experiential learning encourages originality and experimenta-
> tion leading to the discovery of innovative approaches to making art.
> Actually, what really fascinates me is the exploration of the creative pro-
> cess—what energizes it—how it functions—and how its universal values
> can have implications for our lives.

As a teacher and a mentor, Halprin feels that her main responsibility
toward her students is to "present the material clearly, so they can under-

stand it without my personality interfering. I don't want to be anybody's guru." The students' task on the other hand, according to Halprin, is to be "nonjudgmental, not to judge themselves or others. Be willing to try new things—to be open-minded." With such an attitude, combined with teaching that does not rely on the ego of the mentor, Halprin believes the students will be able to get in touch with their own creative approach and to deepen their art and life experience.

Halprin's students found her emphasis to be extremely helpful. Simone Forti describes her experiences with Halprin as follows:

> When she was exploring and trying things with us, that's where I started experiencing those moments of elation in those improvisations where it just felt so beautiful. And it would just happen and roll. And what I've been talking about as dance state, I found it in her classes. We were a lot in that dance state. And my life just changed.

Halprin's experiential approach offered Forti an inspiring scaffolding within which she could explore her own movement patterns. Sally Gross, another Halprin student in our sample, remembers similar situations in Anna's studio:

> I think I had seen her in New York. I also knew that she experimented as a choreographer, and I was drawn to that. She seemed to have faith in what people were willing to try, willing to do, and that was very freeing.

Before studying with Halprin, Gross had studied with Alvin Nikolais in New York for many years. Although she found his teachings extremely influential and sees Nikolais as one of her important mentors, she was also intimidated by the way he taught dance and choreography:

> I don't know how to explain this. Having come out of Nikolais, where you had to do three compositions a week. I'm grateful that we had to do it; but at the time it was very threatening. I felt I was being judged and it was painful to perform and to be criticized.

However, at Halprin's studio, Gross did not feel the same way:

> I'm sure the potential for being judged was there at Halprin's too, but I didn't feel it, maybe because I knew I wasn't going to stay there. I knew that I was going home to NYC; perhaps it's just that the atmosphere there was open and people genuinely seemed to be bringing themselves to it. And I think she too, as a teacher, was strongly influenced by what was being done around her.

According to the testimonies of her students, Halprin succeeded in her goal of providing an environment in which individuals were free to explore their own creativity. In doing so, she distilled a way of teaching and creating that contrasts with Balanchine's vertical style of mentoring. This method shies away from mentor-centered aesthetics and hierarchical relationships, emphasizing instead individual exploration of creativity and artistry.

The other participants in our horizontal modern dance sample were hesitant to raise their mentors on a pedestal, and when acting as a mentor, they were careful not to adhere to the traditional role of a mentor with unlimited power:

> I don't have a guru, but I certainly have people in my life who have contributed to my becoming who I am, as an artist and as a person. I am grateful for their contributions. (Lesley Satin)
>
> My choreography doesn't exist because somebody said, "here are the rules; follow the rules." . . . I feel like it is with the dancers that I do the work. (Sally Gross)
>
> I work with my dancers in a respectful way. I treat my dancers the way my parents treated me, by example. I don't yell at them, I don't berate them, I don't use my director's license to destroy their egos. I despise the traditional infantalization of dancers into girls and boys. I call them gentlemen. I think I say women. I shy away from ladies; it has other connotations. They give me so much respect that I can afford to be informal. (Trisha Brown)

Stephen Petronio in turn was unwilling to call his important influences, or even himself, as mentors altogether:

> I don't honestly know what mentor means. I don't encourage that kind of relationship with my dancers. They work with me and they see my process. I am very honest and open with them and they are very involved, but I try never to preach. I think that the dancers who will choreograph will figure out what it is for them and I certainly encourage them. They can definitely watch my process up close and are invited to be active in it. I ask them to rise to the occasion constantly. You know Trisha asked me to rise to the creative process many times without directly pointing the way and I flourished in that context. You go and you apprentice with someone and you watch and you get the goods, you see their wisdom and so forth and then it's up to you.

In other words, Petronio associates the word *mentor* with the historical, traditional idea of a mentor, the know-all figure that installs his wisdom in the mentee. Petronio feels that, for his purposes, such a mentoring relationship is not helpful. The word has negative connotations for him and he is not willing to connect himself to that image. Instead, he prefers a more "passive" relationship in which the mentee picks up what he needs without the mentor dictating what he should pay attention to.

The participants in our horizontal sample deliberately avoid the absolute position of power that is associated with traditional mentors such as Balanchine. They seem to be aware of the possible negative aspects of a mentoring relationship, and try to avoid them: first, by being aware of their own position of power; and second, by appreciating the power their mentees have in taking responsibility for their own creative exploration and growth.

In case of this horizontal mentoring, the knowledge or tradition that is being passed on is really an attitude toward or a method for creating rather than a technique or vocabulary. By placing the mentee in the position of the interpreter as well as a creator, the choreographers in our sample want to encourage their mentees to be proactive and to explore their own as well as the choreographers' movement.

Individual Creativity as Tradition

None of the choreographers in our sample has developed a codified technique like Balanchine. Nevertheless, experiential learning and emphasis on individual creativity were important to the participants in our horizontal sample. Such interest was inspired by Halprin's and other mentors' method of teaching as well as the choreographers' own independent interest in alternative teaching and in creating experiences.

> [I hope to convey my dancers] a commitment to dance, to experiment, a commitment to experimentation, an emotional investment in it, and for them to feel that they can contribute. That they can—I use a lot of the dancers' material, but it has to be a two-way relationship. (Wendy Perron)
>
> Exploring is important. I love to explore. . . . You have to keep on exploring. It's like the ground keeps melting under you. . . . I want them [the students] to explore an aliveness in their kinesthetic awareness . . . That the experience is interesting to them creatively. That the atmosphere is friendly. And that there aren't any injustices. (Simone Forti)

Further, contrary to Balanchine's carefully controlled teaching and choreographing method, the choreographers in the modern dance sample seem to prefer to teach and create in the role of a facilitator rather than a director.

> So the level of apprenticeship is, yes, how can I encourage the people that I'm attracted to, to work with me, but also that the work is about apprenticing one's own work. And that the material I teach is not exclusively to me, but that it's like how you use these skills for yourself. (K. J. Holmes)

Thus the choreographers are interested in generating an atmosphere in which the students can find their own creativity: Such a milieu in turn acts as a source of inspiration for them as choreographers. To cultivate a sense of individual responsibility, the choreographers allow their mentees a high degree of freedom in their exploration and are careful that their demeanor does not intimidate their students. Such an arrangement suited the mentees in the horizontal sample very well: Contrary to Balanchine's dancers, all of the participants were also interested in working as a choreographer as well as a dancer.

However, if the role of the mentor is more that of a facilitator, how do the students learn what the mentor has to offer? For example, how does Forti teach her mentees the skills she knows if she is, as Kaye describes, "the most nondisciplinarian . . . really she takes care of herself and she sort of lets you take care of yourself." Indeed, we found that instead of exact instructions of how to execute a task, the goal of the choreographers was to be "transparent" or clear in one's thinking and behaving so that the attentive mentee could pick up what he or she needed by observing the mentors.

Transparency as a Method of Learning and Teaching

As mentioned earlier, the choreographers in our sample do not teach a specific technique that they have developed themselves. Instead, they combine influences from many different sources in their teachings. They usually provide guided exercises in which the students use their own movement to explore a theme or a concept that is given to them by the choreographer. Ultimately, the mentees learn the style of the mentor through learning and performing the mentor's choreographies.

Sometimes, as it was in the case of Forti, the choreographers avoid direct instruction and feedback altogether. Here Kaye continues to explain Forti's teaching method: "She wasn't a conscious teacher, she was so absolute about what she did that it was more an active imitation and inspiration in a way." Thus Kaye learned mainly through observing Forti's uncompromising work ethic and artistry rather than through guided learning. Indeed, both Forti's mentees in our sample, Pooh Kaye and K. J. Holmes, found that Forti's ability to make these qualities visible was instrumental to their development:

> I think it was more her attitude, her way of being an artist that was inspiring. Her ability to be open and yet extremely disciplined, open to ideas, but very disciplined about exploring them when she started working on something. (Pooh Kaye)
> I don't think she comes with a lot of ideas that she's giving out. You're watching her think and give you the idea that she's making up at the moment . . . I would say she has a, I don't know, she's got like this, I don't know, like this way of opening to things and then totally embodying them. . . . I think she really remains pretty transparent. . . . There is not a lot of hiding. I think that watching her thought process is really clear, and seeing that through her body, which is what her performance work is, too. You're just watching this person think through their body, and that's amazing, what she comes up with. . . . And [by watching] her associations, you're seeing her make sense and logic, so the transparency is watching this logic develop. (K. J. Holmes)

Thus Forti communicated to her students by embodying the craft and indeed, even her thinking in a convincing manner. By being disciplined in her own exploration and clear in her choices, Forti was able to communicate to her students equally well, if not better, than by explaining her intentions verbally.

Such transparency in one's actions and thinking was frequently mentioned by the choreographers in our sample. Indeed, dance is the art of the body and sometimes words may not be adequate to explain the layered physical reality. Like a picture that can say more than a thousand words, movement can communicate more than could be explained verbally. Therefore it is not surprising that, like Balanchine, the choreographers in our modern dance sample rely heavily on their physicality and movement for transmitting their ideas.

Transparency, however, implies absolute honesty and openness in one's own working and creating habits, and willingness to share them. Balanchine preferred the dancers not to contemplate his motivations and the sources of inspiration for his choreographies, because he believed such knowledge interfered with the purity of his dancers' interpretations of his works. The modern dance choreographers in turn strove toward being as open as possible in their creative process because their dancers actively contribute to the creation of the new pieces.

Transparency requires trust and commitment between the mentor and the mentee so that the choreographers feel comfortable exposing their creative habits to somebody else. On the part of the mentees, transparency requires a keen eye and sensitivity to the nuances of the work and of how it is being created. Indeed, in horizontal mentoring, such give-and-take proves vital for successful creative connection between the mentor and the mentee.

Network of Mentors and Peer Mentoring

Contrary to the vertical model exemplified by Balanchine, the artists in our horizontal sample did not have a single mentor who was instrumental to the development of their own artistic style. Instead, the choreographers talked about the influence of multiple individuals that included teachers, other artists, individuals from other disciplines, as well as other choreographers and peers. When asked whether the participants could name the most important influence on their career, most were unable to give just a single name.

> I don't think that any one person had the greatest influence on me; I was inspired by many people and ideas of the 1960s. (Sally Gross)
>
> No, there wasn't a single most. At different stages in my life there were different people who were important. (Wendy Perron)
>
> The single greatest influence. That's really tough. I don't think there is one (aside from adrenaline and the notion of mortality). (Stephen Petronio)

However, even if the participants were able to mention one person as the most influential one, they also stressed that there had also been other influential mentors:

> Jimmy was the most influential. But other people have been influential, too, including people I've worked with. (Leslie Satin)
>   Well, I would have to say that Simone was a very major influence. And then the other influence of equal proportion were my contemporaries. (Pooh Kaye)

Thus each of the choreographers had a wide "cast of characters" who influenced their professional development in different ways. Further, as demonstrated by Satin's and Kaye's quotations, the data revealed a relatively unexplored characteristic of mentoring; namely the importance of peer mentors. Mentoring relationships between peers have not received much attention in scholarly literature previously. Kram and Isabella (1985) discussed the possibility of peer mentoring in the context of business management. They pointed out that the relationships between individuals of the same age range are often more easily available than relationships between senior and junior members of the domain. These authorities suggested that peer relationships may offer mentoring opportunities that should not be overlooked or underestimated. Nevertheless, the implication is that peer mentoring is merely an alternative if traditional mentors are not available.

According to our findings, the participants often considered their peer mentors to be at least as important as the more traditional mentors they named. For example, when Trisha Brown was asked who she considers to be her mentors, Brown named her peer group, not her earlier formative dance teachers:

> And, then, artistically, I would say, the key colleagues in the Judson Church Dance Theater—David Gordon, Yvonne Rainer, Steve Paxton, Deborah Hay and Simone Forti, who was not at Judson. I worked with her before and I worked with her during Judson when she was not eschewing Judson. It didn't matter, I still worked with her. And those people were—I mean, the 60s were a time for dance to be looked at more carefully and I think those people were brilliant. The people that I just mentioned I know to be very brilliant. We were the world for a while.

Brown felt that with her peers she was creating new genres, new "worlds," and in that process she developed as an artist and creator. Brown further compares her peer mentoring to the "traditional" mentoring relationships and explains what in her opinion is the difference:

> So, in a sense, what you can witness here in relationship is a lifetime of exchange and support, mutual support. So to take it out, mentoring means something because an experienced person is teaching, but you take two experienced people and have them talking.

Thus for Brown the benefit of her peer mentors is that the relationship is of equal exchange. Neither of the participants towers over the other, both are equally experienced. With such a setup, Brown has enjoyed enormously satisfying, lifelong mentoring relationships: "I'm still in touch with these people very closely, so they've been a lifelong artistic team, whether actively or in my mind. They're my little handful of people I make work for."

Indeed, in horizontally oriented practices, peer mentoring relationships may offer an appropriate ground for development and growth because they usually lack the power imbalance of the more traditional mentoring connections. The artists get the benefits of mentoring support and guidance without having to surrender to somebody else's aesthetic prominence and possibly idiosyncratic reality. Peer mentoring may also amplify the collective power of the generation to influence and change the genre. Further, the more democratic relationships may alleviate the possible negative aspects that are associated with the more hierarchical mentorial connections.

The drawback with peer mentoring relationships may be competition between the counterparts because they both essentially work at the same plateau. Peer mentoring relationships may also not provide unconditional support that the successful traditional mentoring relationships do. Nevertheless, because in horizontal practices the focus is on individuality and independent innovation, the artists working in these practices may not need "hand-holding" every step of the way: Indeed, some may prefer having more independent mentoring connections.

DISCUSSION

Our investigation of vertical mentoring, as exemplified by Balanchine, and horizontal mentoring, as exemplified by Halprin and her disciples, revealed clear differences between the two mentoring styles. Vertical mentoring epitomizes the traditional idea of a mentor. Balanchine as a mentor was the source of absolute authority to his mentees, a mentor that was endlessly admired and worshipped. Horizontal mentoring offers an alternative picture of mentoring in the arts. Instead of the authoritarian approach to mentoring, Halprin and her students prefer a more democratic model of mentoring. As mentors they consciously avoid the position of absolute power and allow their mentees a high degree of individual freedom. As mentees, they look for relationships in which they can use their own creativity and artistry rather than embody somebody else's tradition.

Both Balanchine and the choreographers in our horizontal sample have structured their creative and mentoring practices to suit their creative goals. Balanchine's creative efforts were concentrated on creating, maintaining, and passing on his personal style of ballet. He developed a rigorous training system for his dancers so that they could refine their interpretative skills of his work. To keep his style pure, Balanchine preferred not to analyze his creative methods and inspirations with his dancers. He was also opposed to his dancers contributing to the choreography or even contemplating his motives for the different ballets. As far as can be ascertained, most of Balanchine's students' ambition was to perfect their skills as a dancer and interpreter rather than to become a choreographer. Being excluded from the creative process did not generally bother them and was not a hindrance to their development as performing artists.

In the horizontal practice a primary goal of the creators is to change the existing body of knowledge. Instead of looking for an immaculate replication of their style, the choreographers in the horizontal sample are interested in the individuality of their dancers and welcome their creative input. To bring their mentees into their creative process, the choreographers strive toward transparency in their working and creating habits. The mentees in turn appreciate such an inclusive approach: They feel their development as an artist is aided if they are allowed to learn and create through their own movement and input. Indeed, all the participants in the horizontal sample have an interest in becoming choreographers as well as dancers, and thus the proactive role in the creative process suited them.

Uninterrupted transmission of ideas and practices is important in vertical mentoring. To ensure such transmission Balanchine discouraged his dancers' possible relationships with other teachers and mentors unless they were chosen by him to appear as guest teachers for the company. He preferred to be the ultimate and exclusive source of knowledge for his dancers. In the horizontal practices, the goal is to change the tradition: The mentoring network can also be looser and varied. In fact, having a network of mentors enhances the opportunity of choosing among different influences when developing one's own artistic voice. Multiple sources of inspiration are important to creativity in horizontal practices because they support the search for individuality rather than conformity. Having peer mentors further enhances such development. It encourages democratic encounters that preserve the individuality of both counterparts while offering valuable mentorial support.

Because of the importance of a single mentoring relationship in vertical practices, the relationships tend to be highly charged. Balanchine as a mentor acquired a position close to God in the eyes of his mentees. Balanchine in turn cherished his dancers' beauty and talent. In fact, an important part of his creative process was to have a muse, always a female ballerina, who would propel him to ever-higher creative accomplishments. The muse in turn would receive unlimited attention and admiration from Balanchine that would help her to develop her fullest artistic and interpretative potential.

However, the intensity of the relationship between Balanchine and his dancers also had a negative side to it. Indeed, because of the power imbalance between the mentor and the mentee, unsuccessful mentoring relationships in vertical practices may have a hindering effect on both the mentee and the mentor. The mentee may feel powerless and stifled by the mentor's control over his or her life. The mentor and the mentee may also become dependent on each other. Such dependency may hinder the mentee's ability to move beyond the mentoring phase and the mentor's ability to create without the presence of the mentee. Unhealthy dependency between the mentor and the mentee may also lead to difficult separation and hostile feelings.

In horizontal practices the artists usually have a network of mentors that include peers, and the mentoring relationships tend to be more democratic. Thus the mentoring relationships in horizontal practices may be less prone to the possible negative aspects of the mentoring connection. However, this pluralism may also take away from the positive experience of being fully guided by a senior member of the field. Peer mentoring might also harbor competitiveness between the counterparts because both the mentor and the mentee may compete for the same opportunities. Nevertheless, because the focus in horizontal practices is on innovation and change, independence in the mentoring relationship may aid in fostering individual creativity.

In sum, our results indicate that fostering creativity through mentoring is shaped by the specific structure and needs of the practice. In vertical practices, such as classical ballet, the emphasis is on preserving the tradition. Thus the mentoring relationships are very important, hierarchical, rigid, and intense. In horizontal practices, such as certain types of modern dance, the focus is on innovation and individual expression. Thus the mentoring network needs to be more fluid to allow the creator a higher degree of individual freedom.

One of the key differences between vertical and horizontal practices is whether any kind of codified technique or tradition is passed on, and whether the intention is to keep the tradition unchanged. In the case of Balanchine the goal was to pass on his work and technique in its purest form and thus the mentoring practices were organized accordingly. Halprin has no codified technique to transfer. Rather, improvisation was an important component of both the creative and performing work. Improvisation, of course, relies entirely on the skills of the improviser, and thus developing individual creative skills was important in Halprin's style of horizontal mentoring.

When looking at other dance traditions, or any other artistic practices for that matter, we can determine whether they are vertical or horizontal (or somewhere in between) in their mentoring practices. For example, because of the importance of codified technique in Martha Graham's modern dance tradition, it is closer to Balanchine's tradition and therefore more vertical than horizontal. Pina Bausch's modern dance tradition in turn is more horizontal because it relies on the individual creative and interpretive input of the dancers. Most traditional dance techniques such as classical Indian dance or Balinese dance are vertical. Improvisational music traditions are most likely to be more horizontal and ethnic traditions more vertical.

Although our study provides an example of mentoring in a specialized context, we believe that the results of our inquiry are beneficial for attempts to further understand the phenomenon in general. Following the vertical–horizontal distinction within the arts, we can apply similar logic in looking at the sciences. For example, the new sciences such as computer science or genomics are more horizontal because no established doctrine or body of knowledge by a senior scientist can be passed on. Thus the mentoring relationships within these sciences are likely to be more democratic, multiple, and varied. Other sciences, such as certain experimental branches of particle physics, are more vertical because they are all focused around a few laboratories in Switzerland and the United States. To be a part of the discipline and to contribute to it, a young scientist needs to know the approach intimately and believe in the efficacy of it, as well as work with the scientists in the places where the experiments are administered. The mentoring relationships within these disciplines are likely to be more vertical; that is, the mentor is seen as the clear source of knowledge and the role of the mentee is to absorb that knowledge.

Other aspects of the horizontal–vertical contrast merit consideration. It is possible that individuals of a more authoritarian bent will be attracted to vertical domains and traditions, whereas those of a more rebellious nature will gravitate toward more horizontal mentoring relationships. Vertical traditions may be more standard in traditional societies (like some European countries or India), whereas newer societies such as the United States or Australia may embrace more horizontal traditions. In addition, certain artistic eras may usher in work that privileges one form of mentoring: For example, vertical mentoring may be favored in classical or neoclassical eras.

Previous research on mentoring has not paid attention to possible differences in the process of mentoring in different contexts. Understanding how specific constraints can affect mentoring in different disciplines is beneficial for our efforts to learn how to foster effective mentoring through education. Further research on the topic will help to expand our account of vertical and horizontal mentoring. Inclusion of more disciplines and comparison between different age and gender groups will help us further decode the specific needs and symptoms, in both the artistic areas themselves and in the psychologies of the participants, that predispose them to more vertical or horizontal mentoring.

REFERENCES

Ashley, M. (1984). *Dancing for Balanchine*. New York: Dutton.

Belle, A. (1995). *Dancing for Mr. B: Six Balanchine ballerinas* [Videofilm]. New York: WarnerVision Entertainment.

Belle, A., & Dickson, D. (1997). *Suzanne Farrell: Elusive muse* [Videofilm]. Santa Monica, CA : Direct Cinema Limited.

Bentley, T. (1983). *Winter season: A dancer's journal.* New York: Random House.

Bishop, W. (1988). Teaching undergraduate creative writing: Myths, mentors, and metaphors. *Journal of Teaching Writing, 7*(1), 83–102.

Blackburn, R. T., Chapman, D. W., & Cameron, S. (1981). "Cloning" in academe. Mentorship and academic careers. *Research in Higher Education, 15*(4), 315–327.

Buckle, R. (1988). *George Balanchine, ballet master: A biography.* New York: Random House.

Caras, S. (1985). *Balanchine, photo album and memoir.* New York: Rizzoli.

Duncan, D. (1996). *Residents: The perils and promise of educating young doctors.* New York: Scribner.

Emenhiser, D. L. (1989). *Mentor-protégé relationships among people in positions of power and influence.* Unpublished doctoral dissertation, Indiana University, Bloomington.

Farrell, S. (1990). *Holding onto the air: An autobiography.* New York: Summit Books.

Gardner, H., Csikszentmihaly, M., and Damon, W. (2001). *Good work: When excellence and ethics meet.* New York: Basic Books.

Gordon, C. I. (1983). *Toward a conceptual framework of the mentor-mentee relationship.* Unpublished doctoral dissertation, Boston University.

Homans, J. (2002). Geniuses together. *New York Review of Books, 49*(20), 32–35.

John-Steiner, V. (2000). *Creative collaboration.* Oxford, England: Oxford University Press.

Kealy, W., & Mullen, C. A. (1996, April). *Re-thinking mentoring relationships.* Paper presented at the annual meeting of the American Educational Research Association, New York.

Kent, A. (1997). *Once a dancer.* New York: St. Martin's Press.

Kirkland, G. (1986). *Dancing on my grave.* New York: Doubleday.

Kirstein, L. (1984). *Portrait of Mr. B.* New York: Viking Press.

Kram, K. E., & Isabella, L. A. (1985). Mentoring alternatives: The role of peer relationships in career development. *Academy of Management Journal, 28*(1), 110–132.

Li, J. (1997). Creativity in horizontal and vertical domains. *Creativity Research Journal 10,* 107–132.

Mason, F. (1991). *I remember Balanchine : Recollections of the ballet master by those who knew him.* New York: Doubleday.

Maxwell, J. A. (1996). *Qualitative research design: An interactive approach.* Thousand Oaks, CA: Sage.

McDonagh, D. (1983). *George Balanchine.* Boston: Twayne Publishers.

Miles, M. B., & Huberman, A. M. (1994). *Qualitative data analysis: An expanded sourcebook* (2nd ed.). Thousand Oaks, CA: Sage.

Powell, B. J. (1999). Mentoring: One of the master's tools. *Initiatives*, 59(1), 19–31.

Rossman, G. B., & Rallis, S. F. (1998). *Learning in the field: An introduction to qualitative research*. Thousand Oaks, CA: Sage.

Shearer, M. (1987). *Balletmaster: A dancer's view of George Balanchine*. New York: Putnam.

Tallchief, M. (1997). *Maria Tallchief: America's prima ballerina*. New York: Holt.

Taper, B. (1984). *Balanchine: A biography*. New York: Times Books.

Taper, B. (1996). *Balanchine: A biography*. Berkeley: University of California Press.

Tracy, R. (1983). *Balanchine's ballerinas: Conversations with the Muses*. New York: Linden Press.

Wallace, D. B., & Gruber, H. E. (Eds.). (1989). *Creative people at work*. Oxford, England: Oxford University Press.

Zuckerman, H. (1977). *Scientific elite: Nobel laureates in the United States*. New York: Free Press.

11

CONCLUDING COMMENTS: CROSSOVER CREATIVITY OR DOMAIN SPECIFICITY?

JEROME L. SINGER

The editors proposed this volume primarily to address the issue of whether creativity is in some way a general trait or an accomplishment based on abilities largely limited to circumscribed areas of human endeavor. All of the chapters were contributed by distinguished researchers in the study of exceptional productions in the arts and sciences. Each has paid attention to our major question but of course has provided original research and commentary ranging from evolutionary theory, social and contextual influences, and fundamental human abilities and interests to the possibilities for training or educationally enhancing creative potential. Our goal in this final chapter is to set the question of human creativity into the broader context of current research in general psychology and to highlight points of agreement and common conclusions as well as new research avenues that are suggested by the contributors.

CURRENT TRENDS IN COGNITIVE–AFFECTIVE AND SOCIAL LEARNING PSYCHOLOGY

Perhaps the major development of the first 150 years of psychology as a formal discipline has been the recognition of the fundamental role of cognitive processes and their links to emotions, motivations, and social processes. Thinking, consciousness, and self-conceptions were central concerns of psychology as it emerged as a unique scientific discipline in the work of Wilhelm Wundt and William James in the 1880s and 1890s. There was a half-century shift from concerns with consciousness from about 1910 to 1960 as psychologists, seeking to find more precise measurement tools and objectively verifiable methods, embraced behaviorism and animal research on learning. Such research eventually opened the way for recognition of the critical role of social learning processes and for careful, replicable research methodologies. Because of the emphasis on overt behavioral responses there was, except in the clinical areas, a neglect of human conscious experience and ongoing thought processes as a feature of information processing and learning. From the 1960s on, however, with the emergence of cognitive psychology, great progress has been made in research methods and accumulated findings about organized knowledge structures, anticipations, plans, and conscious processes in the acquisition, storage, and retrieval or reshaping of our information. The ties between cognition and our emotional system have also been recognized and are increasingly a subject of study.

The human being can be regarded as an information-seeking, information-processing organism. We need to assign meanings to the ambiguities we confront in each new physical or social setting. Our emotional system is closely linked to the rate, ambiguity, and complexity of the new information we must process from moment to moment. Our established schemas or scripts, along with our wishes and fantasies, lead us to anticipate what we may confront in the next room or in the next social encounter. We rarely get it exactly right, but we seem to be wired up so that moderate degrees of incongruity arouse interest and curiosity, motivating further exploration until we can match the new data with some array of prior schemas. Then we laugh, smile, or experience relief. More extreme degrees of incongruity or disconfirmation of expectancies evoke fear, and the persistence over time of such unexpected information that cannot readily be assimilated evokes anger, distress, or sadness (Mandler, 1984; Singer, 1974, 1984; Tomkins, 1962). Kihlstrom and Hoyt (1990) have shown how one can identify particular functions for conscious and unconscious processes and, in keeping with much research on the self-concept, how a special role is played by the relevance of information or beliefs about the self or of memories defined as autobiographical.

We propose that there are three major sources of stimulation that serve as settings for our encounters with new information. These include the physical or social environment outside our physical selves, although this "real world" takes on a personal meaning on the basis of our experiences and the complexity of our differentiated schemas, scripts, and prototypes for defining it. A second source of stimulation is from the ongoing activity of our memory system: our stream of consciousness, which provides us with fleeting associations, elaborate and sometimes frightening fantasies, and odd but generally intriguing night dreams. This is the domain that was once the special region for psychoanalytic exploration. Finally, the ongoing machinery of our bodies presents us with a continuing series of signals, some fairly readily interpretable as in alimentary, digestive, or excretory functions or reactive pains, but many mere twitchings or, in the case of autonomic or central nervous system functions (such as brain waves), largely outside an awareness level that permits effective communication to others. Evidence of conditioning of bodily activities or of voluntary control through biofeedback (often still without verbal labeling or descriptive awareness) suggests that such signals can be discriminated but not encoded into a lexical or imagery system that permits the formation of schemas.

In effect, part of the human dilemma is that we must maneuver our way through life from moment to moment choosing which stimuli we wish to attend to automatically or with more conscious effort. Generally, we give highest priority to our own physical and social milieu (what Neisser, 1988, has termed the *ecological self*) because survival necessitates, for example, that we look before crossing city streets. We must, of course, slip back into the private self of memory or fantasy to help us interpret new experiences, but this is often an overlearned, automatic process. We can, however, give more attention to our memories, wishes, and fantasies if our external demands are reduced by redundant settings and overlearned situations such as routine chores, solitary environments, and waiting rooms. Centrally generated stimuli can divert our attention from the physical environment, as when we pass a flower shop while riding on a bus and suddenly remember that it is Mother's Day; or even without external cues, as when the face of one's most recent romantic flame stares up at one from a pile of printouts of data analyses. Body signals generally receive lowest priority except when a persistent urge to urinate leaves one wiggling and twisting while trying to conduct a serious conversation or when a pang of muscle pain suddenly interrupts a pleasant reverie about a future victory in tennis.

There has also been increasing awareness that, as James (1890/1950) so well described it, processing of our stored information continues throughout our day and, as laboratory research now makes clear, through our sleep as well (Antrobus, 1991, 1999; Domhoff, 1996; Hartmann, 1998). Bruner (1986), Epstein (1999), and Lewin (1986–1987) have drawn together numerous research threads on the nature of thought to propose two styles of conscious mentation that we all show: a narrative, representational and largely imaginal style on the one hand; and a more rigorous, orderly, logical, and verbal style on the other.

Epstein's research, for example, provides evidence for distinguishing an Experiential from a Rational system of thought. The former is characterized by relatively automatized, effortless, emotionally linked processing. The Experiential mode includes "vibes" from the past which may, however, be influenced by the conscious evaluation of current situations. In this Experiential system, there is a reliance on narrative, on concrete imagery, and on metaphor. The Rational system is more analytic, logical. It is characterized by abstract vocabulary, numbers, and symbols (Epstein, 1999).

The human stream of thought may shift between the narrative–experiential mode (which generally predominates for most of us) and the paradigmatic–rational system, which requires more focused effort and can only be sustained for limited periods before more imaginal, storytelling thought intrudes. The narrative style characterizes much of our day and night dreaming but logical problem solving can emerge even in sleep mentation.

IMPLICATIONS FOR CREATIVITY

We can now begin to see some of the ways in which creativity may derive from the basic ways in which we process new and stored information and the emotions we experience as we struggle to assimilate novel stimuli into our anticipations on the basis of prior schemas and scripts. The very nature of how we think involves an endless dialectic sequence in which we enter new rooms, look at preliminary sketches, try a few notes on a piano or guitar, or confront a mathematical formula and juxtapose this novelty with well-established, easily retrieved schemas. The well-established schemas or scripts of our early experience, overlearned and well-trained, may exert a *conservative* pressure on us (J. L. Singer & Salovey, 1991) so that novelty and potential creative thoughts may be quickly dismissed and forgotten or, even if noted down, as poets, composers, or scientists have reported, disregarded for periods of time. But the imaginative possibility pervades our lives and in this sense, creativity in the "little c," described by Runco in his chapter (see chap. 2) should never be ignored. Our fleeting daydreams or nightdreams reflect the inherent creative potential within all of us. Social forces, as Abuhamdeh and Csikszentmihalyi suggest (see chap. 3), may generate zeitgeists, or cultural atmospheres, that make possible the emergence or later acceptance of particular creative achievements. The sociological studies of Farrell (2001) highlight how "collaborative circles" of painters like the French Impressionists; novelists like Henry James, Stephen Crane, Joseph Conrad, Ford Madox Ford; or feminists like Elizabeth Cady Stanton, Susan B. Anthony, and Lucretia Mott overtly and subtly opened possibilities for the creative accomplishments of each member of the group. The contributors to this volume focus primarily on Creativity ("big C"; see chap. 8, by the Root-Bernsteins), major novel accomplishments in the arts and sciences, but they reflect at various points, recognition of the foundation of novel production in daily life. We believe there are dozens of daily instances when parents think of unusual ways to entertain restless children on rainy days, when merchants conceive novel approaches to lure in customers, when lovers imagine and arrange unexpected gifts for each other. Possibilities abound for us to move from habit, what William James called "the great flywheel of society,"(James, 1890/1950, p. 121) the conservatism of our schemas and action scripts, to risky new thoughts and moves (see Simonton, chap. 6, on stochastic processing) that surprise ourselves and others.

This volume emphasizes socially recognized major creative accomplishments, however. These occur within domains of intellectual or artistic pursuit that require, as most of our contributors agree, at least 10 years of concentrated preparation, study, or training in some discipline. Even in the case of remarkable youthful achievements such as are found in music or mathematics, the training years are still necessary. Although Mozart, Mendelsohn, and Schubert started musical training and showed skills in very early childhood, their first really creative works did not emerge until they were at least 16 or 18 years of age—that is, with 10 years of study behind them. Gauss and Galois, who produced creative work in mathematics just as they moved from adolescence to adult age, had worked for years before in their field. Kaufman and Baer (see chap. 1) pose the problem of domain specificity in a challenging fashion in their chapter providing evidence that even persons of high intellect, or g, may not show c, or a creativity that truly crosses domains. As they put it, could Hawking's talents in physics have led to a comparable accomplishment in poetry? They advise a successful pop singer and composer like Madonna, smart enough to study math, to "keep her day job"!

Lubart and Guignard (see chap. 4) elaborate on Kaufman and Baer's points by specifying the components of domains and pointing to how these impose constraints on cross-domain creativity even though there is continuing evidence of general potential for novel productivity. Their work suggests Sternberg's model of *effective* intelligence, in which analytic, practical, and creative components must interact for optimal adaptation. Production of a socially valued creative product not only depends on novel or divergent thought (creativity), but also involves an ordered, self-critical analysis (analytic) and, as Abuhamdeh and Csikszentmihalyi's (see chap. 3) research on artists shows, an ability to promote one's work and call attention to it in a particular domain (practical intelligence).

Feist (see chap. 5), writing from an intriguing evolutionary perspective, sets forth a model of a limited number of domains of human scientific and artistic endeavor: the psychological self, physics, biology, linguistics, mathematics, art, bodily–kinesthetic, and musical. Development of extraordinary creativity may involve a combination of a person's constitutional readiness and fairly specific social encouragement within a familial or cultural atmosphere that is accepting and nourishing. The technical differences between the domains necessarily introduce further constraints on "crossover creativity."

Simonton (see chap. 6) carries further the dialectic of creative risk taking and domain constraint in his elegant, quasistatistical analysis of how creative achievements in the sciences, and in somewhat different fashion in the arts, involve elements of randomness and chance. Such accomplishments also depend on particular—by now well-demonstrated—personality characteristics: a capacity for producing and tolerating novel associations, openness to experience (which includes acceptance of one's daydreams and other features of consciousness), diversity of interests or hobbies, preference for complexity or for the asymmetric, and willingness to accept ambiguity. The creative personality within various domains has also shown what appears like psychopathology but what is more likely to be an openness and curiosity about the often random nature of one's own ongoing stream of thought in fantasies or dreams. What Simonton calls an "attention failure" might be seen as a willingness not to screen out the randomness of private experience and revert to the conservatism of preestablished schemas by intentional avoidance or reversion to clichéd thought. Creative individuals in various domains have spent their "10 years of mastery," but often they devote less effort to overlearning or completely mastering technical facility. This "looseness" allows them to be more open to the stochastic possibilities so that they do not succumb to excessive analysis and overcorrection. Simonton also calls attention to different criteria in the evaluation of scientific versus artistic creative productions, thus necessitating different degrees of focused skill masteries.

Henderson (see chap. 7) brings to our attention a group of creative individuals who are often neglected by creativity researchers in their tendency to focus on great painters, sculptors, or composers, or on theoretical physicists, chemists, or biologists. She describes the less well-known group of inventors, those who produce the technology of outer space equipment, of computers, and of other physical and chemical products we tend to take for granted. She highlights the issues of establishing one's identity, usually in a fairly restricted domain, as an *inventor*, someone searching for novel solutions on a daily basis. She points up not only the planfulness but also the emotional excitement of their endeavors and, in a sense, bridges some of the gaps between the "little c" creativity and the lofty achievements of an Einstein and a Michelangelo.

With the Root-Bernsteins' contribution (see chap. 8) we find a major effort to cut even more specifically across domains to a focus on particular processes that characterize scientific as well as artistic achievement. These investigators dispute the so-called two-cultures notion separating scientists and artists. They bring together five types of evidence to show that proven creative individuals, whether in the sciences or the arts, are polymaths, with unusually broad patterns of interests, avocations, and talents. They offer anecdotal and biographical evidence of scientists who also excelled in music, literature, or other humanistic activities, such as Louis Pasteur, Humphrey Davy, Ramon y Cajal, all of whom were fine painters; Roald Hoffmann, the chemist, who was a published poet and playwright; Alexander Borodin, who was one of Russia's premier chemists and also one of the nation's finest composers. Painters of renown including Ingres, Klee, and Matisse also manifested considerable musical talent. One of the greatest literary stylists of the 20th century, Vladimir Nabokov, following in his father's footsteps, was also a distinguished lepidopterist.

The Root-Bernsteins also point out that the psychological profiles of artists and scientists show considerable overlap compared with control groups, differing chiefly in the greater willingness of scientists to work in structured settings. Arts activities and interests as well as visual and spatial imagery and memory prove to be good predictors of scientific achievement. Of special importance, tying scientific and artistic creativity to the "little c" of human creative potential based on the fundamental cognitive–affective processes described at the outset of this final chapter, is the evidence that achievers in both fields describe similar approaches. They use careful observations, draw on mental imagery and fantasy, check their efforts through abstraction, and also draw body-awareness and empathy. Both groups assert that their interests in science have stimulated their artistic achievements or that artistic vocations and curiosities have fostered their scientific work.

Of special importance is the Root-Bernsteins' delineation of the common thinking tools that creative individuals in the arts and sciences draw on: imagery, careful observation, and patterning, as well as efforts at analogizing or modeling. These mental tools not only point to specific, fundamentally overlapping processes in creativity but also direct our attention toward the approaches to enhancing creativity through training that are emphasized by Plucker and Beghetto in chapter 9 and by Keinänen and Gardner in chapter 10.

Plucker and Beghetto independently summarize the accumulated agreement in defining creativity as an achievement that is *novel* and *useful* within a particular social context, and they provide an indication of why creativity necessarily appears to be domain specific (i.e., one must accumulate the background experience and make a time commitment to work intensively on one or a series of achievements in a domain). But an attitude of *wanting* to be creative, a sense of creativity as a decision process (Sternberg, 2002) cuts across domains. These contributors go on to some specific ways in which one can introduce creativity training into educational settings in a fashion that allows for flexibility that can later be applied toward creative efforts within domains. Keinänen and Gardner (see chap. 10) carry this thrust into detailed accounts of effective mentoring by teachers or by specialists with their apprentices to show how the dimensions of horizontal or vertical orientation can be effective in fostering creativity in a variety of domains.

In summary, training for creativity as a general orientation is a real possibility as the research of Renzulli (1994), Singer and Lythcott (2002), Sternberg (2002), as well as the concluding chapters of this volume suggest. One must grant that the highest levels of creative achievement are generally attained only in one specific domain by individuals. These same achievers may demonstrate strong creative potential in other areas, but social contexts, the 10-year rule, and the stochastic elements of risk and chance may constrain comparably outstanding accomplishments across domains. As our contributors show, however, creativity can cut across domains because both artistic and scientific creative persons use common tools: their imaging abilities, analogic and abstract thought, mental modeling, and sharp observation of the world around them. They show a common sense of excitement in confronting new information and novelty, and they try as much as possible to avoid being constrained by the conservative nature of their overlearned schemas and scripts. They are risk takers in several domains even if their greatest success is limited. As one of the 20th century's finest poets, Rainer Maria Rilke, wrote in an unpublished fragment (1968):

> As long as you catch what you yourself threw into the air,
> all is mere skill and petty gain;
> only when you unexpectedly become the catcher of the ball
> that the Goddess, your eternal playmate,
> threw toward you, toward the center of your being
> in a precisely calculated curve, in one of those arcs
> reminiscent of God building bridges;
> only then is being able to catch the ball an ability
> to be cherished—
> not yours but a world's. And if you
> were to have that strength and courage to return the throw,
> nay, even more miraculous . . . if you had forgotten about
> strength and courage
> and had already thrown . . . as the year
> throws birds, the migrating flock
> that an older warmth flings
> across seas to a younger—only
> through your daring is your play genuine.
> You neither make throwing easier nor harder
> for yourself. From your hand issues
> the meteor that races towards its place in the heavens.

REFERENCES

Antrobus, J. S. (1991). Dreaming: Cognitive processes during cortical activation and high afferent thresholds. *Psychological Review, 98*, 96–121.

Antrobus, J. S. (1999). Toward a neurocognitive model of imaginal thought. In J. A. Singer & P. S. Salovey (Eds.), *At play in the fields of consciousness* (pp. 3–28). Mahwah, NJ: Erlbaum.

Bruner, J. S. (1986). *Actual minds, possible worlds.* Cambridge, MA: Harvard University Press.

Domhoff, G. W. (1996). *Finding a meaning in dreams: A quantitative approach.* New York: Plenum Press.

Epstein, S. (1999). The interpretation of dreams from the perspective of cognitive-experiential self theory. In J. A. Singer & P. S. Salovey (Eds.), *At play in the fields of consciousness* (pp. 51–82). Mahwah, NJ: Erlbaum.

Farrell, M. (2001). *Collaborative circles: Friendship dynamics & creative work.* Chicago: University of Chicago Press.

Hartmann, E. (1998). *Dreams and nightmares: The new theory of the origin and meaning of dreams.* New York: Plenum Press.

James, W. (1950). *Principles of psychology.* New York: Dover. (Original work published 1890)

Kihlstrom, J., & Hoyt, I. (1990). Repression, dissociation and hypnosis. In J. L. Singer (Ed.), *Repression and dissociation* (pp. 181–208). Chicago: University of Chicago Press.

Lewin, I. (1986–1987). A three-dimensional model for the classification of cognitive products. *Imagination, Cognition, and Personality, 6*(1), 43–54.

Mandler, G. (1984). *Mind and body.* New York: Norton.

Neisser, U. (1988, August). *The self: An ecological analysis.* Keynote address presented to the Twenty-Fourth International Congress of Psychology, Sydney, Australia.

Renzulli, J. S. (1994). *Schools for talent development: A practical plan for total school improvement.* Mansfield Center, CT: Creative Learning Press.

Rilke, R. M. (1968). [Poetic fragment]. Cited in E. Fink, The oasis of happiness: Toward an ontology of play. *Yale French Studies, 41,* 19–30.

Singer, J. L. (1974). *Imagery and daydream methods in psychotherapy and behavior modification.* New York: Academic Press.

Singer, J. L. (1984). *The human personality.* San Diego, CA: Harcourt Brace Jovanovich.

Singer, J. L., & Lythcott, M. (2002). Fostering school achievement and creativity through sociodramatic play in the classroom. *Research in the Schools, 9*(2), 43–52.

Singer, J. L., & Salovey, P. S. (1991). Organized knowledge structures and personality: Person schemas, self-schemas, prototypes and scripts. In M. J. Horowitz (Ed.), *Person schemas and maladaptive interpersonal patterns* (pp. 43–79). Chicago: University of Chicago Press.

Sternberg, R. J. (2002). Encouraging students to decide for creativity. *Research in the Schools, 9*(2), 61–70.

Tomkins, S. S. (1962). *Affect, imagery, and consciousness.* New York: Springer.

AUTHOR INDEX

Numbers in italics refer to listings in the references.

Farrell, S., 172, *192*
Faste, R., 107, 118, *122*
Faust, D., 93, 96
Fehr, H., 134, *148*
Fein, D., 66, 67, 80
Feist, G. J., 11, 13, *16*, 58, 62, 72, 74, 78, 87, 94, 96
Feld, S., 51, *56*
Feldhusen, J. F., 155, *165*
Feldman, D. H., 69, 80
Ferguson, E. S., 138, *142*, *148*
Fetterman, D. M., 118, *122*
Filippelli, L. A., 117, *122*
Finke, R. A., 12, *16*, 89, 96, 157, *166*
Fiske, S. T., 96
Fodor, J. A., 78
Ford, M. E., 112, 113, 114, 116, 118, *122*
Fox, L. H., 68, *81*
Freeman, C., 78
Freeman, M., *39*, *41*
Fromm, E., 35, *41*

Gagné, F., 154, *164*
Gallup, G. G., 66, 82
Galton, F., 83, 86, 96
Gardner, H., 4n, 5, *11*, 14, *16*, *18*, 60, 62, 67, 69, 69, 70, 71, 72, 78, 82, 144, 145, *148*, 154, 160, *164*, 170, *192*
Garnier, H., 135, 136, 147, *150*
Gelman, R., 58, 61, 78
Gentile, C. A., 7, *15*
Getz, I., 107, *122*
Getzels, J. W., 13, *16*, 32, *41*, 72, 73, 77, 78, *122*
Getzels, U. J. W., *39*, *41*
Gleick, J., 78
Glick, I. D., 72, *75*
Glück, J., 10, *16*, 44, *54*
Goertzel, M. G., 94, 96
Goertzel, T. G., 94, 96
Goertzel, V., 94, 96
Goldberg, D. E., 89, 96
Goldberg, M., 70, 71, *79*
Goleman, D., 60, 65, 78
Goodyear, I., 66, 76
Gopnik, A., 78
Gordon, C. I., 179, 180, *192*
Gough, H. G., 10, *16*, 90, 94, 96
Grammar, K., 65, *81*
Gray, C. E., 48, *54*
Gray, W. D., 67, *81*
Greenberg, C., *37*, *41*

Greenberg, M., 131, *147*
Gruber, H., 33, *41*, 141, 144, *148*
Gruber, H. E., 5, 6, *16*, *19*, *193*
Grunstein, M., 64, 77
Guilford, J. P., 12, *16*, 58, 78, 90, *97*
Guillemin, R., 129, *148*
Gustafson, S. B., 51, *55*

Hadamard, J. R., 89, *97*, *148*
Hall, W. B., 73, 78
Halpern, D. F., 157, *164*
Han, K. S., 7, *17*, 53–54, *54*, 154, *164*
Harrington, D. M., 33, *42*, *54*
Hartmann, E., 197, *203*
Hatch, T., 65, 78
Hauser, A., *31*, *42*
Hayes, J. R., 5, *17*, 84, 91, *97*
Hébert, T. P., 117, *122*
Heerwagen, J. H., 62, 80
Heilbrun, A. B., Jr., 10, *16*
Helmholtz, H. von, 89, *97*
Helson, R., 73, 78, 98, 133, *148*
Henderson, S. J., 104, 107, 108, 109, 112, 113, 116, 117, 118, *122*, *123*
Hennessey, B. A., 115, *123*
Henry, B., 120, *123*
Hermelin, B., 133, *148*
Herron, M., 118, *121*
Herschel, W., 129, *148*
Hesse, H., 7n, *17*
Hickok, G., 69, *79*
Hindle, B., 143, *148*
Hirstein, W., 71, 80
Hjerter, K., 129, 131, *148*
Hocevar, D., 9, 9n, *17*, 52, *54*
Hoepfner, R., 12, *16*
Hoffmann, R., 129, *148*
Homans, J., 177, *192*
Hong, E., 135, *149*, 154, *165*
Horn, J. L., 73, *81*
Hou, C., 70, 71, *79*
Howe, M. J. A., 67, 69, *79*
Hoyt, I., 196, *203*
HP invent, 104, *123*
Huber, J. C., 86, 87, *97*, 104, *123*
Huberman, A. M., 118, *124*, 172, *192*
Humphreys, L. G., 133, *148*
Hung, S. S., 71–72, 82
Hutchinson, E. D., *131–132*, *148*

IBM research news, 104, *123*
Infeld, L., 88, 96

155, *156*, 160, 161, 162, *166*, *167*,
201, *203*
Stewart, A. V., 158, *165*
Stipp, D., *125*
Stone, J., 131, *150*
Stone, V., 66, *76*, *82*
Storr, A., 32, *42*
Storr, R., *35–36*, *42*
Stott, C., 66, *76*
Strosberg, E., 142, *150*
Strykowski, B. F., 71–72, *82*
Stuss, D. T., 66, *82*
Sulivan, K., 133, *147*
Szladits, L., *150*

Tagano, D. W., 156, *167*
Tallchief, M., 172, *193*
Taper, B., 176, *176*, 177, *178*, 180, *193*
Tardif, T. Z., 5, *18*
Taylor, S. E., *96*
Teach, R., 158, *166*
Tellegen, A., 91, *101*
Terman, L. M., 68, *82*
Thomas, D., 85, *98*
Thorndike, E. L., 60, *82*
Todjman, S., 49, *55*
Tomkins, S. S., 196, *203*
Tooby, J., *82*
Torrance, E. P., 12, *18*, 105, *125*
Toynbee, A., 25, *30*
Tracy, R., 172, *193*
Tramo, M. J., 61, *82*
Tweney, R. D., 89, *101*

Unger, F., 10, *16*, 44, *54*
Urdan, T., 115, *125*

Vaid, J., 157, *167*
Vallery-Radot, M., 129, *150*
Van Hook, C. W., 156, *167*
Van't Hoff, J. H., 134, *150*
Vasari, G., 32, *42*, 83, *101*
Veroff, J., 51, *56*
Vitz, P. C., 142, *150*

Vollard, A., 37, *42*
Vosburg, T., 105, *125*

Waddington, C. H., 142, *150*
Wagner-Döbler, R., 86, 87, *97*
Walberg, H. J., 71–72, *82*, 117, *122*
Walker, A. M., 32, *42*
Wallace, D. B., 5, 6, *16*, *19*, *193*
Wallach, M. A., 13, *19*
Waller, N. G., 91, *101*
Walters, J., 69, *82*
Wanner, R. A., 85, 86, *96*
Ward, H. B., 137, *150*
Ward, T. B., 89, *96*, 157, *166*, *167*
Ward, T. S., 12, *16*
Watercutter, A., 106, *125*
Waugh, C., 131, *147*
Weber, R. J., 104, *125*
Weisberg, R. W., 5, *19*, 84, *101*
Weiss, S., 110, *125*
Weston-Smith, M., 145, *147*
Wheelwright, S., *76*
Whelan, M., 28, *30*
White, K. G., 87, *101*
White, M. J., 87, *101*
White, R. K., 135, *150*
Whitney, D. M., 9, *18*
Wiener, N., 68, *82*
Wilson, G. D., 73, *82*
Wilson, T. D., 89, *98*
Winner, E., 133, *147*, *150*
Wise, L. L., 68, *82*
Wolfflin, H., 34, *42*
Wright, R., 104, *125*
Wuthrich, V., *91*, *101*

Yaniv, I., 88, *99*
Yao, G., 133, *148*

Zeldow, P. B., 73, *82*
Zenasni, F., 49, *55*
Zigrosser, C., *143*, *150*
Zuckerman, H., 171, *193*
Zythrow, J. M., 84, *97*

SUBJECT INDEX

impact on scientists, 135, 136
scientific, of writers, 131–132

Balanchine, George (vertical mentoring), 173, 174–181
  absolute authority in, 188
  authoritarianism of, 176, *177*, 178, *179*
  ballerina wives of, 180
  blurring of mentee–mentor line in, 180–181
  control of training classes, 175–176
  creation, maintenance, passing down personal style, 188–189
  demands of
    absolute commitment, 176
    ego surrender, 177
    perfection, 175
  expectations of, 175–176
  as guru, 176–177
  mentoring relationship gone awry, 178–180
  muses of, 180
  passing on a style, 175–177, 188–189
  setting an example, 177–178
    ballet as craft *vs.* as art, 177–178
    by demonstration, 178
Barron-Welsh art scale
  aesthetics and scientific creativity and, 134
Big C creativity, eminent, 158
Biology
  implicit, 60–61
Black, Sir James, 138, *139*
Brennerman, L., *58, 78*
Brown, Trisha
  on peers as mentors, *187*, 188

Career decision making
  of inventors, 112
Chance
  in creativity, 84–85
  in generation of products, 92
Children
  artistic talent in, 71
  autistic, 66–67
  creative development of, 49
  natural history and talent in, 67
  originality of, 24
  risk-averse, 50
Choreographers
  multitalents of, 131
Clark, Sir Kenneth, *134, 147*

Cognitive-affective and social learning psychology, 195–198
  shift from consciousness to behavior, 196
  social learning process, 196
Cognitive components of creativity, assessment of, 51–52
Cognitive integration models
  of process, 25–26
Cognitive overlaps
  between artists and scientists, 133–134, 138
Cognitive styles
  of scientists
    correlation with avocations, 135–136
Collaborative circles
  individual achievement and, 198
Componential model of creativity, 7–8
Components of creativity
  cognitive, assessment of, 51–52
  weighting and interaction of, 53
Composers
  multitalents of, 130–131
Computer simulation programs
  rediscovery *vs.* discovery with, 89
Conation
  and creativity across life span, 50–51
Constraints
  on creative scientists *vs.* creative artists, 94
  creativity and, 44
  stochastic, 94–95
Content
  experience and, 34, 35
  linear *versus* painterly, 33–34
  process and, 34, 35
  representational *versus* abstract, 33–34
Conti, R., *7, 8, 16*
Coon, H., *7, 8, 16*
Cost-effectiveness
  of inventions, 106
Cranberg, L. D., *66, 77*
Creative personality. *See* Personality, creative
Creativity
  analysis of, 155–160
  artists' definitions of, 44
  attributes for, 45–47
  characteristics of
    domain-general and domain-specific, 158–159
  components of, 45, 51–52, 53

constraints in, 44
correlation of artistic and scientific, 128–143
  arts proclivities and scientific success, 134–137
  commonality of tools for thinking in, 138–141, 202
  scientists as artists and artists as scientists, 129–132
  shared psychological profiles and, 132–134, 201
  use of interactions of, 141–143
creative as adjective *vs.*, 28
criteria for, 58
definitions of, *4, 43–45, 156, 166*
domain-general–domain-specific controversy and, 44–45, 153–154
domain-specific. *See* Specificity
elements of
  ability and process, 156
  novelty and usefulness, 157, 201
  observable outcome, 157
  social context, 157–158
general. *See* General creativity
generality or specificity question and, 4–6
historical perspective on, 83–84
implicit theories of, 9, 10, 11
investment theory of, 45–47
lifespan changes in, 50–51
novelty in, 43–44
probabilistic nature of, 95
resources for, 45–46
  personal and potential, 46–47
as stochastic process
  definition of, 84
systems model of. *See* Systems model of creativity
value of, 29
Creators
  as judges of own product, 92–93
  need for feedback from audience and peers, 93
Cross-domain creativity, 144–145
Cross-domain performance, 8–9
Csikszentmihalyi, M., *39, 41*

d'Ambroise, J., *178*
Davis, S. N., *5, 6, 16*
Development
  artistic
    artistic success and, 39–40

of creativity
  biopsychosocial factors in, 50
  in children, 49
Discovery
  independent, simultaneity of, 86
  multiple. *See* Multiple discovery
Discovery learning
  influence on invention, 118, 119
Discretion
  in personal creativity, 23–24
Distribution
  of creative products
    across career, 86–87
  of potential, 26–27
  of products
    across career course, 93
  of talent, 71–72
Divergent thinking
  training in, 51
  vs. convergent thinking, 49
Domain
  definition of, 58
Domain-general–domain-specific controversy
  both/and positions in conceptualization of, 160–161
  educational implications of, 162–163
  openness to information and experience and, 162
Domain-general–domain-specific hybrid position
  educational implications of, 162–163
    flexible thinking for transfer, 162–163
    interaction of ability and context, 162
Domain-generality
  cross-domain factors in, 8–9
Domains
  bridging and linking of, 147
  elements of
    as constraints on cross-domain creativity, 199
  fluid integration of
    for creative thought, 73–74
  of mind. *See* Mind, domains of
    talent and creativity mapping onto, 71
  neurophysiological and psychological mechanisms of, 75
  potential and, 29
  vs. modules, 58

Graham, Martha, codified technique of, 190
Greenberg, C., *37, 41*
Gross, Sally
  on mentors, *186*
Gruber, H. E., *5, 6, 16*

Halprin, Anna (horizontal mentoring), 173–174
  emphasis on individuality of pupil, 182–183
  mentor and teacher of, *181*
  on task of student, *182*
  as teacher and mentor
    experiential approach of, 182
    nonjudgmental, *182*
    open mindedness, 181–182
Hauser, A., *31, 42*
Hayden, F. S., *143*
Heisenberg, Werner, on abstraction, *139*
Hesse, H., 7n, *17*
Holmes, K. J.
  on Forti, Simone, as mentor, *185*
  as mentor, *184*
Home environment
  and invention, 118
Horizontal faculties
  of scientists and artists, 144–145
Horizontal mentoring. *See also* Halprin,
    Anna (horizontal mentoring)
  choreographer as facilitator in, *184*
  democratic model of, 188
    attitude or method for creating in,
      184
    Brown, Trisha, *183*
    Gross, Sally, *183*
    Haprin, Anna, 181–183
    Petronio, Stephen, *183*
  exploration and, *184*
  individual creativity as tradition, 184–185
  observation in, 185
  by peers, 186–188
  transparency in, 185–186
  as two-way relationship, *184*
Hutchinson, E. D., *131–132, 148*

Ideas
  conception and expression of, 141
Imaging
  by artists and scientists, 138–139
Implicit theories, 9, 10–11, 12
Incompetence

from self-sealing behaviors, 162–163
Information
  creativity and, 198
  memory activity or stream of consciousness, 196–197
  processing of as stream of consciousness, 197
  sources of stimulation for
    physical or social environment, 196
Integrated activity sets, 144
Intelligence, 45, 46
  and creativity, 13
  practical, 118–119
Intentionality, 23
Interpretation
  personal, 25
  weighting of factors in, 25–26
Interpretive capacity, 23, 28
Inventing talent
  formative experience and, 118–119
  nature *vs.* nurture and, 120
Invention
  defined, 104–107
  impact of, 106
  terminology and, 104
  unique features of
    cost-effectiveness, 106
    impact, 106
    novelty, 105
    patents, 106–107
    utility, 105–106
  vs. innovation, 104
  vs. other forms of creativity, 105
Inventors
  characteristics of, 120
  creative achievement and motivational
    correlates, measures for, 112–113
  creativity and, 107–108
  demographics of
    age and, 110
    education level, 111
    ethnicity, 111
    gender in, 110, 111
    minorities in, 111
    in past, 110
    today, 110–111
  Internet and, 103
  motivational systems theory in, 112
  motivation of
    intrinsic *vs.* extrinsic, 114–115
    personal goals in, 113–115
  profiles of 21st century

for corporate inventors, 108–109
for independent inventors, 108, 109
psychological studies of
living systems framework for, 112, 113
psychology of, 111–120
public interest in, 104
role identity as, 200
gender differences in, 109–110
importance of, 109
and motivation, 109
social learning theory and, 112
studies of
framework for, 112
method in, 108–109
results of, 109–111
Investment approach
to creativity, 45–47
of risk-averse children, 50

Jensen, Johannes, on science fostering art, 142

Kahn, S. F., 39, 41
Kaufman, J. C., 4, 5
Kaye, Pooh
on Forti, Simone, as mentor, 185
on mentors, 187
peers as mentors, 170–171
Kimmelman, M., 35, 37–38, 42
Kirkland, Gelsey, 179
on Balanchine as mentor, 175
Knowledge, 45–46
Kovalevskaya, Sophya, work in literature and mathematics, 145, 149
Kruger, J., 162–163, 163, 165

Language domain, 61
Linguistics
implicit, 61
Linguistic talent, 70
Little c creativity, everyday, pedestrian, 158
Lucie-Smith, E., 35, 42
Lyons, L., 35–36, 42

Market place needs
inventor solutions to, 108
Mathematics
implicit, 61
Mathematics domain, 61
precocity in, extreme, 68–69
talent in, 68–69

McDonagh, D., 177, 192
Mental disorders
in artists, 36–37
Mentee
in vertical mentorship, 189–190
Mentor
description of, 169
as facilitator, 184
as personification of wisdom, 169
traditional model of, 188
Mentoring
in arts
domain-specific structure and needs in, 171
effective, 201
horizontal. See Horizontal mentoring
partners in, 170
passive approach to, 183
by peers, 186–188
process in different contexts, 191
relationships in
pitfalls and abuse of, 179–180, 181
studies of, 170–191
research method in, 172
samples in, 172–174
traditional, 169
vertical. See Vertical mentoring
Mentor network, 170, 186
Miller, H. D., 129
Mind
evolution from implicit knowledge to explicit modes of thought in, 75
evolution of domains of, 58–64. See also Evolved domains
art, 62
evolved, 62–64
language, 61
music, 61
natural history, 60–61
numerosity and seriation, 61
physical objects and spatial relations, 60
proposed by various authors, 59
social–emotional, 58, 60, 199
Morris, D., polymath writer and zoologist, 146, 149
Motivation
creativity and, 13
of inventors, 114–115
emotion in, 112, 116–117
personal agency or self-efficacy in, 115–116

constraints on, 32
creative
    self-report questionnaire for, 9
    studies of, 9–10
individuality and, 40
mental disorder and, 36–37
relationship with style, 36
representational–abstract dimension, 36
Personality differences
    between art and science domains, 72–73
Personality traits, 32
    across-field work and, 47–48
    of artists *vs.* scientists, 72–73
    commonality of, across domains, 72
    covariance with creativity, *11, 16*
    creativity-relevant, 13, 15
    field dependence of, 47–49
    within field work and, 47–48
    generality-specificity and, 47–49
    genetic predisposition for, *versus* development of, 49–51
    self-report questionnaires for, 52
Personal knowledge
    transformation of, 141
    translation of, 141
    from use of mental tools, 140–141
Petronio, Stephen
    on mentors, *186*
Physical environment
    as source of information, 196–197
Physical-technical domain
    talent in, 66–67
Physics
    implicit, 60
    talent in, extreme, 66
Picasso, Pablo, on abstraction, *139*
Planck, M., *134, 149*
Plucker, J. S., 6, *17*
Poisson distribution
    of multiple discoveries, 85–86
    of products, 86–87, 94
Polanyi, M., on personal knowledge, *140, 149*
Polymaths, 146
    examples of, 200–201
Polymathy
    in artists, *129*
    in arts, 129
    and creativity, 131–132
    and success, 144
Pop Art

Expressionism and, 38
Potential. *See also* Multipotentiality
    assessment of
        cognitive measures in, 51–52
        performance-based, 53–54
        self-report questionnaires in, 52
    for creativity, 46–47
    and discrepancy in performance, 26–27
    distribution across bell curve, 26–27
    interpretive capacity and, 28
    objectivity and, 26–28
    recognition of, 24, 25
    vs. performance, 28–29
Potential, enhancement of, 29
Practical intelligence
    in artistic development and success, 39, 199
Pretz, J. E., *4, 5*
Probability
    of creative productivity, 85, 86, 87, 95
    of multiple discovery, 85, 86–87, 95
Problem solving
    in artistic creativity, 107
    creativity as form of, 84, 88
    in inventing, 107
    logical, 88
    motivation behind, 108
    process as, 84, 88
    random or incongruous stimuli and, 89
Process
    for abstract style, 34, 35
    affective dimensions of, 117
    artistic development and, 39–40
    comparison of expressionist and photo realist experience and style, 35–36
    creativity-relevant, 45
    interrelationship with ability, 156
    linear-painterly dimension and, 35
    as logical problem solving, 88
        close-end problems and, 88
    observable, 157
    person and, 12
    as problem solving
        open problems and, 88
    products and, 12
    relationship of style and experience in, 35–36
    for representational style, 34, 35
    self-reports about, 89
    stochastic constraints on, 94–95
    stochastic operation of, 88–89

transformation of subjective knowledge
in, 141
Productivity
across career course, 86–87
assumed in creativity, 24
problems with, 24–25
quality as function of quantity in, 87,
88
random combinatorial process in, 87–
88
as stochastic phenomenon, 87
task commitment for, 160, 161
Products
best single, 87
criteria for
originality *vs.* adaptive/functional
character of, 93
definition of, 24–25
as extension of past achievements, 37
inventors of
corporate, 109
individual, 108
multidimensional and configurational
nature of
creators and, 92–93
novelty of, 44
observable, 157
Poisson distribution of, 86–87
and potential, 26–27
prolixity-quality ratio and, 92
of stochastic creativity, 92–94
Psychological profiles
common to scientists and artists, 132–
133
Psychology
implicit, 58, 60
Psychopathology
and artistic creativity, 36, 37, 40
artistic personality and, 36–37, 200
and constraint on artistic creativity, 94
Psychoticism
correlation with creativity, 90–91
Pye, David, *142*

Quality
as function of quantity, 94

Remy, M., *146, 149*
Risk
in generation of products, 92
Risk taking
in children, 50

of creative persons, 202
domain constraint and, 199–200
domain-specificity of, 47
in elderly, 50–51
Rodin, R., *140*
Root-Bernstein, M., *138, 139,* 140, 141, *150*
Root-Bernstein, R. S., *138, 139, 140, 141,
145, 150*
Rothenberg, *35*
Runco, M. A., *11, 18, 22, 30*

School environment
context for socialization and personality development, 50
and development of creativity, 49
and invention, 118
Science fostering art
in Jensen, 142
in Steinbeck, 142
Sciences
creativity in
arts and crafts avocations and, 128
psychological tests for, 134
vertical *vs.* horizontal mentoring in, 191
Scientific domain(s)
mathematical, 68–69
physical-technical, 66
in autistic children, 66–67
giftedness in, 66
talent in, 66
social sciences, 65–66
talent in
natural history/biological science, 67
theoretical physics and, 66
Scientific success
arts proclivities and, 134–137
correlation of artistic hobbies/avoca-
tions with, 135
Scientists as artists, 129–132
Scripts and schemas
effect on creativity, 198
Seagoe, M., *135, 150*
Self-efficacy
of inventors, 115–116
Self-promotion
in artistic development and success, 39
Self-report questionnaires
for assessment of creativity, 52
in creative personality research, 9–10
problems with, 52
Self-reports
of creative process, 89

Self-report scales
  for general creativity, 6
Seuphor, M., *16, 42*
Skill(s)
  achievement and
    inventor, 112, 117
  creativity-relevant, 7–8, 13, 15
  domain-relevant, 45
  domain-specific appearing as domain-
    general, 12–14
  general
    operation on domain-specific level,
      14
  thinking *vs.* communicating, 145
Smith, C. S., *140*
Snow, C. P., *127, 150*
Snyder, Gary, on translation of personal
    knowledge, edit *141*
Social context
  acceptability of novelty and, 158
  in definition of creativity, 157–158
  manifestation in domain specificity,
    159–160
Social disability
  autism and impulse control problems,
    65
Social–emotional domain, 58, 60
Social environment
  development of creativity and, 50
  as source of information, 196–197
Social forces
  creative achievement and, 198
Social intelligence domain
  disability in, 65–66
  giftedness and talent in, 65
Social sciences, 65–66
  talent in, 65
Specificity
  eminent performance and, 48
  restriction of outside perspectives, 161
Sprinthall, R., *26–27, 30*
Stanley, T. J., *68, 76*
Sternberg, R. J., *4, 5, 11, 12, 16, 18, 19*
Stochastic model
  of multiple discovery, 85–86
  of scientific creativity, 85–86
Storr, R., *35–36, 42*
Strong vocational interest tests
  correlation of artist, musician, author
    with scientist or engineer, 134
Style
  and artistic personality, 36–37

cognitive, 35–36
  handing down
    in vertical mentoring, 175–177
  of introverts *vs.* extroverts, 36
  personal
    creation, maintenance, passing down
      of, 175–177, 188–189
  relation to experience, 35–36
Systems model of creativity, 32–39
  domain in, 33–34, 41
  field in, 33, 37–39
  individual in, 36–37
  personality implications of, 36–37

Talent(s)
  in artistic domains, 69–71
  correlative, of artists and scientists, 144
  distribution of, 71–72
  domains of
    mapping onto domains of mind, 71
  domain-specificity of, 64–72, 74
  inventing, 67–68
    development of, 120
  linguistic, 70
  in mathematical domain, 68–69
  in music, 69–70
  overlapping domains of, 71
  in scientific domains, 67–68
  single pool for artists and scientists, 134
  in visual arts, 70
Taper, B., *177, 178, 193*
Tardif, T. Z., *5, 16, 18*
Task analysis
  for creativity within field and across
    field, 48
Task commitment
  for productivity, 160, 161
Task motivation, 13, 14, 45
Task-specific training
  effect on transfer, 162
  nontransferability of, 162
Teachers
  as role models, 49
  transparent, 185–186
Ten-year rule
  for domain mastery, 91–92
  domain-specific achievement and, 199
  for domain specificity, 4n, 5
  in inventor study, 117
  stochastic possibilities and, 200
Terman, L., *135, 150*
Thinking/thought

divergent *vs.* convergent
and development of creativity, 49
experiential *versus* rational system of,
197–198
Thinking tools. *See* Tools for thinking
Tools for thinking
abstracting, 139
of artists and scientists, 144, 201
body thinking, 140
common to scientists and artists, 138–
141
empathizing, 140
imaging, 138–139
observing, 138
pattern recognition, 139–140
Toynbee, A., *25, 30*
Tradition
individual creativity as
in horizontal mentoring, 184–185
passing on
in vertical mentoring, 175–177, 189
in vertical *vs.* horizontal mentoring,
189, 190
Training
in divergent thinking, 51
for enhancement, 51
task-specific
effect on transfer, 162
Tramo, M. J., *61, 82*
Transfer
task-specific training effect on, 162
Transformation, of subjective knowledge,
141
Transformational capacity, 23
Translation, of subjective knowledge, 141
Transparency

as method of learning and teaching,
185–186
requirements for, 186
in thinking and actions, 185

Understanding
intuitive, 141
synthetic form of, 141
Usefulness, as criteria, 58
Utility
of an invention, defined, 105–106

Vasari, G., *32, 42*
Vertical mentoring. *See also* Balanchine,
George, (vertical mentoring)
traditional concept of, 188
in traditional societies, 191
Visual art domain, 62
Visual arts talent, 70
Vollard, A., *37, 42*

Weisberg, R. W., 5, 16, *19*
White, R. K., *135, 150*
Williams Syndrome
musical ability in, 69–70
Woolf, Virginia, on pattern recognition, *139*
Work
enjoyment and satisfaction with
in inventing achievement, 116–117
Work environment
impact on innovative achievement, 118
Writers
science avocations and vocations of,
131–132

Zigrosser, C., *143, 151*

ABOUT THE EDITORS

Robert J. Sternberg is best known for his theory of successful intelligence, investment theory of creativity (developed with Todd Lubart), theory of mental self-government, and balance theory of wisdom as well as for his triangular theory of love and his theory of love as a story. Dr. Sternberg is the author of more than 900 journal articles, book chapters, and books and has received about $20 million in government grants and contracts for his research. He is past-president of the American Psychological Association (APA) and editor of *Contemporary Psychology*. He received his PhD from Stanford University in 1975 and his BA summa cum laude, Phi Beta Kappa, from Yale University in 1972. He has won many awards from APA and other organizations. He has been president of four APA divisions and has served as editor of *Psychological Bulletin*.

Elena L. Grigorenko holds a PhD in general psychology from Moscow State University (1990) and a PhD in developmental psychology and genetics from Yale University (1996). Her professional experiences include conducting research, teaching psychology, and designing educational curricula. Dr. Grigorenko has published more than 100 books and articles, and she is currently associate editor of *Contemporary Psychology*. Dr. Grigorenko has worked with American, Russian, Indian, and African children. Her main interests are individual differences, child development, and exceptional children. Currently, Dr. Grigorenko is associate professor at Yale and Moscow State University.

Jerome L. Singer received his doctorate in clinical psychology from the University of Pennsylvania. He is a professor of psychology at Yale University, where he served for many years as director of the graduate program in clinical psychology and also as director of graduate studies in psychology. He is codirector, with Dr. Dorothy G. Singer, of the Yale University Family Television Research and Consultation Center. He is a specialist in research on the psychology of imagination and daydreaming. Dr. Singer has authored more than 200 technical articles and has written or edited more than 15 books. He is a fellow of the American Psychological Association (APA). He has been president of the Eastern Psychological Association; president of the Society for Personality and Social Psychology of the APA; chair of the Board of Scientific Affairs of the APA; and president of the APA Society for the Psychology of Aesthetics, Creativity, and the Arts. Currently he is editor of the journal, *Imagination, Cognition and Personality*.